The Rock Garden Plant Primer

THE ROCK GARDEN PLANT PRIMER

Easy, Small Plants for Containers, Patios, and the Open Garden

Christopher Grey-Wilson,

B.Sc. (Hort.), Ph.D., V.M.H.

Timber Press
Portland • London

Half title page, *Erodium*; frontispiece, *Helianthemum* cultivars;
page 5, *Platycodon grandiflorus*; page 6, *Aquilegia flabellata* var. *pumila*.

Photographs are by the author unless otherwise indicated.

Published in 2009 by Timber Press, Inc.

The Haseltine Building   2 The Quadrant
133 S.W. Second Avenue, Suite 450   135 Salusbury Road
Portland, Oregon 97204-3527   London NW6 6RJ
www.timberpress.com   www.timberpress.co.uk

Printed in China

Library of Congress Cataloging-in-Publication Data

Grey-Wilson, C.
    The rock garden plant primer : easy, small plants for containers, patios, and the
open garden / Christopher Grey-Wilson. — 1st ed.
        p. cm.
    Includes bibliographical references and index.
    ISBN 978-0-88192-928-7
  1. Rock plants. 2. Rock gardens. I. Title. II. Title: Easy, small plants for containers,
patios, and the open garden.
    SB421.G684 2009
    635.9'672—dc22
        2009006148

A catalog record for this book is also available from the British Library.

For my mother
Jean Marie Grey-Wilson

Contents

Preface

ROCK GARDEN PLANTS fit into today's gardens extremely well, indeed where space is limited these bright, cheerful, and quite varied plants come into their own. It is not necessary to have a formal rock garden with hefty lumps of rock or to create a mock mountain vista in the garden in order to grow them. Raised beds can be an integral part of the overall garden design and are ideal for growing a whole range of rock plants. While a beautifully planted old stone trough bursting with color can be an arresting sight, there are many kinds of containers (including some very realistic artificial troughs) available that are suitable for many different rock plants. These can make splendid features for patios, terraces, or courtyards, while they can also be incorporated with ease into other parts of the garden.

Gardening and plants fascinated me from an early age, when I would help my grandfather in his London garden. From those early days I was destined for a career that involved plants, this taking me to read a degree in horticulture at London University and then on to the Royal Botanic Gardens Kew as a young botanist. While at university in the early 1960s, one of my tutors, Mary Page, introduced me to the world of rock garden plants and took me along to meetings of a local group of the Alpine Garden Society in Kent. I joined the society almost straight away and have been an avid member ever since, indeed the society's editor for the past eighteen years. This fascination with alpine plants brought me to Switzerland in my second year at university to work during the summer vacation in the famous nursery of Correvon and Son on the outskirts of Geneva, a traditional nursery in those days growing a wide range of alpine plants, many growing there in the rock garden, in raised beds, on tufa walls, and in troughs. Monsieur Aymon and Heidi Correvon took me very much under their wings and during that summer encouraged me to travel around the Swiss Alps as much as time allowed. I have been traveling around mountains in various parts of the world ever since.

One point that has to be cleared up at the onset is the use of the words *alpine* and *rock* in relation to these exquisite little plants. In Europe the term *alpine* is widely used to cover all small hardy plants that can be grown in gardens, hence the Alpine Garden Society. The term *alpine* in this context is used in a very lax manner and encompasses all small plants whether they come from mountain or lowland areas. In strict botanical parlance, the term *alpine* refers to all those plants that grow above the tree line in mountains around the world accepting, at the same time, that at extreme northerly and southerly latitudes many of these plants grow low down, sometimes even at sea level. In North America the term *alpine* instead means many discreet little plants, often cushions or small tufts, that inhabit high mountain regions and are tricky to grow and maintain in cultivation: the terms *rock garden plant* or *rock plant* are widely used to cover all those little plants that are available to the gardener, many easily grown and adaptable. Hence the American equivalent of the Alpine Garden

Opposite: *Trollius acaulis*

Society is logically the North American Rock Garden Society.

It is easy to get baffled by terminology, but whether you live in Europe, North America, Japan, New Zealand, or elsewhere, the world of rock garden plants and alpines is a fascinating and colorful one. It is easy to get hooked on these delightful little plants and, like any addict, the more you delve into their world the more fascinating it becomes. The range of rock garden plants available today is huge and, if plants are not available from commercial sources, there are always enthusiasts willing to give or exchange plants. Likewise, the prime societies and clubs concerned with these plants around the world have extensive seed exchanges, often offering plants not available elsewhere. (Some of these societies and clubs are listed at the back of the book.)

The entries included in the A to Z section are in many ways personal choices; however, they do reflect the diverse range of colorful and exciting small plants (rock garden and alpines) grown in gardens. This is not a book about tricky or difficult plants, rather one that extols the virtues of the easier and more freely available rock garden plants. Only in very exceptional circumstances is a plant included that is rare in cultivation or unavailable in the horticultural trade, otherwise all the plants are freely available. In addition, there are very many excellent small plants suitable for rock gardening in the broad sense, and also readily available, not included here. It would, for instance, be easily possible to fill the pages with gentians, primulas, or saxifrages alone. Although shrubs are not in general included, exceptions are made for indispensable small shrubs and shrublets, especially daphnes. Nor are bulbs, in the strict sense, included, but important tuberous groups such as anemones, cyclamen, and corydalis are. As far as possible, the most up-to-date scientific name for a particular plant is given, while important synonyms are presented immediately after the accepted name: these are cross-referenced in the index. Cultivar names are included in single quotation marks. Those without quotation marks represent groups or grexes as recognized by the Royal Horticultural Society and other organizations. Except where indicated, all the plants mentioned in the A to Z section are fully hardy to at least zone 6.

This book is intended to bring the fascinating world of rock garden plants to greater public attention and to convince gardeners that there is a place in every garden for a collection of these plants, which will give pleasure for many years to come. Today, an excellent range of readily grown rock garden plants is available at garden centers and nurseries. It is fun to go along and select the plants yourself. If you are unsure about a plant, check this book for guidance, although, in most instances, the proprietor will be only too willing to advise you on your choice. You can also attend chapter or group meetings of your local rock garden or alpine club and meet fellow enthusiasts. There you will certainly make some good friends, be able to exchange plants and seeds, and learn more about this exciting group of plants. Although my taste in plants is fairly catholic, my interest in alpines continues unabated and there is still so much to see and learn. I hope this book will encourage many more people to grow these delights in their own gardens.

Opposite: *Cyclamen hederifolium*

Introduction

To SEE PLANTS growing in the mountains, sometimes at very high elevations, is one of the great joys in life. You don't have to know the name of the different plants you come across to appreciate their beauty. What strikes one most is their compactness, the majority low-growing, forming tufts, mats, or hummocks, many with apparently disproportionately large, showy, and colorful flowers. They are without doubt among the most beautiful of any group of flowering plants, and it is often difficult to believe that many inhabit such bleak, often exposed and windswept places. Also fascinating is the wide range of habitats in which mountain plants are found and, although some species are adapted to a wide range of conditions, others have fairly exacting requirements. Go to any mountain region and you will see plants growing in meadows and marshes, along the margins of streams, on rocky slopes, cliffs, screes, and moraines, while some even manage to survive on the tops of high ridges and peaks in the harshest environment of all.

Yet many of the plants grown in the rock garden also come from lower elevations, growing in similar habitats but also in or on the margins of woodland. There are many fine woodland plants, including hardy ferns, in the rock gardener's repertoire, their prime feature for inclusion being their size. The possibilities are compounded by the very nature of the rock and soil, for many rock plants are adapted to either acid or alkaline rocks, rather few being catholic in their soil requirements. Perhaps most intriguing of all is the fact that so many of these little plants, drawn from many corners of the world, can be grown in lowland gardens side by side, provided that they are given certain conditions, but these are on the whole quite easy to provide.

A rich alpine meadow brimful of colorful mountain plants forms a stark contrast to the snow-clad Caucasian mountain backdrop, in northwestern Georgia, above Ushguli.

Rock Plants in the Garden

THESE PLANTS CAN be grown in a variety of situations in the garden (lists are included at the end of the book giving examples of rock garden plants for sun or shade, moist or dry conditions, and so on). A feature can be made of a single stone trough or other container attractively planted with a group of rock plants. A rock garden, with rocks, large or small, with pathways, associated pools or rivulets, pockets, ledges, and crevices for a wide selection of different plants can be a major feature, but it is not always practical or feasible, either because of the space required or from the cost point of view. But a rock garden, however nice, is not a prerequisite for growing these plants: retaining walls holding back soil on a slope, raised beds of various shapes and sizes, and a multitude of different sorts of containers are all equally effective. It is important, from the aesthetic point of view at least, that these vari-ous structures are incorporated into the over-all design of the garden. After all raised beds or retaining walls can be very attractive features in their own right, and when combined with pathways, a pool, or patio, an important focal point is created.

Choosing the right aspect and providing the plants with the conditions in which to flourish is the key to success when it comes to growing rock garden plants. Many are no fuss-ier than other groups of plants in the garden. The great joy is their compactness and bright colors: there are a large number that can be grown with ease in the garden, and it is quite astonishing how many can be accommodated in a relatively small space. For instance, a con-tainer or trough measuring 2 × 1 m (6 × 3 ft) could, with the right selection, accommodate forty or more plants, giving interest through many months of the year.

Good Conditions for Most Rock Garden Plants

MOST ROCK GARDEN plants, but certainly not all, require an open sunny position in the garden, away from overhanging trees. Some dappled shade during the hot midday hours is acceptable to many, but too much shade will result in open growth and a lack of, or at the

. . . .
A 2-m (6-ft) slate trough in the author's garden is colorful in early summer with *Phlox subulata* cultivars, with part of a rock garden beyond. Such features can fit harmoniously into the general landscape of the garden and provide focal points of interest at different times of the year.

least reduced, flowering. An open, moisture-retentive, yet very well-drained compost is im-portant and, for most, an alkaline or neutral pH will be fine, although there are some rock plants that will only thrive in acid conditions. If the garden soil is naturally loamy, then the incorporation of some fine sharp grit may be all that is necessary to accommodate the plants, provided it has been freed of any injurious weeds, particularly the perennial ones. How-ever, it may be necessary to make up a com-post suitable for filling in pockets in the rock garden or for raised beds and containers. A good standard mix is one part by volume sterilized loam or good garden soil, one part humus (peat was used extensively in former times but its use is much frowned upon today; a friable, sieved garden compost will work just as effectively), and one to two parts horticultural grit or coarse (sharp) sand. The amount of grit or sand can be varied according to the plants being grown: thus plants that are drought-resistant and need acute drainage can have extra grit or sand, while those requiring more moisture in the compost require less grit and more humus, and so on.

Some form of irrigation may be required, especially during long hot summers, but under average conditions most rock plants need no more water than most other garden plants, indeed some deteriorate if subjected to excessive moisture. This is most apparent in the winter months when some choice cushions may rot if the conditions become too soggy. An effective way of protecting these vulnerable plants is to place a glass cloche overhead for the inclement months or at least a sheet of glass or plastic secured overhead.

Hardiness

Most rock garden plants, indeed the majority included in this book, are hardy to at least zone 6 (–23 to –18°C; –10 to 0°F). Some may well be far hardier still. For rock plants, as with many plants, hardiness is not just a matter of temperature, as other factors play an important role. These include aspect, shelter, soil type (some soils, especially sandy ones, are naturally warmer than others), late frosts, amount of rainfall (particularly in very wet areas), and even provenance of the plants involved. A few

rock plants are more susceptible to winter temperatures that fall below –5°C (23°F). However, the chief reason for winter fatalities among these plants is more likely to be excessive moisture. That is why the majority thrive best in very well-drained, gritty compost, and why a dressing of rock chippings around the collar of many is essential to keep the plant's vulnerable neck as dry as possible.

Books like this can give a rough guide to hardiness, but only by trial and experimentation can you really find out how a particular plant will grow at a certain site. This is all part of the fun of gardening. If I am not sure of the hardiness of a particular plant and I have enough plants, then I try them in different parts of the garden, under varying conditions. It is often surprising just which plants will prove to be hardy, for there is nothing like trial and error to find out. Nonetheless, it is worth getting the right conditions, for it is very disheartening to acquire a little gem of a plant and watch its slow or rapid demise solely because it has been given the wrong conditions or simple preparations have not been undertaken. Plants are like pets: well cared for and nurtured, they will respond as you would want.

Soil Type

The majority of rock garden plants will thrive in neutral to alkaline soil (pH 7 or higher). Some such as celmisias, the autumn gentians, and soldanellas require an acid compost (pH below 7). In gardens with an alkaline soil, acid-lovers can be grown in troughs or containers with a suitable acid compost. While it is easy to modify an acid soil to an alkaline one by adding lime, the reverse is not possible.

Aspect

An open sunny site suits the majority of rock plants, although some shading during the heat of the day (provided by nearby trees or buildings) can be beneficial and prevent scorch or excessive dehydration. Don't worry if you have a fairly shady garden, for there are many rock plants, especially the smaller woodlanders and ferns, that thrive in shade or partial shade.

Rainfall

Natural rainfall is ideal, as it is for all garden plants. However, in low-rainfall areas or during drought periods, some form of artificial watering will be necessary. Tap water varies enormously from one area to another. The main thing to avoid is drenching acid-loving rock garden plants with highly alkaline water.

Types of Rock Gardens

ALL THE FEATURES presented below can add a huge amount of interest to the garden. While each has its own particular characteristics, all are aimed at giving varying groups of rock plants the right niche in which to thrive, while at the same time producing something that is beautiful and adds interest to the garden for many months of the year.

When creating a rock garden or scree bed the ground should first be cleared, making sure that all perennial weeds are eradicated, otherwise they will come back to haunt you. It is also important to ensure that any compost used is weed-, pest-, and disease-free.

Rock Garden

These can be any size from a small island border to a much grander affair with pathways and rivulets. A slope gently bedded with rocks can provide numerous niches for plants. Very hot dry positions are unsuitable unless you are growing a collection of drought-resistant rock plants. Rock gardens with a north or northwest aspect can be very effective, the slope min-

imizing to some extent the extreme temperature fluctuation of a south-facing slope (in the Northern Hemisphere, that is).

Rock gardens are expensive to build and labor-intensive, but there is no finer way of showing off a collection of rock plants. The choice of rock is a personal one, although limestone and sandstone are the most favored. Most gardeners will want to use local rock, if available, for the haulage fee over any distance can be alarmingly prohibitive.

The rocks can be positioned in various ways. Many gardeners like to produce a well-ordered rock garden in which all the pieces of rock are laid out like a natural outcrop, with well-defined strata. A modern trend is to lay them in vertical lines (see the following crevice garden description). However, if you go to the mountains, many natural rock gardens are far more disorganized, with rocks and fragments strewn about in a rather haphazard manner. In the end, you are trying to create an interesting and pleasing feature in the garden and one that will suit a wide variety of plants.

When placing rocks, especially the larger

A view of one of the famous rock gardens built at the Chelsea Flower Show, London, over the years by the Alpine Garden Society. The use of large rocks and the softening effect of contrasting plants makes for year-round interest.

ones, incline them slightly backward into the soil. This will allow rain to run into the rocks rather than away from them, thus keeping the plants' roots well supplied with water. Rocks should be properly stabilized: the larger ones must not tilt or rock when stood on, otherwise accidents may occur, especially if children play in the garden.

A scree bed edged with old bricks provides a colorful early-summer display featuring an assortment of small hardy geraniums, achilleas, and pinks (*Dianthus*).

Scree Garden

In nature, scree is the rocky detritus that accumulates at the base of cliffs and steep slopes. Scree, which has perfect drainage, can harbor a fascinating array of rock plants. Moraines, detritus produced at the sides and ends of a glacier, are very similar and, like scree, once stabilized can support a range of interesting plants. The scree (or moraine) garden aims to create such conditions by mimicking sloping areas with varied sizes of rock fragments laid over the soil. The layer of fragments needs to be at least 15 cm (6 in) deep; some gardeners make it two or three times this thickness. Many taprooted or extensively rooted rock plants thrive in these conditions once they are able to get

established, although planting in screes can be quite difficult. Scree, as with the crevice garden and tufa, can be a part of the rock garden or essentially the infill for a raised bed.

Some rock gardeners advocate the use of sand beds, which serve more-or-less the same function as a scree bed, providing perfect drainage for the plants. The sand should be a coarse, angular one. Builder's sand is generally not acceptable because it is too fine-grained, nor is coastal sand, which may contain injurious amounts of salt unless it has been thoroughly cleansed.

Crevice Garden

In recent years the crevice garden has become popular. First advanced in the Czech Republic, then Holland and elsewhere, it has now made inroads into Britain and North America. Crevice gardens or crevice beds can be very pleasing, although they can take a lot of time to prepare at first. The prime principal of the crevice garden is that pieces of vertical or ascending rock are sandwiched close together to form numerous vertical fissures into which small plants can be established. The ideal rock for this is one that makes flat shards, perhaps 5–10 cm (2–4 in) thick; even broken paving slabs and old tiles have been used by some to great effect. Many of the small and choicer hardy rock plants really thrive in such conditions.

Raised Bed

Raised beds have always been important to the rock gardener. Apart from looking pleasing to the eye, a raised bed can be an important feature in the overall garden design. In many ways, raised beds solve the problem of rock plants and critical drainage, for by raising the surface above ground level excellent drainage is achieved. Raised beds, which can be anything from knee to waist height, can be constructed of brick, stone, or wooden slabs or sleepers and can be filled in with a good compost or scree mixture. They can be landscaped with small shrubs and pieces of rock. Gaps left in the vertical walls allow extra niches for crevice plants. An important feature of raised bed is that they make gardening much more accessible for disabled gardeners, especially those in a wheelchair.

Personally, if I had only a single feature in the garden for growing rock plants it would be a raised bed, for they can provide interest throughout the year. Furthermore, they can be any shape and size to fit the landscaping of the garden. The proportion of the bed needs to be considered in relation to the other garden features. For instance, a raised bed along the side of a patio or terrace or along part of a pool margin can work very well. A good starting point is one that is about 2–3 m (6–9 ft) long and 1.5–2 m (4½–6 ft) wide, with a height that can vary from 20 to 30 cm (8 to 12 in), although anything up to 75 cm (2½ ft) is feasible. However, filling large deep beds requires a great deal of compost. In deep beds the lower third or even half can be filled with rubble (old broken bricks, bits of concrete, stone, or whatever is at hand), but care must be taken that it is well beaten down to avoid large air pockets. The compost also needs to be firmed down with great attention as the filling process continues. This is particularly important around the edges. Slightly overfill to allow for later settling. It is often recommended that large raised beds are not planted until several weeks have elapsed after filling, to allow the settling pro-

Raised beds can be composed of various materials including wood, stone, and old bricks, as seen here. Raised beds provide excellent drainage and just the conditions in which to grow a wide selection of rock garden plants and small hardy bulbs.

cess to take effect. More compost can be added if necessary just before planting commences.

Dry Retaining Wall

On slopes or banks the soil can be kept from slipping by building walls, either mortared or of the dry stone type. The tops of such walls, as well as any crevices designed in their construction, make ideal places to grow a range of rock plants. It is often difficult to establish plants in an existing wall, and far easier to place them in suitable niches as the wall is built. Air pockets behind retaining walls, which can stunt plant growth, can be avoided as building proceeds by firming and pushing down compost into all the spaces at regular intervals. Plants need to be watered in carefully until they are properly established, which is usually indicated by renewed growth.

Humus Bed

In the old days the peat bed was a key feature in many rock gardens. Peat allowed a far greater range of plants to be grown, particularly acid, moisture-loving, and woodland plants. However, the environmental degradation caused by peat extraction from the wild has caused many gardeners to discontinue its use. In reality a lot of plants do not like pure peat and a bed with a really good friable garden compost or leafmold (or a mixture) often proves a better alternate, especially in regions where peat is a dwindling and precious commodity. Peat beds were often confined by blocks of peat, but in the humus bed logs or sleepers are just as effective. Unlike all the other categories included here, humus beds are best not sited in full sun, but in dappled shade. Some sort of watering system can be incorporated as the area is developed, for the humus bed requires ample water, more so than any other area in the rock garden. Natural rainwater is ideal if it can be stored.

Alpine Lawn

Mountain meadows studded with plants can be irresistible, and attempts to recreate such wonderful areas in the garden have proved

. . . .

Alpine lawns like this one at Wurzburg Botanic Garden, Germany, are difficult to achieve in the average garden, but the effect can be astonishingly beautiful, even when common plants like dandelion (*Taraxacum*), lawn daisy (*Bellis*), speedwells (*Veronica*), and forget-me-nots (*Myosotis*) dominate.

very difficult over the years. It is all a matter of selecting the right plants, especially small grasses, and getting a good balance, but the results can be disappointing to say the least. The best examples are probably seen when only small tussock grasses (different fescues, for instance) are interplanted with low mat-formers, such as thymes, sedums, and vetches. The end result should be a patchwork of color and one that is excellent for insects. Small bulbs can be used in conjunction with such plantings but vigorous plants are best avoided. Alpine lawns are a matter of trial and error and getting the balance right on your garden's particular soil, but it can be great fun trying.

Troughs and Containers

Where space is limited, a trough or container can be a charming addition to the garden, especially when planted with a selection of small rock plants. Treat the container as a miniature garden, adding pieces of rock or tufa to create interest. Troughs are also ideal for growing some of the choicer rock plants, where conditions can be more readily controlled. For instance, it is easier to protect plants during the winter in a trough than in the rock garden.

A corner of a small stone trough in early spring with an assortment of floriferous saxifrages.

Troughs should preferably be at least 30 cm (1 ft) deep so that plants have plenty of room to develop a good root system and not dry out too rapidly. Shallow troughs are excellent for drought-resistant rock plants: a collection of houseleeks (*Sempervivum*) can look very effective in a large, shallow trough.

Tufa

Tufa is an extraordinary rock composed of thick deposits of calcium carbonate, like stalactites or stalagmites but on a grander scale. It is relatively light, easy to bore holes in, and ideal for many rock plants, especially the more discreet and cushion-forming kinds. A single large piece of tufa planted with an assortment of plants can punctuate the rock garden. Tufa is available in some areas but it usually has to be sought out and is not particularly cheap. It can be used for the construction of tufa walls or used in smaller pieces on raised beds or in troughs. Pieces should be buried by up to one-third of their bulk to work effectively: the rock is porous and will draw up

A small rock garden cleverly incorporating several troughs and blocks of tufa merging with an area of rocky detritus provides ideal niches for many different and discreet little rock plants.

moisture from the ground, thus keeping the plants well supplied.

Freshly quarried tufa is yellowish, often soft, and rather crumbly, but the surface quickly weathers and grays to become rock hard. It is best placed in an open, airy, well lit position, to provide niches of various aspects for a range of plants. Any small tufa debris can be added to compost or used for topdressing. Small pieces of tufa can be used to enhance a trough or other container with plants sandwiched between the pieces. Boring large lumps of tufa is not difficult using a drill or even an old screwdriver or chisel. Holes should be about 7.5 cm (3 in) deep and about 2.5 3 cm (1 1⅓ in) diameter, inclined downward at about a 45° angle. Young plants or newly rooted cuttings work best, rather than attempting to cram in pot-bound specimens, which can be easily damaged in the process and take longer to establish.

A large tufa block like this one can accommodate an exciting range of different rock plants and makes an impressive feature in any garden, whether set alone or grouped with other pieces of tufa.

Alpine House and Frame

Growing rock garden plants under cover in unheated frames or specially built or adapted

glasshouses allows a gardener to grow a greater range of rock plants, especially some of the trickier species that need more exacting conditions. They are also excellent places in which to grow a collection of bulbs or to raise plants from seed or cuttings. For those just starting to grow rock plants, the alpine house is probably one step too far. Enjoy your rock plants in the open garden and in a few years, if you find you want to develop your hobby, then the alpine house may prove an irresistible option. The one advantage of an alpine house is that you can dive into them during those wet winter or spring days and enjoy the plants in a dry environment.

Ponds and Rock Gardens

Water is an irresistible feature in any garden. While a pool can be aesthetically pleasing, a cascade tumbling down across rocks into a pool can be even better, providing movement

Pools and rock gardens are indispensable companions and allow a wide range of plants to be grown, as seen here at Glen Chantry, in Essex.

in the garden and that wonderful murmuring sound that only water makes. Cascades, falls, and pools can all be incorporated into the rock garden as it is constructed and, if you do not want to construct these from scratch, there are lots of kits and preformed ponds available today. Marshy areas adjacent to water can provide interesting spots for bog-loving primulas, cotton grasses (*Eriophorum*), and monkey flowers (*Mimulus*) and other water-marginal plants, such as some of the irises, sarracenias, and butterworts (*Pinguicula*). Water has the added feature of attracting birds and various insects (particularly dragonflies) into the garden, as well as frogs and toads, which are great at mopping up unwanted pests. Larger pools can also be stocked with fish.

Where to start

Many of the rock garden plants that are available today, especially in garden centers and other retail outlets, are as easy to grow as other garden plants. There is no mystery to growing them. Preparing special areas for rock plants

undoubtedly increases the range that can be grown. While a rock garden can be an exciting and eye-catching feature in the garden, it is perhaps not the best starting point. If you just want a few colorful rock plants, then a trough or container comes first. It can be great fun going down to the garden center or nursery and choosing a selection of plants. Many will be in flower, making selection that much easier, while in the best establishments clear labeling will tell you the conditions that each requires, as they do with a great range of other garden plants. Moving on from troughs and other types of containers, the next step up is certainly a raised bed. These can be an important part of the overall garden design and many rock plants can be accommodated in such a bed measuring, say, 4 × 1.5 m (12 × 4½ ft). Once your enthusiasm has been fired and you have experienced growing a range of these plants, then the next move is certainly constructing a piece of rocky landscape in the garden to show off your plants. Yes, rock gardens can be pricey and time consuming to build but, in the end, are worth every scrap of time and energy expended.

Caring for Rock Garden Plants

Watering

Alpines require water like any other plants in the garden. While most hate fierce hosing, many modern watering systems allow for fine spray application, which is ideal. Water only really needs to be applied in dry periods. While an irrigation system can be incorporated into large rock gardens, it really is not necessary for

smaller areas. Certainly troughs and containers can be watered using a conventional watering can. While rainwater is ideal, tap water will often have to be used. It is worth storing rainwater in water butts (barrels) and tanks, important in today's changing climate. The pH of tap water should be checked to ensure it is not too alkaline for acid-loving plants in the garden. Newly planted areas will requires careful watering until the plants have become established, but avoid the temptation to overwater, for some rock plants hate too much.

Topdressing

The vast majority of rock garden plants look good and respond well to a good topdressing of rock chips. This not only looks pleasing but also serves to suppress weeds and to keep the vulnerable neck of many plants relatively dry, thus avoiding the problem of neck or crown rot. Dressings can be placed around the plants after planting, but it can also be done annually or whenever required. Many rock chip types are available today, some quite ghastly: it is wise to choose one that matches the color of

other rocks employed in the rock garden, raised bed, or trough, otherwise the finished product will never look quite right and will be a source of constant irritation. Rock chips no more than about 12–15 mm (½–⅗ in) are the best and most effective to use. They also have the advantage of keeping cats off the soil.

Winter Protection

Although many rock plants are fully hardy as far as temperature is concerned, susceptibility to excessive moisture can prove to be a problem, and plants may succumb, especially during the winter months, through rotting of the crown or fungal infection of the leaf rosettes. Cushion plants can be especially susceptible. Although the vast majority of the plants listed in the A to Z section of this book require no winter protection whatsoever, several do, especially in those areas with a high winter rainfall and little or no snow cover. Protection can be easily provided by placing a cloche over the plants or a pane of glass or acrylic secured overhead to keep rain off. Plants are best kept well aerated from the sides as a foggy, enclosed atmosphere may only exacerbate the problem. Any protection should be firmly secured, or it may be carried away in a winter storm.

Treating Pests and Diseases

Pests and diseases are no more prevalent in rock garden plants than any other group of plants in the garden; however, because the plants are naturally smaller it may be sometimes difficult spot potential troubles before they develop too far. Undoubtedly, good hygiene around areas planted with rock plants will help and keeping detritus, especially fallen

Aquilegia flabellata var. *pumila*, a dainty little columbine, is an excellent rock garden and raised bed plant, seeding around happily in many gardens.

leaves, away from plants is important for it can harbor various pests and diseases.

If, like me, you hate the use—especially the overuse—of pesticides and other chemicals in the garden, then vigilance is the best practice, although there are increasing numbers of more natural and biological controls on the market today. Making a garden a good place for wildlife can have a significant effect on pests, for predatory insects such as ladybirds (ladybugs), various birds, and even toads are excellent at seeking out and devouring a wide range of pests.

. . . .

Even concrete, once weathered and carefully constructed, can provide perfect raised beds or large troughs, like this one at the Old Vicarage, East Ruston, Norfolk.

Slugs and snails often lurk under leafy plants or in rock crevices and can be a real nuisance, especially to newly planted young specimens. They are especially troublesome with seedlings, even seeking them out in cold frames and greenhouses. Clean cultivation will help reduce the problem. Birds will clear out quite a few slugs and snails from the garden, but undoubtedly one of the best methods of control is to go into the garden in the evening or early morning and pick them off by hand and dispose of them.

Along with the slugs and snails, aphids are perhaps the most widespread garden pests. Aphids suck the plant's sap, resulting in contorted and yellowing growth and reduced vigor. On small plants like rock plants this can

be devastating. There are many different remedies on the market ranging from systemic sprays to eco-friendly options. Ladybirds can be very beneficial, and the grubs in particular will eat large numbers of aphids as they roam over the plants. In addition, some aphids cause problems by infesting the roots or crown of the plant: unseen they can cause a lot of damage. Aphids and other sap-sucking insects may also transfer viruses from plant to plant; primula species are particularly vulnerable, but other plants can also be prone.

The vine weevil is an insidious pest. Telltale crescent-shaped bites in leaf and petal margins, made by the adult weevil, may indicate trouble. The grubs often lurk belowground creating havoc, and it may be too late for the plant by the time the warning signs appear aboveground. Badly affected plants are best removed and any cuttings taken, the rest destroyed. At the same time, it is wise to scoop out the soil where the plant grew and destroy or sterilize it, as some grubs are almost certain to remain in the compost.

Mice and voles can be a problem by eating buds and stealing fruit. They can be especially troublesome in frames and alpine houses and can devastate pots of newly sown seed. Humane and less humane traps and poison baits are widely available, although a friendly cat can do just as well.

Many birds are very beneficial in the garden; however, some will peck at rock garden plants or pull off flowerbuds. In severe cases, some sort of scaring device or netting may be the answer. I tend not to grow those plants that are most prone to such irritating damage. After all, there are plenty of other plants from which to choose, and birds are such an important component of any garden.

Mildew is not a huge problem on rock garden plants, but both downy and powdery types may attack seedlings, especially if they are kept too moist or were too densely sown in the first place. Damping-off is caused by *Pythium debaryanum*, a soil-borne fungus that attacks seedlings at soil level and causes them to collapse. Infected plants are best destroyed and the compost discarded. Under glass, rock plants and the majority of seedlings require ample ventilation and this will help ward off potential mildew problems. In the glasshouse, botrytis may be problematic, being especially prevalent in cool, damp summers. Botrytis infection starts as small orange or yellow spots on leaves, buds, and petals. These become gradually larger until much of the surface is enveloped in a gray mould. In severe cases some chemical control will have to be resorted to, otherwise the plants will be killed.

Rots can cause trouble with rock plants in the open garden as well as those grown under glass. The rock plants most at risk are cushion or hummock formers or those with soft woolly or velvety rosettes. The first sign of problems may be the collapse of all or part of the plant, by which time all may well be lost. Under glass, cleanliness around plants and excellent ventilation will help alleviate any problems. In the open garden a wet autumn or winter are critical times. A cloche or pane of glass placed over vulnerable plants will help ward of crown rot by keeping the neck of the plant relatively dry. Adequate rock chips placed around the vulnerable necks of plants will also help.

Viruses can affect many plants but are not

A colorful display of alpines on a low raised bed in the Dell Garden, Bressingham, the garden of the late Alan Bloom, one of England's most famous and flamboyant gardeners.

especially prevalent among rock plants. Mottling or streaking of foliage and aborted flowers may indicate virus infection, which is spread principally by aphids and other leaf-sucking insects, although some are undoubtedly transferred by hand or by dirty knives or secateurs or pruning shears. Plants that are obviously virus-infected are best destroyed.

Deadheading and Seed Collecting

REMOVING DEAD FLOWERS, withered leaves, and dying stems is all part of the gardener's annual routine. Some gardeners methodically snip off stems once they have flowered, but I am not one of those. I like to see the developing seedheads and some, like those of the pulsatillas, geums, and thrifts (*Armeria*), have decorative fruits that provide interest well after the plants have ceased flowering. For many rock plants it is impractical to deadhead, as the flowers are held close to or among the foliage; however, deadheading of plants like pansies and violas certainly helps prolong the flowering season, the plant putting its energy into producing more flowers rather than fruits.

An important consideration is whether you want seed of a particular plant, in which case fading flowers have to be tolerated until the fruits have developed and the seed can be collected. Seed collecting from your own plants is a fulfilling pastime, especially of the scarcer plants in your collection. A word of caution here, though: seed from an individual cannot always be expected to come true to type, and the offspring may be quite variable. Certain rock plants hybridize very readily in the garden, particularly if several different ones are grown in close proximity. This applies especially to some plants, including pinks (*Dianthus*), columbines (*Aquilegia*), pasque flowers (*Pulsatilla*), toadflaxes (*Linaria*), violets and pansies (*Viola*), and some saxifrages and campanulas. So seed needs to be collected with caution. Having said this, hybrid seed can sometimes produce some very interesting plants. For many rock plants seed will produce fairly consistent results and even some named cultivars will produce predominantly, if not one hundred percent, similar individuals.

Collected seed should be thoroughly dried before being stored. It can be placed in envelopes that are clearly marked on the outside as to their contents and date of collection. Packeted seed can be stored in a dry cool place until it is required. Many gardeners place the packets in seal-tight plastic containers and put these in a domestic refrigerator. The viability of seed varies a great deal from plant to plant and depends on the storage conditions. While some certainly needs to be sown fairly soon after harvesting (at the latest by the following spring) others will keep quite happily for several years without apparent loss of viability. Many members of the primrose family (Primulaceae) fit in the first category, while poppies (*Papaver*) fit the second. Normally, plants produce far more seed than is required, but excess seed makes excellent gifts for gardening friends or for seed exchanges.

Propagation

REARING YOUR OWN plants is a rewarding pastime in itself. Apart from saving money, it can provide plenty of healthy young plants, not only for your own garden but as gifts or barter with like-minded gardening friends or even for local plant sales. Some say that you are only a true gardener if you raise your own plants from seed or by other means. However, it is not always possible or practical to propagate your own plants. If you just want a few, then it is easier to go down to the local nursery or garden center to purchase them.

Seed

Although the seed of some rock plants is best sown the moment ripe, most will be fine sown in late winter or early spring. A good sterile seed compost and clean pots are essential requirements for success. Always sow thinly and topdress sown pots with very fine grit, which will protect the seeds and help keep them moist. Sown pots can be placed in a shaded or partly shaded cold frame or greenhouse to await germination. Apart from bulbous subjects, most seedlings are best pricked out into individual pots the moment they have produced one or two true leaves. Many rock plants are large enough to be planted in the garden toward the end of their first summer, otherwise they must wait until the following spring.

Many named cultivars do not come true from seed or may be sterile, so that cuttings or division are the answer. It is also important to remember that, although many rock plants come true to type from seed, others (especially hybrids and selections) will probably not: the results will be mixed, some will be rubbish best quickly discarded, and some may produce excellent plants.

Cuttings

Cuttings provide an excellent way of increasing stock if you cannot be bothered with the fiddle of sowing seed. While seed can provide far too many plants on occasions, cuttings can be regulated to provide the number you want. Cuttings can generally be taken any time from midsummer until early autumn. Hygiene again is critical to success. Although a heated propagating frame is important to some growers, it is not essential for success and many manage very well with simple pots and plastic bags. The key to success is using clean pots and a good gritty mix and being careful not to overwater. Cuttings should be potted on the moment they have produced a good root system.

Division

For clump or carpeting rock plants that root down freely, division is a ready means of increasing stock. This can generally be undertaken before the plants come into growth in the spring or after they have ceased growing in late summer and early autumn. Division, like cuttings, is a fine way of keeping plants growing vigorously and in good health.

Types of Rock Garden Plants

Herbaceous Perennials

One of the largest groups of rock plants, herbaceous perennials are those that die down each season, flowering on the current season's shoots. They in fact merge with larger herbaceous perennials in the garden, indeed many familiar perennials such as anemones, campanulas, gentians, hypericums, and salvias range from smaller species ideal for the rock garden, raised bed, or container to the larger ones seen in the general flower border. Easy and first-rate rock plants in this category are *Aquilegia* species, *Campanula carpatica*, *Gentiana septemfida*, *Geranium subcaulescens*, *Hacquetia epipactis*, and *Incarvillea himalayensis*.

Cushion Plants

Many high-mountain plants form cushions, which come in various shapes and sizes from small neat, symmetrical buns to large irregular hummocks. They can be soft, hard, or spiny to the touch, rather open in growth or dense. The flowers can be solitary and held close to the cushion or they can be carried on stalks well above the foliage. The foliage of cushion plants is generally aggregated into rosettes that are crammed together in the cushion. Many different genera have evolved the cushion habit, which is perfectly adapted to extreme mountain conditions; however, the cushion habit is not confined to high-altitude rock plants, for many examples can be found from low altitudes, especially in those with a Mediterranean or continental climate. Typical genera with cushion-forming species are *Alyssum, Androsace, Arabis, Draba, Saxifraga*, and *Sempervivum*. Cushion rock plants often make ideal trough and container plants.

Matted Rock Plants

Another common adaptation among mountain plants is ground-hugging mats, which spread over or between the rocks or in stony meadows. Some matted plants spread and root down as they go (making propagation relatively simple), while others radiate from a single crown. Typical mat-forming plants include *Androsace studiosorum, Houstonia caerulea, Pratia pedunculata*, and species of *Thymus*.

Rosette Plants

Many rock plants form distinctive and prominent leaf rosettes, sometimes solitary or more commonly with a number of leaf rosettes crammed together. In the most spectacular case, like *Saxifraga longifolia*, the rosettes are extremely handsome and regularly symmetrical. In this instance, the rosette builds in size for several years before the plant flowers, seeds, then dies. Commonly grown rock plants of rosette habit include *Haberlea rhodopensis, Horminum pyrenaicum, Lewisia cotyledon*, and *Ramonda myconi*. Many rosette plants of this type make excellent plants for rock or wall crevices.

....

A small corner of a May rock garden, with the rounded evergreen bush of *Daphne ×susannae* 'Cheriton' bursting into bloom. In front *Polygala calcarea* 'Lillet' and the deep blue trumpets of *Gentiana acaulis* contrast form and color with the daphne.

Annuals

Although some annuals are found among rock plants, they are not particularly common and certainly very few seem to find a space in the rock garden. However, some are easy-to-grow and cheerful plants that can often be used as space fillers for summer interest. *Limnathes douglasii* and *Omphalodes linifolia* fit this category perfectly. Annuals may often self-sow

but excess plants are readily removed and discarded. Unlike the others categories listed here, direct sowing where the plants are to flower is advised.

Dwarf Shrubs

Many dwarf shrubs, both deciduous and evergreen, are often incorporated into the rock garden, indeed they can form important features and focal points. Supreme among the dwarf shrubs are daphnes, dwarf conifers, and the smaller rhododendrons, the last two of which are very large and complex categories with numerous named cultivars. Although dwarf conifers and rhododendrons are excluded from this volume, their importance should not be

overlooked. Other first-rate dwarf shrubs include *Deutzia gracilis* 'Nikko', *Erinacea anthyllis*, *Genista lydia*, *Polygala chamaebuxus*, and *Salix lanata*.

Bulbs

Bulbous plants, including those with rhizomes and tubers, form an important part of the mountain flora and are well covered in a number of excellent books. The smaller bulbs are very useful adjuncts to other plants in the rock

A medley of spring color in the author's garden with *Corydalis* (*Pseudofumaria*) *ochroleuca* in harmony with *Geranium tuberosum*, with daphnes (*D.* ×*napolitana* and *D.* ×*burkwoodii*) in the background.

garden. Many produce overbearing foliage that can look untidy, especially in the rock garden, and may swamp other plants; however, species of *Crocus*, *Galanthus*, *Iris*, *Scilla*, the smaller narcissi, and tulips look very fine in the rock garden setting and provide plenty of interest, especially in the spring. Bulbs in the true sense belong to the monocotyledon division of the flowering plants and are not covered in this volume. However, there is a range of dicotyledonous tuberous plants that perfectly suit the rock garden, including *Corydalis*, *Cyclamen*, *Eranthis*, some anemones, and buttercups (*Ranunculus*) and some of these will be found in the A to Z section of the book.

Companion Plants

ROCK GARDEN PLANTS work very well in association with other plants. Many dwarf shrubs help to give emphasis to plantings. On acid soils rhododendrons are greatly prized, and

Spring bulbs, especially the smaller ones, are ideal companions to the coarser rock plants: *Euphorbia myrsinites* spills in front of hyacinths and various daffodils, making a colorful and cheerful scene.

there are numerous small species and culti-vars that fit into the rock garden landscape very well. On neutral or alkaline soils daphnes (several are included in the A to Z section) are suitable substitutes and equally effective.

In addition, there is a host of small conifers highly suited to rock gardening. Many are evergreen, adding height and shape to rock gardens and raised beds, while the smallest are ideal for punctuating troughs and other con-tainers. Be sure that you acquire genuinely dwarf conifers, for some will quickly outgrow their allotted space.

Ferns are a very important adjunct to the rock gardener's menu. Indeed there are numer-ous small alpine or mountain ferns ideal for combining with rock garden plants, especially on raised beds and in troughs and other con-tainers. Many small ferns are excellent crevice plants, while some of the larger ones are good companion plants in the rock or scree garden or in the woodland border.

Bulbs also play a very important role in the rock garden, while many can also be grown in containers. Many of the larger bulbs are too gross to mix with rock plants, as are those with coarse large leaves that can easily swamp neigh-boring plants. Of the true bulbs (monocoty-ledons) the finest genera for use in combina-tion with rock plants are *Allium* (smaller ones), *Chionodoxa, Crocus, Erythronium, Fritillaria, Galanthus, Iris* (smaller ones), *Leucojum, Lil-ium* (smaller ones), *Narcissus* (smaller ones), *Scilla*, and *Tulipa* (smaller ones). Of the dicoty-ledonous tuberous plants, *Anemone, Cyclamen, Eranthis, Oxalis*, and *Ranunculus* figure prom-inently and several of these are mentioned in the A to Z section.

Rock Garden Plants A to Z

Achillea

A genus of composites (Compositae or Asteraceae) generally with aromatic, dissected or toothed foliage, usually with numerous small, rayed flowerheads crammed into flat heads. Most are too large and coarse for the rock garden but several of the smaller are worth consideration, particularly as they flower in summer and are highly attractive to insects.

They thrive in full sun in a gritty, well-drained compost. Propagation is easy by division in early spring or after flowering. Seed sown in early spring germinates freely but can give very mixed results, especially as the species tend to hybridize in the garden environment.

Achillea ×lewisii

A charming little hybrid between two European species, *A. clavennae* and *A. tomentosa*. Plants form small tufts to 25 cm (10 in) tall in flower, with narrow, finely fringed, gray or silvery gray leaves. Flowerheads small, but in broad corymbs up to 5 cm (2 in) across, cream to yellow or whitish; early to midsummer. Prefers a dry gritty soil in plenty of sunshine. 'King Alfred' rather deeper yellow flowers borne on a somewhat smaller plant, fading with time; 'King Edward' yellow aging to cream.

Adonis

A wonderful buttercup relation (Ranunculaceae) with striking white, yellow, or red, multi-petaled flowers. There are about 20 species scattered in Europe eastward through Asia as far as Japan. Some are arable field annuals but the finest are clump-forming herbaceous perennials. Adonises, or pheasant's-eyes as they are sometimes called (this name refers to the annual red-flowered species), have finely divided

Opposite: *Daphne arbuscula*

Achillea ×lewisii 'King Alfred'

Adonis 'Fukujukai' (syn. *A. amurensis* 'Fukujukai')

A sterile hybrid between *A. amurensis* and *A. ramosa* originating in Japan but widely available elsewhere. It forms neat clumps in time to about 25 cm (10 in) tall in flower, with bipinnately divided leaves bearing narrow-elliptic, toothed segments. The bowl-shaped flowers appear with the developing foliage and are golden yellow with a bronze reverse, about 5 cm (2 in) across, with up to 30 petals; early to midspring. Requires a leafy soil and dappled shade to prosper.

Adonis vernalis

Götland and central Europe east to the Urals. A clump-forming plant to 20 cm (8 in) tall in flower, generally taller in fruit, with bright green, bipinnately dissected foliage, with linear segments. Flowers saucer-shaped to flat, bright yellow, to 7.5 cm (3 in) across, with up to 20 elliptical petals; early to midspring. A sumptuous plant when well grown, requiring a sunny, sheltered position for its flowers to open fully.

leaves and mostly solitary flowers. The fruit is a collection of small achenes.

They are excellent plants for the rock garden or semi-woodland conditions, the smaller for raised beds or pan culture, a well-drained compost being their chief requirement. Adonises can be propagated from seed, preferably sown the moment it is ripe or in late winter. The clump-forming perennials can be divided with care just before they come into growth in early spring or, alternatively, after flowering.

Aethionema

A beautiful genus of cresses with some 70 species scattered in the Mediterranean region and western Asia, where they are predominately plants of rocky habitats. Aethionemas range from evergreen subshrubs to perennials and a few annuals, with simple, narrow, gray- or blue-green leaves. The four-parted flowers, typical of crucifers (Cruciferae), are usually numerous, borne in dense to lax racemes. The fruit is a two-parted elliptic or heart-shaped capsule.

Aethionema ×warleyensis

Aethionemas are ideal for the rock garden or raised bed, with the smaller more discreet perennial species making excellent trough or sink plants. They thrive in most ordinary well drained soils or compost, especially if limestone chippings are added. Plants can be trimmed back to the foliage after flowering, unless, that is, the seed is required. Propagation from seed sown in late winter or early spring will produce excellent results. Alternatively, especially good forms can be raised from cuttings of vegetative shoots taken in the summer.

Aethionema grandiflora (syn. A. pulchellum)

Turkey, Iraq, and northern Iran. A woody-based, tufted perennial to 30 cm (1 ft) tall with erect to ascending stems bearing numerous alternate, gray-green, narrow-oblong leaves, 10–15 mm (⅕–⅗ in) long. Flowers pink, 10–18 mm (⅖–⅔ in) across, borne in long racemes in late spring and early summer, sometimes later.

Aethionema saxatile (includes A. graecum)

Southern Europe, Turkey. A small rather lax, spreading perennial to 15 cm (6 in) tall in flower. Lower leaves oval but the upper ones progressively more lanceolate or linear, rather thick and fleshy, glaucous. Flowers white or pink, 5–10 mm (⅕–⅖ in) across, borne in rounded racemes that elongate as successive flowers open; spring and early summer.

Aethionema ×warleyensis

The parentage of this hybrid is uncertain, although it is thought to be A. armenum and A. grandiflorum. The plant is a woody-based, bushy perennial to 15 cm (6 in) tall with glau-

cous linear foliage to 1 cm (⅖ in) long. The racemes of rich rose-pink flowers are carried in profusion in late spring and early summer, each flower about 1 cm (⅖ in) across. This hybrid first appeared spontaneously in the garden at Warley Place in Essex, the home of the distinguished gardener Ellen Willmott. The plant is usually sold under the name 'Warley Rose'. A darker form with crimson magenta flowers, 'Warley Ruber' is sometimes available.

Alchemilla

A large and complicated genus with at least 250 species confined primarily to the temperate Northern Hemisphere, but with some species found further south on the higher mountains in the tropics, especially Africa. They are tufted to creeping perennials and evergreen or deciduous, with attractive rounded to kidney-shaped, palmately lobed, toothed leaves. The tiny yellow or greenish yellow, four-parted flowers are generally borne in large clusters just clear of, or amid, the foliage.

Alchemillas are excellent plants for the rock garden or border, where their foliage is just as attractive as the flowers, sometimes more so. Most thrive in any well-drained soil in a sunny or partly shaded site. Propagation is easiest by division of mature clumps, although self-sown seedlings will often appear in the garden.

Alchemilla alpina

Northern Europe south to the Alps and Pyrenees, Greenland. A tufted perennial with a tough, rather leathery base, to 20 cm (8 in) tall. Leaves rounded in outline, 2–5 cm (⅘–2 in) across, digitately lobed, with five or seven oblong lobes that are deep green above but silvery with silky hairs beneath. Flowers in small, branched clusters, yellowish green; late spring and early summer. Much confused with *A. conjuncta* in cultivation and rarer in cultivation.

Alchemilla conjuncta

Southwestern Alps, Jura Mountains. Rather similar to the previous species, but a larger, more robust plant to 30 cm (1 ft), with larger, less deeply divided leaves with seven lobes. Flowers numerous, yellow-green, in dense clusters; late spring and early summer.

Alchemilla mollis

Europe. A very beautiful plant, to 40 cm (16 in), suitable for the larger rock garden but also an excellent border plant. Leaves rounded, grayish or bluish green, softly hairy, to 10 cm (4 in) across, with 9 or 11 shallow lobes. Flowers yellow, in large, branched clusters during late

Alchemilla alpina

Alchemilla mollis

spring and summer. Looks particularly effective close to water.

Alyssum

A genus of about 150 species in the cress family (Cruciferae or Brassicaceae) scattered in the Mediterranean region, western Asia, and Siberia. The most desirable are small tufted mountain plants, but the genus does also contain small annual species of little interest to gardeners. The perennial species have small gray-green or blue-green, simple leaves with forked hairs. The flowers are usually yellow and are four-parted, being followed typically by small, two-parted, elliptical to globose fruit capsules. The well-known yellow alyssum of gardens has been transferred to the genus *Aurinia*.

These plants are best grown in a rock garden or on a raised bed in a gritty well-drained, preferably alkaline, soil in full sun. Seed can be sown the moment it is ripe or in early spring. Alternatively, late summer cuttings afford a good means of increasing particularly fine forms.

Alyssum montanum

Central and southern Europe. A rather variable plant often spreading to about 25 cm (10 in) across, occasionally more, or more upright. Leaves oblong to spathulate, to 2 cm (⅘ in) long, with a variable number of white hairs, the uppermost leaves more linear. Flowers bright yellow, 4–6 mm (⅙–¼ in) across, with neatly notched petals, borne in dense clusters at first, but these elongate as the fruits develop. 'Berrgold' golden, a particularly fine and compact form.

Alyssum spinosum

Alyssum spinosum (syn. *Ptilotrichum spinosum*)

Northern Africa, southwestern Europe. An intricately branched, softly prickly, mound-forming subshrub to 50 cm (20 in) across. Leaves lanceolate to obovate to 2.5 cm (1 in) long, gray-green, adorned with scaly, silvery hairs. Flowers borne in great abundance in short racemes just clear of, or among, the foliage, white to pink, each flower only 6 mm (¼ in) across. 'Roseum' has rich rose-pink flowers.

Anagallis

A genus of some 20 species primarily in the Mediterranean region and tropical Africa, several being widespread weeds of cultivation; these include the well-known annual scarlet pimpernel, *Anagallis arvensis*, with flowers in scarlet or occasionally blue or pink. In the same family as *Lysimachia* (Primulaceae), the plants bear small, opposite, sometimes alternate, untoothed leaves and solitary, long-stalked flowers from the upper leaf axils; these are rather flat or campanulate and five-parted. The fruit is a small many-seeded capsule that dehisces by means of a small cap.

The two included below are readily raised from seed or cuttings. *Anagallis tenella*, in particular, roots down readily, and self-rooted pieces are easily detached and grown on.

Anagallis monellii (syn. *A. linifolia*)

Southwestern Europe. A tufted to matted evergreen perennial to 20 cm (8 in) tall, with deep green lanceolate to linear leaves up to 15 mm (3/5 in) long, opposite or whorled on the stem. Flowers produced in abundance, usually deep gentian blue, sometimes paler, pink or red, 10–15 mm (⅖–⅗ in) across; summer. Inhabits dry, sunny places in the wild, often on rather sandy soils, and this is what it needs in the garden. 'Wesnacomp' (Blue Compact), 'Blue Light', and 'Skylover' are three good blue selections; brick red 'Waterperry' is sometimes available, as is the scarlet-flowered 'Sunrise'. As with all pimpernels, the flowers open widely in bright light but close by late afternoon.

Anagallis tenella

Western Europe, including England. Very different from the previous, being a prostrate carpeter of boggy habitats in the wild. Shoots very slender, readily rooting down, bearing opposite or alternate, elliptic to rounded, rather pale green leaves, 5–10 mm (⅕–⅖ in) long. Flowers flesh pink, erect, narrow-campanulate, 10 mm (⅖ in) long; late spring and summer. 'Studland' has rich pink flowers.

Anchusa

A genus of about 35 species of herbs mostly too large for rock garden conditions. They are bristly members of the borage family (Boraginaceae), mostly with forget-me-not blue flowers. The species range from annuals to biennials and short-lived perennials. The smallest species, *A. cespitosa* (often misspelled *caespitosa*), is an ideal trough plant but most often seen in a pot in the alpine house or frame.

Anchusa cespitosa requires a sunny position in a well-drained gritty, alkaline compost.

Anagallis monellii

Anagallis tenella 'Studland'

If grown outside, it is advisable to place overhead protection, such as a pane of glass or similar, to keep off excess winter wet, otherwise the crown of the plant is prone to rotting. Propagation is from seed, if available, but more often from root cuttings in late winter or rosette cutting in the summer, being careful not to overwater either until a good root system has formed.

Anchusa cespitosa

Western Crete. A truly delightful little tufted perennial not more than 7.5 cm (3 in) tall, with rosettes of bristly, deep green, linear leaves to 10 cm (4 in) long, which mostly lie flat on the ground. Flowers deep blue, 12 mm (½ in) across, borne in dense clusters in the center of each leaf rosette in late spring and early summer.

Androsace

Commonly known as rock jasmines, this important rock garden genus contains slightly over 100 species, a number among the very choicest of rock plants for the connoisseur to grow. They range from annuals to biennials and perennials, many of the perennials forming mats or cushions. The majority have small entire or variously lobed or toothed leaves in rosettes, in some these are crammed together into tight hummocks. The flowers can be solitary or several, or again clusters borne in umbels on a common stalk. The individual flowers vary in color from white to pink or purple, rarely yellow or red. The corollas are rotate, with a short tube and five spreading, rounded lobes, leaving a tiny hole, like a forget-me-not flower,

. . . .

Anchusa cespitosa

in the center, this often yellow or orange margined. The fruit is a small multiseeded capsule.

The easy androsaces are excellent and beautiful eye-catching plants for the rock garden and raised bed. The tight cushion species make superb plants for pot culture in an alpine house or for troughs or blocks of tufa in the open garden. They all require a well-drained gritty compost in sun or part shade and need to be carefully protected from aphids (a regular systemic insecticide is recommended) and excessive winter wet. Any dead, dying, or infected shoots should be carefully removed as soon as they are spotted. Seed should be sown the moment it is ripe or as quickly as possible after and kept in a cold frame. Cuttings can be struck in a pure gritty sand, using single rosette shoots or small tufts.

Androsace alpina

European Alps. A neat cushion-forming plant up to 25 cm (10 in) across, rarely much more, with numerous crammed, green or gray-green, globular leaf rosettes. Leaves elliptic to linear, 5–10 mm (⅕–⅖ in) long. Flowers one or several per leaf rosette, on very short stalks, pink or

white with a yellow eye, 7–9 mm (⅓ in) across; spring. A fine plant for trough or raised bed culture, but prone sometimes to die off in patches.

Androsace carnea

Alps and Pyrenees. A tufted or cushion-forming plant to 15 cm (6 in) tall in flower, with rosettes of stiff, narrow-elliptic, pointed leaves to 30 mm (1⅕ in) long, generally smaller. Flowers pink or rose, 5–8 mm (⅕–⅓ in) across, borne in umbels above the foliage in spring.

Androsace alpina

Androsace carnea subsp. *laggeri*

Subsp. *laggeri*, from the Pyrenees, is the prettiest variant with magenta-pink flowers and needle leaves only 10 mm (⅖ in) long; subsp. *rosea* from the Massif Central, France, with rose-pink, largish flowers and leaves to 25 mm (1 in) long, is the easiest in gardens and will often self-sow.

Androsace hirtella

Southern France (Pyrenees). This species forms compact rounded, gray-green cushions to 10 cm (4 in) across composed of numerous tight rosettes of linear to oblong leaves, about 8 mm (⅓ in) long on average, covered in erect hairs. Each rosette produces one or two very short-stalked white flowers, 5–7 mm (⅕–¼ in) across in spring. One of the best of the cushion species for growing outdoors on tufa or in a trough; however, any batch of seedlings will produce a range of forms, some with good-sized flowers, other poorer and best discarded. Often confused in cultivation with hybrids between this species and the far more difficult to cultivate *A. cylindrica*, an inhabitant of the western Pyrenees.

Androsace laevigata (syn. *Douglasia laevigata*)

Northwestern United States; Oregon and Washington. Plants form a lax to rather dense mat of flattish rosettes of dark green, glossy, oblanceolate leaves, 5–20 mm (⅕–⅘ in) long, sometimes toothed on the margin. The deep pink to deep rose red flowers are relatively large, 10–18 mm (⅖–⅔ in) across, have an orange throat, each umbel bearing up to 10 flowers on a common stalk to 7.5 cm (3 in) long; spring and early summer. 'Gothenburg' compact and richly colored.

Androsace lanuginosa

Western Himalaya. A mat-forming species making lax plants by means of leafy, reddish stolons that terminate in a open leaf rosette, spreading to 50 cm (20 in). Leaves elliptic, to 2.5 cm (1 in) long, gray-green, silky with hairs. Flowers lilac-pink with a greenish yellow eye, 8–12 mm (⅓–½ in) across, borne in umbels on a common stalk 5–10 cm (2–4 in) high. Var. *leichtlinii* is more vigorous, forming tangled mats to 90 cm (3 ft) across. Both flower in late spring and summer, sometimes into early autumn.

Androsace mucronifolia

Western Himalaya, western Tibet (Xizang). A mat or low hummock-forming species to 30 cm (1 ft) across, composed of numerous rather rounded deep green rosettes each up to 10 cm (⅖ in) across. Leaves rather leathery, elliptic to obovate, not more than 6 mm (¼ in) long, adorned with stiff cilia along the papery margin. Flowers white to deep pink, with a yellow eye, 6–8 mm (¼–⅓ in) across, borne in small umbels of up to six on a common stalk shortly above the rosettes; spring and early summer.

Androsace sempervivoides

Western Himalaya. Closely related to *A. mucronifolia* but a stoloniferous plant with more open, flattish rosettes to 2.5 cm (1 in) across, the leaves broad-spathulate, to 14 mm (⅗ in) long. Up to 10 pink or pinkish mauve flowers are borne in an umbel on a common stalk up to

7.5 cm (3 in) long, each flower 8–12 mm (⅓–⅖ in) across and delightfully scented; spring and early summer. An excellent scree bed plant for full sun. 'Susan Joan' a compact and well-colored selection.

Androsace studiosorum

Western and central Himalaya. A mat-forming stoloniferous perennial with both winter and summer rosettes, the former dense and surrounded by a ruff of larger old dead leaves, the

name *A. sarmentosa* in cultivation. 'Chumbyi' and 'Doksa' too are fine, floriferous selections.

Androsace villosa

Western Europe eastward to western Asia and the Himalaya. A quite variable plant but in cultivation forming grayish mats or low cushions to 20 cm (8 in) across, occasionally more, composed of numerous globular rosettes. Leaves linear to elliptic, to 12 mm (½ in) long, tipped with long whitish hairs. Flowers white with a yellow eye, sometimes aging pink with a red eye, 6–10 mm (¼–⅖ in) across, borne in small umbels on a common stalk to 3 cm (1⅕ in) long; spring and early summer. An excellent raised bed or scree plant, best protected from excessive winter wet in the open garden.

Anemone

A moderate-sized genus with about 120 species found in most temperate regions of the world, especially those of the Northern Hemisphere. They range from vigorous clump-forming perennials to dainty woodland and alpine species. Anemones have tuberous or rhizomatous rootstocks and simple, pinnately or palmately divided leaves. The flowers are either solitary or a number borne in an umbel; in either case they are subtended by a ruff of leaf-like bracts. The anemone flower is petalless, but the sepals, 5 to 20 in number, are colored and petal-like. The center of the flower is dominated by a boss of showy anthers and the ovary. The fruits, or achenes, are borne in a tight head.

Anemones are generally easy to grow: the smaller ones are ideal for the rock garden,

summer rosettes 2–3 cm (⅘–1⅕ in) across, with small outer leaves (from the winter rosette) to 16 mm (⅔ in) long, while the inner leaves are much larger and elliptic-lanceolate, to 70 mm (2⅘ in) long. Flowers pink to deep rose, 7–9 mm (about ⅓ in) across, up to 20 in an umbel on a common stalk up to 15 cm (6 in) long. One of the finest and most colorful androsaces for the average garden. *Androsace studiosorum* is often found under the incorrect

Anemone blanda

Anemone magellanica

raised beds, and containers, although some of the Asian species require specialist treatment in the bulb frame or greenhouse. Those listed here can be propagated readily from seed, which is best sown the moment it is ripe. Seedlings are slow to develop and are best left undisturbed for the first year.

Anemone apennina

Southern Europe (Corsica east to Greece). A colony-forming rhizomatous perennial to 20 cm (8 in) tall in flower. The basal long-stalked leaves often appear after the flowers and are trilobed, the three main lobes toothed and further lobed, hairy beneath. The flowers are solitary, bright blue or occasionally white, 2.5–3.5 cm (1–1⅖ in) across, with 8 to 14 sepals; spring. Var. *albiflora* white. Double-flowered forms are also available.

Anemone blanda

Balkans and Turkey. Similar to *A. apennina*, but a more substantial plant with stouter tubers and blunter leaves that are glabrous beneath. Flowers somewhat larger, 3–5 in (1⅕–2 in) across with 12–18 sepals; late winter and spring. A plant of rocky slopes and open woodland in the wild, where it is a harbinger of spring. In cultivation it is very easy, widely available, and often acquired as a dried tuber from garden centers and nurseries. *Anemone blanda* can form substantial colonies in time, so is unsuitable for smaller areas. 'Atrocaerulea' deep blue; 'Blue Mist' pale blue; 'Pink Star' medium pink; 'Radar' bright pink with a white center; 'Violet Star' violet; 'White Splendour' white, extra-large.

Anemone magellanica (often included in *A. multifida*)

South America. An upright perennial forming clumps to 30 cm (1 ft) tall in flower. The tufts of basal leaves are deep green and hairy, trilobed, with lobed and toothed segments. Flowers three or four borne on stiff, erect, hairy stems, white to cream, occasionally greenish, 2.5–4 cm (1–1⅗ in) across, with most often six sepals; late spring and early summer. Fruitheads woolly, globose. Readily grown from seed, but it does not respond to moving or division once established.

Anemone narcissiflora

Central and southern Europe eastward into western Asia. A variable, rather robust, tufted perennial to 40 cm (16 in) tall in flower. Leaves palmately lobed, with the prime segments further divided, deep green, somewhat hairy. Flowers in umbels of up to eight, occasionally more, each white, sometimes pink-flushed outside, to 4 cm (1⅗ in) across, with five or six oblong sepals; late spring and summer. Not always easy to please in the garden but best in a pocket in the rock garden. Young plants establish far better than older or pot-bound specimens. However, it is a very beautiful anemone in its larger-flowered forms and worth every effort to grow.

Anemonella

A North American genus containing a single species that looks superficially like a rather delicate anemone. The species is a woodland plant and requires a moist, humus-rich soil and dappled shade in the garden. It also makes a very fine pot or container specimen. For best results the seed should be sown the moment it is ripe or, alternatively, stored for an early-spring sowing. Plants can also be divided when dormant, this being the best means of ensuring propagation of good forms.

Anemonella thalictroides

Eastern North America. A clump-forming plant spreading in time to some 30 cm (1 ft) across, 10–15 cm (4–6 in) tall. Leaves olive green, biternate, with up to nine ovate, shallowly three-lobed leaflets, all borne on a slender stalk. Flowers in lax clusters with a whorl of six leaflet-like bracts beneath, about 20–25

Anemone narcissiflora

Anemonella thalictroides

mm (⅕–1 in) across; tepals white or pink, 5 to 10, but often 6, oval and spreading; spring. 'Betty Blake' double, cream; 'Cameo' double, pale rose-pink, slightly greenish in the center; 'Oscar Schoaf' ('Schoaf's Double') double symmetrical pompons, rose pink.

Anthemis

A genus with about 100 species centered on Europe but extending into East Africa and western Asia. They are perennials and shrubs, some cushion-forming, with finely dissected leaves. Flowerheads are daisies with white or yellow rays.

The species described below requires a sunny warm site in which to succeed and some protection from excessive winter wet. Propagation is from seed sown in early spring or by basal cuttings of strong new growth in late spring and summer. Trimming back plants after flowering helps to promote a good bushy plant.

Anthemis punctata subsp. *cupaniana*
(syn. *Anthemis cupaniana*)
Sicily. A woody-based perennial to 60 cm (2 ft) across, forming a lax low mound. Leaves silky with whitish hairs, bipinnately lobed, 5–12.5 cm (2–5 in) long. Flowerheads with a yellow disk and pure white rays, 5–6 cm (2–2⅖ in) across; late spring and summer. The type species, *A. punctata* subsp. *punctata*, native to North Africa, is a larger, coarser, plant less suitable for the rock garden.

Anthyllis

Collectively known as the kidney vetches, the genus has some 20 species ranging from the Canary Islands and Europe to western Asia and North Africa. They include annuals, perennials, and subshrubs that thrive in cultivation on most well-drained soils and full sunshine. The leaves are alternate and generally pinnate with few to many small leaflets, while the typical peaflowers are borne in tight clus-

Anemonella thalictroides 'Betty Blake'

Anthemis punctata subsp. *cupaniana*

ters with stalkless, leaf-like bracts at the base. A light gritty soil and plenty of sunshine are the prime requirements. Plants are best raised from seed sown in late winter or early spring.

Anthyllis montana

Alps and mountains of southern Europe. A tufted, woody-based perennial with spreading to rather sprawling stems making moderately dense clumps to 60 cm (2 ft) across, sometimes more. The leaves, which are mostly crowded at the base of the plant, are pinnate with 17–41 lanceolate leaflets that are silky with hairs all over. The purple flowers, each 10–15 mm (²⁄₅–³⁄₅ in) long, are held in dense globose heads; summer. Subsp. *jacquinii* has pink flowers.

. . . .

Anthyllis montana in a meadow, southern France.

Aphyllanthes

The genus, which has a single species confined to southwestern Europe, is a member of the lily family (Liliaceae) but is sometimes placed in its own family, Aphyllanthaceae. Whatever its family, the species is a delightful and somewhat unusual rock plant that does very well outdoors in the rock garden or raised bed given a gritty well-drained soil, but it is not particularly fussy as to soil type. To flower well, however, it demands a sunny, sheltered warm or even hot position.

Plants deteriorate in response to root disturbance once established, and it is wise to seek out young vigorous plants in the first instance to establish in the garden. However, plants can, with care, be propagated by divi-

sion in spring as plants come into growth or from seed when available.

Aphyllanthes monspeliensis

Portugal and Spain eastward to Italy and Sicily. Plants form rush-like, deep green tufts to 30 cm (1 ft) tall. The leaves are reduced to papery sheaths while the true leaf function is taken on by the slender green stems. The funnel shaped flowers, 2–3 cm (⅘–1⅕ in) across, are produced in small stemless clusters at the tips of some stems, each cluster surrounded by several small reddish brown, overlapping bracts; tepals blue with a deeper midvein, oval, sometimes notched at the apex; summer.

Aphyllanthes monspeliensis

Aquilegia

The columbines are a delightful and deservedly popular genus containing larger herbaceous perennials and small tufted alpines. About 70 species are found right across the Northern Hemisphere at both low and high altitudes. Many of the smaller species make excellent plants for the rock garden, raised bed, troughs, and other containers, reveling in sun or partial shade. Columbines have a basal tuft of generally biternately compound leaves; stem leaves are generally rather few and smaller. The five-parted flowers can be solitary or several borne in a branched inflorescence. The sepals are usually elliptical, spreading and petal-like, the same color as the true petals or different. The inner segments (petals) have a broad limb and are produced backward into a short to long, straight to hooked spur, each flower having five spurs. The fruit consists of a collection of pod-like follicles.

Most columbines are fairly easy to grow, although one or two of the high alpine species have more exacting requirements. A moist, gritty, yet well-drained compost suits the majority. They are best planted out as young plants, for old, pot-bound specimens are often slow to establish. Most species, despite being perennial, tend to be short-lived, and regular raisings from seed are needed to maintain them. However, the species are notoriously promiscuous in the garden and hybrids are very common; some of the hybrids can be very attractive. Seed is best sown in late winter and early spring.

Aquilegia alpina

Alps and northern Apennines. An erect perennial to 70 cm (28 in) tall in flower, often less, with biternate leaves, the leaflets 1–3 cm (⅖–1⅕ in) long, gray-green, usually trilobed. Flowers several, nodding, bright blue, 5–8 cm (2–3⅕ in) across, with straight or slightly curved spurs to 2.5 cm (1 in) long; summer. Often confused with the common columbine, *A. vulgaris*, in gardens, but a more beautiful plant with larger flowers. In the wild it inhabits meadows, rocky places, and woodland margins at 1500–2500 m (5000–8300 ft).

Aquilegia bertolonii

Southeastern France and northern Italy. A dainty species to 25 cm (10 in) tall in flower with biternate leaves, the leaflets often trilobed. Flowers nodding, violet-blue, to 3 cm (1⅕ in) across, up to four per inflorescence, the spurs relatively short, 10–15 mm (⅖–⅗ in) long, often hooked at the tip. Another excellent small species for trough or raised bed culture.

Aquilegia canadensis

Canada and eastern United States. A rather slight plant with slender stems to 40 cm (16 in) tall in flower, with dark green, biternate leaves, the leaflets 1–2 cm (⅖–⅘ in) long. Flowers several per stem, nodding or half-nodding, with

red sepals contrasting with lemon yellow petals and spurs, the spurs straight, about 2 cm (⅘ in) long; summer. A plant of woodlands and rocky places in the wild, requiring dappled shade in the garden. 'Nana' a dwarf form not more than 20 cm (8 in) tall.

Aquilegia ecalcarata (syn. Semiaquilegia ecalcarata)

Western China. A rather elegant, slender-stemmed, short-lived perennial to 40 cm (16 in) tall in flower. Leaves biternate, green, often flushed with purple, the leaflets somewhat lobed, to 2.5 cm (1 in) long. Flowers borne in airy sprays, nodding, purplish red, 2–3 cm (⅘–1⅕ in) wide, the petals pouched or slightly spurred at the base; late spring and summer. 'Flore Pleno' semi-double flowers.

Aquilegia flabellata

Japan, Korea, eastern Russia. Plant to 50 cm (20 in) tall in flower, but variable. Leaves relatively few, with trilobed leaflets up to 4 cm (1⅗ in) long, glaucous, more obviously so beneath. Flowers nodding, rather dumpy, 3–4 cm (1⅕–1⅗ in) across, with bluish purple sepals and cream to white petals, the spurs hooked, 1–1.5 cm (⅖–⅗ in) long; spring. Var. *pumila* is similar but not more than 20 cm (8 in) tall; var. *pumila* forma *alba* ('Nana Alba') pure white. Several series are available. Cameo Series: 'Cameo White', 'Cameo Blue', 'Cameo Blush', 'Cameo Pink and White', 'Cameo Rose'; Jewel Series: 'Amethyst', 'Blue Jewel', 'Pink Jewel', 'Pink Topaz'. Var. *pumila* is an excellent trough and container plant and normally comes true from seed.

Aquilegia flabellata var. *pumila*

Aquilegia formosa

Western North America. Very similar to *A. canadensis*, but flowers broader and with shorter spurs; summer.

Aquilegia pyrenaica

Pyrenees. A dainty species of pastures and rocky places rather like a scaled down version of *A. alpina*, not more than 25 cm (10 in) tall in flower, with small biternate leaves. Flowers nodding, solitary or few in a branched inflorescence, deep blue overall, 3–4 cm (1⅕–1⅗ in) across, with straight spurs up to 2 cm (⅘ in) long; late spring and early summer. An excellent trough or raised bed plant.

Aquilegia saximontana

United States; Colorado. Another small species, not usually exceeding 20 cm (8 in) in height with gray-green, biternate leaves, the leaflets 1–1.5 cm (⅖–⅗ in) long. Flowers half-nodding, 1.5–2.5 cm (⅗–1 in) across, with deep lavender-blue sepals contrasting with the yellowish petals, the spurs slightly curved and hooked, not more than 8 mm (⅓ in) long; late spring and early summer. A very reliable and easy plant for raised beds and troughs, where it will self-sow on occasion.

Arabis

A genus of about 120 species mostly confined to the northern temperate region but extending south into the African mountains. Many are weedy species scarcely worth cultivating, but the genus does contain several first-class perennial rock garden plants. These are tufted

Aquilegia formosa

Aquilegia pyrenaica

to mat-forming plants with most of the leaves in lax basal rosettes, covered in a down of star-shaped (stellate) hairs. The flowers are borne in racemes that elongate as successive flowers open; these are typical four-parted crucifer flowers with separate sepals and petals. The fruit is a long slender pod that splits into two when ripe.

The three listed below are only suitable for the outside garden, where they are among the showiest and most floriferous rock garden plants in the spring. They can be readily grown on most average, well-drained soils and a sunny site. Propagation is from seed, or good color forms are readily increased from rosette cuttings taken in late summer. Division in summer or autumn offers another means of increase. Plants can be clipped back after flowering to keep them in shape.

Arabis alpina subsp. *caucasica*

Caucasus. The most widespread species in cultivation, which makes grayish or whitish mats of rosettes to 60 cm (2 ft) across, sometimes more, but not more than 25 cm (10 in) tall in bloom. The downy leaves are obovate, tapered at the base, to 7.5 cm (3 in) long, and with a few blunt marginal teeth. The racemes of white, 15 mm (3/5 in) flowers are congested at first but gradually become laxer; spring, sometimes a few later flowers. 'Flore Pleno' double white; 'Pink Pearl' medium rose; 'Rosea' deep rose; 'Schneehaube' (SNOWCAP) pure white, large flowers; 'Snowdrop' white; 'Variegata' white, leaves with cream variegations.

Arabis ×arendsii

A widely available plant that is a hybrid between the widely grown and variable *A. alpina* subsp. *caucasica* and the far lesser known Turkish *A. aubrietioides* and intermediate in character. Plants form lax tufts to 20 cm (8 in) tall in flower with leaves rather like those of the former parent and racemes of flowers in various shades of pink; spring. 'Rosabella' soft pink.

Arabis blepharophylla

United States; California. A tufted to cushion-forming plant up to 20 cm (8 in) in height. Leaves oval, often broadest above the middle, downy, usually coarsely toothed, 2– 8 cm (4/5–3 1/5 in) long. Flowers rose-purple, 12–18 mm (1/2–3/4 in) across, borne in lax racemes in spring. 'Frühlingszauber' with richly colored flowers is the most widely grown cultivar.

Arenaria

A moderate sized genus with about 150 species, commonly referred to as sandworts, from northern temperate and arctic regions. Many are weedy annuals or biennials, but some are

Arabis alpina subsp. *caucasica* 'Rosea'

delightful little tufted or mat-forming or cushioned perennials worthy of a place in any rock garden. All sandworts have paired leaves and five-parted (occasionally four-parted) flowers, either solitary or in cymes. The petals are characteristically rounded or elliptic and without a notch or cleft at the apex.

Most species require a well-drained soil, the choicer ones scree or raised bed conditions in a sunny position (except *A. balearica*, see below). Propagation is by seed sown in late winter and early spring or by division in early spring, before flowering, or in late summer.

Arenaria balearica

Balearic Islands. A dense mat-forming perennial tightly pressed to the ground and not more than 5 cm (2 in) tall in flower, with creeping, very slender stems that root down at the nodes. The tiny, rounded leaves, to 4 mm (⅙ in) long, deep green; solitary white flowers, 6–10 mm (¼–⅖ in) across, project well above the mat on thread-like stems; spring and summer. Requires damp shady places in which to thrive, especially close to water or on old walls or paving.

Arenaria montana

Southwestern Europe. A tufted or mat-forming, gray-green plant to 30 cm (1 ft) across, sometimes more. Leaves oblong to lanceolate, 1–2 cm (⅖–⅘ in) long, covered in short curly down. Flowers solitary or several, pure white, 15–20 mm (⅗–⅘ in) across, borne on stems up to 10 cm (4 in) tall, the sepals with fine membranous margins; spring and early summer. An easy and accommodating plant excellent for crevices between rocks or on large raised beds.

· ·

Arenaria balearica

Arenaria montana

Arenaria purpurascens

Pyrenees and northern Spain. A fairly discreet, tufted to mat-forming plant to 20 cm (8 in) across with narrow elliptic or lanceolate leaves 5–10 mm (⅕–⅖ in) long, hairy on the margin at the base. Flowers solitary or two to four in a cluster, pale purple, sometimes whitish, about 13 mm (½ in) across, with purple anthers; mid to late summer. A good trough plant. 'Elliott's Variety' rich purple.

Armeria

This genus is comprised of about 80 species from the northern temperate region and South America allied to *Plumbago* and commonly called thrifts. They are generally hummock-forming evergreen perennials, often with masses of linear to elliptic or lanceolate leaves, all at the base of the plant. The five-parted flowers are crammed together into tight heads at the top of a wiry stem, often well above the foliage. The single-seeded fruits bear a small papery parachute at one end, which is formed from the calyx.

Delightful and generally accommodating plants that range from sea level species to those of high mountain habitats. They grow best in a well-drained, gritty compost and plenty of sunshine. Propagation is by spring-sown seed or cuttings taken in late summer and overwintered in a cold frame or similar. Their neat habit makes them ideal plants for raised beds and troughs, as well as for the general rock garden.

Armeria juniperifolia (syn. *A. caespitosa*)

Central Spain. A tight cushion-forming plant to 30 cm (1 ft) across, sometimes more, with deep green linear leaves 5–15 mm (⅕–⅗ in) long, with a ciliate margin. Flowers pink or pinkish purple, in tight globose heads 10–15 mm (⅖–⅗ in) across, borne on stems rarely more than 2.5 cm (1 in) tall; spring and early summer. Perhaps the finest thrift for the rock garden. 'Alba' white; 'Beechwood' deep pink on stems to 10 cm (4 in); 'Bevan's Variety' deep rose-pink clusters on stalks to 5 cm (2 in) tall; 'Six Hills' like 'Beechwood' but pale pink.

Armeria maritima

Widespread across Northern Hemisphere and South America. The common thrift is found in both coastal habitats and the mountains and is, as a consequence, a quite variable species with several subspecies recognized, especially in the mountains of Europe. It forms tough gray-green to bright green hummocks or mats to 60 cm (2 ft) across. Leaves linear, up to 12.5 cm (5 in) long. Flowerheads pink to reddish purple, up to 25 mm (1 in) across, borne on a wiry stem 5–20 cm (2–8 in) long; late spring and summer. 'Alba' white; 'Bloodstone' blood red; 'Dusseldorfer Stolz' (Dusseldorf Pride) purplish red; 'Laucheana' rich pink; 'Perfection' extra-large heads of bright pink; 'Rubrifolia' red leaves and purple-red flowers; 'Ruby Glow' ruby red; 'Vindictive' startling pinkish red.

Artemisia

The wormwoods consist of some 300 species of pungent herbs and shrubs with variously dis-

Armeria juniperifolia 'Bevan's Variety'

sected leaves and panicles of small, rayless, groundsel-like flowerheads, often produced in the summer or autumn. The genus is widespread in the temperate Northern Hemisphere and in South Africa and South America.

Many are not particularly garden worthy or are too large and coarse for the rock gardener. However, the one listed below is a true delight, requiring a sunny site and a well-drained gritty compost to thrive. Propagation is by division in early spring just before growth commences or by means of late summer cuttings.

Artemisia schmidtiana

Japan, eastern Russia. A tufted plant with a short-creeping rhizomatous rootstock, to 30 cm (1 ft) tall with well-branched stems. Leaves silvery, bipalmately divided, 3–4.5 cm (1⅕–1⅘ in) long, with filigree divisions, silky with down. Flowerheads dull yellow, about 5 mm (⅕ in) across; summer. 'Nana' a dwarf form half the size with strikingly silver foliage; an excellent rock garden plant.

Asarina

This genus is a close relation of the snapdragons (*Antirrhinum*) and sometimes included within that genus. *Asarina* contains about 16 species from Central and North America and southern Europe. They are trailing or clambering plants with paired, often rather fleshy, leaves that are often triangular in outline. The two-lipped, snapdragon-like flowers are borne one to two per node. The small, two-parted fruit capsules contain numerous seeds.

The only hardy species is included below. It is a splendid plant for dry places in the rock garden or for rock walls in sun or part shade; it will often thrive in dry places below conifers. Plants may be killed in particularly cold winters, but they generally self sow and seedlings can be expected to appear. Propagation is from seed sown in early spring, or late spring or summer cuttings of vigorous young, leafy shoots.

. . . .

Armeria maritima

Artemisia schmidtiana 'Nana'

Asarina procumbens (syn. *Antirrhinum procumbens, Maurandya asarina*)

Western Alps and Pyrenees. The creeping snapdragon produces prostrate stems up to 60 cm (2 ft) long, which sometimes form lax mats. The yellowish or grayish green hairy leaves are kidney-shaped, to 6 cm (2⅖ in) wide, with a shallowly lobed and toothed margin. Flowers white with pale purple veining and a yellow lip, 3–3.5 cm (1⅕–1⅖ in) long; late spring to autumn. 'Nana' an especially dwarf and compact form excellent for raised beds and large troughs.

Asperula

A delightful genus of about 100 species of annuals, perennials, and dwarf shrubs often confused with the goosegrasses (*Galium*). Asperulas are distributed primarily in the Mediterranean region and western Asia, some venturing onto the mountains of central Europe. They possess square stems and slender leaves in whorls of four to eight. The small flowers are borne in whorls or heads, often in masses, and consist of a short to long tube and four, occasionally five, spreading lobes. Fruit is small, with paired smooth lobes.

The genus contains some beautiful and eagerly sought rock garden plants, as well as plants for the specialist alpine house. Most are excellent plants for raised beds and troughs, looking especially effective in rock crevices or established on a block of tufa. Many are rather susceptible to winter wet and need to be protected from excess rain during this period. A well-drained gritty, alkaline compost suits the majority, along with an airy, sunny or partly shaded site. Propagation is by seed (when available) sown in late winter, division in autumn, or from summer cuttings. Plants rarely set seed in cultivation but can be induced to do so by careful hand-pollination.

Asperula arcadiensis (*A. suberosa* of gardens)

Greece; Peloponnese. A delicate-looking, soft, gray-hairy plant forming lax mats or cushions to 30 cm (1 ft) across. Leaves in whorls of six normally, these linear to narrow-elliptic, 5–10 mm (⅕–⅖ in) long, enveloped in soft hairs. Flowers in small heads, with a ruff of leaves immediately beneath, clear pink, 8 mm (⅓ in) long, borne profusely in late spring and summer. Grows well outside but best protected from winter wet with a pane of clear glass or similar.

Asperula sintenisii

Turkey. A densely tufted to cushion-forming species to 15 cm (6 in) across, the stems only 2.5 cm (1 in) long, spreading to erect. Leaves

Asarina procumbens

blue-green, linear to narrow-oblong, 4–8 mm (⅙–⅓ in) long, with a slender spiked apex. Flowers deep pink, solitary or paired at the upper nodes, about 10 mm (⅖ in) long; late spring and early summer. A denizen of limestone rock crevices and ledges at 1600–1800 m (5300–6000 ft) in the wild.

Aster

A sizeable genus with about 250 species confined to the Northern Hemisphere and South America. The majority are clump-forming perennials with basal leaves and leafy stems bearing one to many daisy flowerheads, often with purple, mauve, or blue rays surrounding a yellow or orange disk.

An important group of plants in the garden, cherished as much for their cheerful flowers as for the fact that they are great at attracting insects, especially species of bee and butterfly. Most will thrive in any good, well-drained, neutral to alkaline soil in full sun. Propagation is easiest by division after flowering or in early spring before growth recommences.

Aster alpinus

Alps and Pyrenees. The alpine aster is a clump-forming plant to 20 cm (8 in) tall, occasionally more. Leaves mostly basal, narrow-lanceolate to spathulate, to 7.5 cm (3 in) long, hairy. Flowerheads solitary, violet-blue, rarely pink or white, about 5 cm (2 in) across; summer. 'Albus' pure white rays; 'Beechwood' blue; 'Dunkle Schöne' (DARK BEAUTY) deep purple; 'Golianth' violet-blue, slightly taller, to 25 cm (10

Asperula sintenisii

Aster alpinus (Photo courtesy of Alpine Garden Society)

in); 'Happy End' semi-double lavender, compact plant; 'Pirmensis' deep rose; 'Roseus' pale pink; 'Ruber' red; 'Superbus' purple; 'Wargrave' pastel lilac; 'White Beauty' pure white.

Aster pyrenaeus

French Pyrenees. Similar to *A. alpinus* but a taller plant to 60 cm (2 ft), with oblong-lanceolate leaves that half-clasp the stem. Flowerheads lilac-blue, to 37 mm (1½ in) across,

plants greatly attractive to butterflies, the leaves forming lax rosettes, often obovate and toothed. The typical four-parted crucifer flowers are borne in racemes that elongate as successive flowers open.

Aubrietas are generally quite easy to grow. Although a number of species are in cultivation, they do not esteem much support, yet the common aubrieta of gardens, *A. deltoidea*, and a plethora of fine hybrids (generally assigned to *A.* ×*cultorum*) are among the most cheerful and brightly colored spring alpines and deserve a place in any rock garden. Furthermore, they are generally very accommodating plants ideal for average well-drained soils, being excellent for dry walls, banks, and edging paths. Although admittedly some get large in time, judicious clipping back will keep them tidy and in check.

Plants can be propagated by late summer division, cuttings taken in the summer, or seed sown in early spring. Plants will often self-seed in the garden, but the progeny cannot be relied upon to resemble their parent.

Aubrieta ×cultorum

A general name that covers the majority of named forms available today. Most are vigorous plants with especially large flowers in a wide range of colors; spring and early summer, occasionally later. 'Aurea' lavender, with golden green leaves; 'Belisha Beacon' deep rose red; 'Blue Cascade' near pure blue; 'Bob Saunders' reddish purple, double; 'Bressingham Pink' pink, double; 'Doctor Mules' purple-blue; 'Elsa Lancaster' deep purple, dwarf with puckered leaves; 'Gloriosa' soft rose; 'Greencourt Purple'

mostly in clusters of two to five; summer and autumn. 'Lutetia' long-flowering, starry, lilac-blue daisies.

Aubrieta

Often misspelled as *Aubretia*, the genus contains just a handful of species from the mountains of southeastern Europe eastward to Iran. They are cheerful mat- or cushion-forming

purple, semi-double; 'Hartswood' rich purple, especially large flowers; 'Henslow Purple' bright purple; 'Joy' mauve, double; 'Kitte Blue' deep purple-blue; 'Maurice Prichard' pale pink; 'Red Carpet' deep glowing red; 'Red Cas-

cade' deep red; 'Riverslea' mauve-pink, later flowering than most; 'Triumphante' blue; 'Variegata' lavender-blue, leaves yellow-variegated; 'Wanda' pale red, double.

Top left: *Aubrieta ×cultorum* 'Doctor Mules'

Top right: *Aubrieta ×cultorum* 'Kitte Blue'

Bottom: *Aubrieta deltoidea*

Aubrieta deltoidea

Southern and southeastern Europe. Common aubrieta is a mounded, sometimes rather straggly, evergreen perennial to 60 cm (2 ft) across,

with gray-green obovate leaves, to 20 mm (⅘ in) long. The racemes of flowers, which are congested at first, range in color from violet to pink or reddish purple, rarely white, 15–25 mm (⅗–1 in) across; spring, intermittently through the summer.

Aurinia

A small genus from central and southern Europe and western Asia of subshrubby, bushy perennials closely related to, and once included in, *Alyssum*, often with gray or silvery leaves. The small, normally yellow, four-petaled flowers are borne in billowy masses followed by small elliptical fruits that split into two when ripe

Aurinias are excellent plants for dry sunny places in the rock garden but perhaps look their best on dry stone walls, being generally too large for raised beds and containers. A gritty well-drained soil is required. Seed sown when ripe or in early spring provides a ready means of increase, although plants will often self-sown in the garden. Young plants transfer quite easily in the garden provided they are well watered in, but older more established plants do not. Taking cuttings of named forms in the summer is also a good means of increase, especially as these do not always come true from seed.

Aurinia saxatilis

Central and southeastern Europe. Commonly known as yellow alyssum, a lax mounded evergreen subshrub to 90 cm (3 ft) across and 30 cm (1 ft) tall in flower. Leaves grayish or whitish with down, borne in lax rosettes, obovate to oblanceolate, to 15 cm (6 in) long, somewhat lobed along the margin. Flowers bright

....
Aurinia saxatilis

yellow, numerous, 4–6 mm (⅙–¼ in) across, borne in large panicles; spring and spasmodically through the summer. 'Citrinum' lemon yellow; 'Compactum' dwarf and denser; 'Dudley Neville' biscuit yellow; 'Plenum' double, bright yellow; 'Tom Thumb' dwarfer even than 'Compactum', to 10 cm (4 in) tall; 'Variegatum' cream-marked, somewhat contorted foliage.

Calceolaria

A large genus of about 300 species confined to Central and South America, particularly Chile and Peru. They range from shrubs to evergreen and herbaceous perennials and annuals, some with basal leaf rosettes but most with paired leaves on the stems. The flowers, borne singly or in small to large cymes, are very distinctive, two-lipped with the lower lip the larger, pouched, often balloon-like, the upper lip smaller but also pouched, sometimes hooded. The fruit is a small two-parted capsule containing numerous seeds.

The genus offers a large number of rock garden species, although relatively few are suitable for unprotected sites in the garden; however, these make admirable subjects for raised beds and troughs in particular. Calceolarias require a light soil but one that does not dry out, for drought is the chief enemy of these plants. Propagation is from seed sown in late winter and early spring; the seed should be only lightly covered and kept moist at all times. Division is possible in the spring as growth commences, while those with leafy stems lend themselves to late summer cutting.

Calceolaria arachnoidea

Chile. A clump-forming plant to 40 cm (16 in) tall in flower, with erect, somewhat branched stems. Leaves mostly toward the base of the plant, oblong-spathulate, 4–10 cm (1⅗–4 in) long, white-downy, with a winged petiole. Flowers dull purple to blackish violet, about 15 mm (⅗ in) across; late spring and summer. In the wild this plant colonizes dry earthy or grassy steppes and snow gullies.

Calceolaria biflora (includes *C. falklandica*)

Argentina and Chile, Falkland Islands. A clump or colony-forming species to 40 cm (16 in) tall in flower, often less, spreading by short rhizomes. Leaves deep green, all in basal rosettes, oblong to lanceolate or almost diamond-shaped, slightly toothed along the margin, to 10 cm (4 in) long, hairy on the veins beneath and with a broad, winged petiole. Flowers several on a slender stem high above the foliage, bright yellow, with rounded pouches, the

. . . .

Calceolaria biflora (Photo courtesy of Alpine Garden Society)

lower up to 2 cm (⅘ in) across, sometimes red-spotted; spring and summer. Found over a wide altitudinal range in the wild from sea level to 2800 m (9300 ft). An easy and accommodating plant in the garden with a long flowering period.

Calceolaria uniflora

Chile and Argentina, particularly southern Patagonia. An absolutely delightful little clump or cushion-forming plant, not more than 10 cm (4 in) tall in flower. Leaves deep green, in dense basal rosettes, oblong-spathulate to almost diamond-shaped, to 7.5 cm (3 in) long, entire to finely toothed on the margin. Flowers solitary or two or three on slender stalks above the foliage, basically orange-yellow freckled with red or chestnut and with a distinctive shiny white horizontal bar in the mouth, the lower pouch forming a distinctive obovate lip, 18–25 mm (¾–1 in) long; spring. Var. *darwinii* has larger, glabrous leaves and flowers, which are consistently solitary. *Calceolaria uniflora* is prone to sun scorch and requires dappled shade as well as an acid, moist, humus-rich compost in which to thrive.

Callianthemum

Charming buttercup relation with a handful of species in Europe and Asia. They have finely dissected foliage and anemone-like flowers with up to 20 narrow petals. The fruit is a small head of achenes.

This genus requires a gritty, humus-rich soil and sun or dappled shade in which to thrive. Propagation is from seed as soon as ripe or soon afterward.

Callianthemum anemonoides

Austria. A very beautiful gem, forming small clumps of rather fleshy, gray-green, pinnately lobed leaves that are only partly developed at flowering time, but eventually 7.5 cm (3 in) long. Flowers solitary, occasionally several on a common stem, 2.5–4 cm (1–1⅗ in) across, white to pale pink, with 12–16 petal-like sepals

Calceolaria uniflora

Callianthemum anemonoides

that have an orange nectary at the base, and numerous yellow anthers; early spring. An excellent plant for the rock garden or raised bed, requiring a gritty, humus-rich soil and a sunny site. Propagation is best from fresh seed, as older, packeted seed tends to give very poor results.

Campanula

The bellflower genus contains about 300 species scattered primarily in the temperate Northern Hemisphere, particularly in the Mediterranean region and European mountains. They range from coarse herbaceous, sometimes invasive, perennials to the neatest of high alpines. A number are monocarpic, spending several years as a leaf rosette before flowering, seeding, and then dying. The majority have variously cupped or bell-shaped flowers, often in shades of blue, while a few have more star-shaped flowers: the petals are fused together to form a long or short, narrow or broad tube. The fruit is a capsule containing numerous tiny seeds.

Bellflowers are best planted in the spring or early summer and are ideal for rock gardens, raised beds, troughs, and other containers. Many of the tussock-forming alpine species look excellent sandwiched between rocks. The more robust, spreading species can be divided after flowering or in the autumn, while the smaller, more discreet species are readily raised from seed. The less robust species and cultivars require regular replenishing by division, otherwise they often decline after only a few years, having exhausted the soil or compost they are

Campanula 'Birch Hybrid'

growing in. Some of the choice alpine species are prone to depredation from slugs and snails and are best protected from excess winter wet when grown in the open garden.

Campanula 'Birch Hybrid'

An interesting and very floriferous hybrid between *C. portenschlagiana* and *C. poscharskyana* and intermediate in character. Plants have a spread of about 45 cm (18 in), forming a mass of deep green leaves. The star-shaped, upward-facing flowers are purple-blue and borne in large trusses on stems 10–15 cm (⅖–⅗ in) long; summer. Less invasive than its parents, this excellent bellflower is readily propagated from rooted side pieces.

Campanula carpatica

Carpathian Mountains. The Carpathian bellflower is one of the most widely grown and easy campanulas, which is often sold as a potted plant. It forms slow-spreading clumps to 30 cm (1 ft) tall, twice as much across, of medium green, oval, sharply toothed leaves. The ascending stems carry several disproportionately

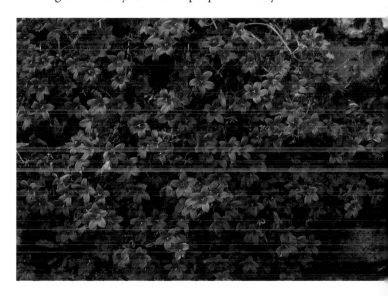

Campanula carpatica 'Blaue Clips'

Campanula cochlearifolia

large, wide bowl- or saucer-shaped flowers, 3–4 cm (1⅕–1⅗ in) across; summer to early autumn. 'Blaue Clips' (BLUE CLIPS) lavender-blue, 20 cm (8 in) tall; 'Bressingham White' extra-large flowers on 15-cm (6-in) stems; 'Riverslea' large purple-blue flowers; 'Turbinata' 15 cm (6 in) tall, bearing one violet flower per stem; 'Weisse Clips' (WHITE CLIPS), extra-large pure white flowers. Double-flowered forms are also grown.

Campanula cochlearifolia

European Mountains. Known as fairy's thimbles, this species soon forms tufts, spreading by thin underground stolons. The small, shiny green leaves are oval to heart-shaped and slightly toothed. Slender arching stems to 10 cm (4 in) tall carry several neat, lavender to

blue, occasionally white bellflowers, each 12–16 mm (½–⅗ in) long; late spring and summer. 'Blue Baby' medium lilac-blue flowers; 'Cambridge Blue' pale powder blue; 'Elizabeth Oliver' double, powder blue; 'Miss Wilmott' lustrous lavender-blue flowers in profusion; 'Tubby' wide blue bells; var. *alba* pure white.

Campanula 'E. K. Toogood'

A fine plant of hybrid origin (probably *C. poscharskyana* and *C. garganica*), forming lax clumps to 50 cm (20 in) across festooned in arching sprays of bright blue, white-centered flowers, each about 18 mm (⅔ in) across; summer.

Campanula 'E. K. Toogood' on a raised bed in the Dell Garden, Bressingham.

Campanula formanekiana

Greece and Macedonia. A very handsome biennial or monocarpic plant taking up to four years to reach flowering maturity, to 30 cm (12 in) tall in flower. Leaves primarily in a large, solitary, basal rosette, ovate, to 15 cm (6 in) long, with a wavy, toothed margin and a winged and toothed petiole, gray-downy overall. Flowers inclined, broad-campanulate, white, often flushed with bluish lilac, 5–6 cm (2–2⅖ in) long, borne in a broad branched raceme; summer. An excellent crevice or raised bed plant,

which needs to be constantly raised each year from seed to keep it in the garden.

Campanula garganica

Western Greece and southeastern Italy. A clump-forming evergreen perennial to 20 cm (8 in) tall in flower, with spreading stems. Basal leaves rounded to heart-shaped, blunt-toothed, often rather bright green. Flowers numerous, blue with a white center, starry, about 20 mm (⅘ in) across, borne in arching sprays just above the foliage; late spring and summer. 'Dickson's Gold' yellow-flushed leaves and blue flowers; 'W. H. Paine' rich blue flowers.

Campanula myrtifolia

Southern Turkey. A delightful and easy little plant that inhabits limestone rock crevices in the wild. Forms quite tough little plants not

more than 5 cm (2 in) tall, bearing small ellip-tic leaves. Narrow bell-shaped flowers, 15 mm (⅗ in) long, lavender or white, borne up to five per stem; early summer.

Campanula portenschlagiana
Dalmatian Mountains. The Dalmatian bell-flower hales from one-time Yugoslavia, where it is a cliff dweller in the wild. Forms spread-ing, sometimes invasive, clumps to 20 cm (8 in) tall, the leaves bright green, heart-shaped, mostly borne in lax basal rosettes. From these arise spreading, leafy, somewhat branched stems bearing a mass of deep lilac-blue, bell-shaped flowers, each 20–25 mm (⅘–1 in) long; summer and early autumn. Easy and reliable plant, excellent for wall and paving crevices. 'Resholdt's Variety' is a more compact, less in-vasive selection.

Campanula poscharskyana
Another species from the former Yugoslavia at home in rocky habitats. Plants form clumps or mats of bright green, heart-shaped leaves. Slen-der spreading or arching, leafy stems to 30 cm (1 ft) long bear branched racemes of upright, starry, lavender-blue flowers, 15–18 mm (⅗–¾ in) across, often paler in the center; late spring to autumn, even in winter on occasions. A very floriferous plant that can prove invasive in some gardens. 'Blue Waterfall' less invasive se-lection with deeper, bluer flowers; 'E. H. Frost' milky blue flowers.

Campanula pulla
Eastern Alps. A delightful little bellflower from alpine meadows and screes, above 1700 m

(5600 ft) in the wild. Forms slow-spreading tufts with rosettes of glossy deep green, heart-shaped leaves. Flowering stems, to 15 cm (⅗ in) tall, bear several narrower leaves and generally a solitary, half-nodding, very deep blue, tubby bell, 18–20 mm (¾–⅘ in) long, summer.

Campanula sarmatica
Caucasus. A rather erect, clump-forming plant to 30 cm (1 ft) tall in flower, occasionally more.

Campanula poscharskyana

Campanula pulla

Campanula sarmatica

Campanula saxifraga

Leaves mostly toward the base of the plant, oblong-ovate, gray-downy, with a heart-shaped base, a double-toothed crisped margin, and winged petiole. Flowers grayish blue, campanulate, 30–40 mm (1⅕–1⅗ in) long, half-nodding, borne in lax racemes; summer. Can be a bit vigorous for the smaller rock garden, but nonetheless delightful.

Campanula saxifraga

Caucasus. A small tufted plant to 10 cm (4 in) tall in flower, with gray-green leaf rosettes, the leaves linear-lanceolate to linear-spathulate, rarely more than 5 cm (2 in) long, with entire to slightly toothed margin, crisped-hairy, especially on the margin. Flowers solitary, ascending, wide-campanulate, violet-blue with a white center, 25–30 mm (1 –1⅕ in) long; summer. An excellent plant for scree conditions

and raised beds. The related *C. aucheri* (from Turkey and the Caucasus) has similar proportions but the leaves are more clearly toothed and hairy, the flowers deeper colored.

Campanula thyrsoides

Eastern Alps, Slovenia. A very distinctive and handsome monocarpic species forming an open rosette of rather pale green, oblong-lanceolate leaves in the first year or two. Flowers borne in a dense columnar spike to 40 cm (16 in) tall, campanulate, pale yellow, 18–20 mm (⅔–⅘ in) long; summer. A rather more intriguing than beautiful plant, but much admired by some growers; will occasionally self-sow.

Campanula zoysii

Southeastern Alps, Dolomites. One of the most distinctive bellflowers, it inhabits limestone cliff crevices in its native haunts. Plants form discrete little clumps scarcely 7.5 cm (3 in) tall in bloom, with most of the elliptic to oval leaves crowded toward the base of the plant. Flowers several, horizontal to upwardly inclined, 18–20 mm (¾–⅘ in) long, narrow-tubular, with a characteristically crimped mouth, very unlike that of any other species; summer. Very prone to slug damage but, nevertheless, an ideal trough plant.

Carlina

A small genus with 28 species of annual, perennial, or monocarpic species distributed from the Azores to Europe, North Africa, and western Asia. They are intensely prickly, thistle-like plants often with brownish flowerheads that are surrounded by a ring of shiny, whitish, silvery or pinkish, linear, entire floral bracts.

Despite their prickly nature, these are delightful plants for dry or even hot sunny sites in the rock garden, preferring alkaline

Campanula thyrsoides

Campanula zoysii

soils, but not particularly fussy about soil type. They are best propagated from seed sown in early spring.

Carlina acanthifolia

Southern and eastern Europe, primarily in the mountains. A bold and handsome monocarpic plant forming a large thistle-like rosette to 60 cm (2 ft) across. Leaves oval, pinnately lobed, gray-green, white-downy beneath. Flowerhead

usually solitary, to 15 cm (6 in) across, sometimes larger, the slender, shiny floral bracts straw-colored to lemon yellow, long-lasting; summer. An unusual addition to the larger rock garden, but one that needs to be constantly raised from seed to keep it in cultivation; plants may take as many as four years to reach flowering size. The flowerheads are often pinned to the doors of a house in the Alps, Pyrenees, and elsewhere as a good-luck symbol, but the dried heads open in dry weather and close in damp conditions, thus acting as nature's barometer at the same time.

Carlina acaulis

Central and southern Europe east to central Russia. A short-lived perennial or monocarpic plant to 15 cm (6 in) tall, with a rosette of thistle-like, pinnately lobed, spiny-margined leaves, to 30 cm (12 in) long. Flowerheads solitary, often sessile, 5–10 cm (2–4 in) across, surrounded by a ruff of leaf-like bracts, the floral bracts wide-spreading silvery white, sometimes pink-flushed; summer. Subsp. *simplex* larger, more clump-forming version with erect stems to 60 cm (2 ft) tall, bearing up to six flowerheads. There are bronze-leaved versions of both the stemless and stemmed subspecies.

Celmisia

A remarkable genus in the daisy family (Compositae or Asteraceae), the species noted for both handsome foliage and striking, generally white, daisy flowers. The genus contains some 65 species that are primarily confined to New Zealand, mostly in the higher mountains, while

. . . .

Carlina acanthifolia

Carlina acaulis subsp. *simplex*

Celmisia angustifolia

Celmisia hookeri

· ·

a few outlying species are located in eastern Australia. They have mats or tufts of small to large simple, often spear-shaped leaves and bracted stems bearing a solitary flowerhead.

Celmisias require a moisture-retentive soil and cool conditions if they are to succeed, along with ample light. Although some are undoubtedly difficult to maintain in cultivation, others are more accessible. However, few mountain plants are bolder and more handsome, especially the large-rosette types, and they are well worth persevering with. Plants are considered to be self-sterile, so several are needed to produce reliable seed; however, as with many composites, only the plump seed produced is viable. This can be sown in early spring. Alter-

natively, cutting or division in late spring and summer are possible options. Celmisias dislike overfeeding, which can result in rotting problems or poor flowering.

Celmisia angustifolia

New Zealand; South Island. A slighter plant than *C. semicordata*, to 25 cm (10 in) tall with grayish leaves that are narrow lanceolate-elliptic, to 5 cm (2 in) long, white-felted beneath. Flowerheads about 3.5 cm (1⅖ in) across, borne on sticky stems above the foliage; summer. Sometimes found under the incorrect name of *C. durietzii*.

Celmisia hookeri

New Zealand; South Island. A very handsome tufted plant with large rosettes of elliptic, spreading leaves to 20 cm (8 in) long, dull green

above, cream-felted beneath and along the margin. Flowerheads the largest in the genus, to 10 cm (4 in) across, shaggy daisies with wide-spreading white rays surrounding a yellowish or brownish disk; summer. Best grown in dappled shade in a rock crevice or on a raised bed.

Celmisia semicordata (syn. *C. coriacea* of gardens)

New Zealand; South Island. A bold and handsome plant to 40 cm (16 in) tall with rosettes of ascending lanceolate leaves, gray-downy above, silvery white and satiny below, to 40 cm (16 in) long. Flowerheads white with a yellow disk, to 6 cm (2⅖ in) across; summer. The Inshriach Group of celmisias are of hybrid origin. Produced in Scotland, they probably represent this species crossed with another New Zealander, *C. traversii*. All are excellent and eye-catching plants.

Chamaemelum

A genus of familiar white daisy plants perhaps better known under the genus *Anthemis*, the chamomiles. Plants thrive in a well-drained gritty soil with added humus and a sunny open aspect. Seed can be sown in late winter. Division in summer provides an easy means of increase.

Chamaemelum nobile (syn. *Anthemis nobilis*)

Western and southwestern Europe. Popularly known as lawn or Roman chamomile, this aromatic mat-forming perennial has fresh green leaves divided into a filigree of narrow segments. The solitary daisy flowerheads are white with a yellow disk, 10–15 mm (⅖–⅗ in) across; summer. An excellent plant for pathways, lawns, or containers, prized especially for its sweetly aromatic foliage: the most aromatic form for lawns is the nonflowering 'Treneague'. 'Flora Pleno' double button-like flowers.

Chiastophyllum

A relation of the stonecrops (*Sedum*) and houseleeks (*Sempervivum*) from western Asia and, like them, equally drought-resistant in the garden. Being a discreet and noninvasive plant, it is ideal for raised beds and troughs or indeed the general rock garden. Readily raised from cuttings in spring and summer.

Chiastophyllum oppositifolium

Caucasus Mountains. A succulent species forming neat, bright green clumps to 20 cm (8 in) tall in flower. Leaves fleshy, mainly basal, rounded to oval, to 5 cm (2 in) long, with a neatly toothed margin. Flowers yellow, 3–5 mm (⅛–⅕ in) long, borne above the foliage in branched inflorescences, drooping at the tips

and catkin-like; early summer. Sun or partial shade in a well-drained position; drought tolerant and excellent for troughs and raised beds. 'Jim's Pride' has variegated foliage.

Clematis

A familiar genus with about 300 species widely scattered in both the Northern and Southern Hemispheres. While most are vigorous climbers, several of the smaller ones have found favor in the rock garden. Clematis are primarily woody climbers and lianas, but some are herbaceous perennials. All have opposite simple or variously compound leaves and flowers with colored sepals, only occasionally with true petals. The decorative fruits consist of a collection of achenes normally with feathery appendages or styles.

Three species are included below, and they thrive in a gritty, moist, loamy soil. While the former is a climber, the latter two are small and tufted, ideal subjects for raised beds, troughs, and other containers. Propagation from seed sown the moment ripe or in late winter affords an easy means of increase. *Clematis alpina* can be propagated during the summer from cuttings, using semi-mature internodal (that is, between the nodes) sections of stem.

Clematis alpina (syn. *Atragene alpina*)
European Alps east to central Asia. Although a climber to 3–4 m (9–12 ft), the alpine clematis is often grown in the rock garden, being excellent for clambering over rocks or shrubs. The leaves are biternate, with elliptic to lanceolate, toothed, green leaflets. The solitary, lantern-

like flowers are borne on slender stalks from the nodes of second-season shoots and are 2.5–4 cm (1–1⅗ in) long, with blue, violet, or purplish sepals with shorter, spoon-shaped white staminodes within, these latter being transitional with the numerous yellow stamens; spring and early summer. 'Burford White' creamy white overall; 'Columbine' white with a hint of blue; 'Francis Rivis' large deep blue flowers with white staminodes; 'Pamela Jack-

man' azure with contrasting cream staminodes; 'Ruby' lilac with white staminodes.

Clematis marmoraria

New Zealand; South Island. A true alpine gem discovered as recently as 1973 in the Nelson Range, where it occupies rock crevices. Plants are dioecious with separate male and female individuals and are in effect dwarf evergreen shrubs. Leaves leathery, deep green and glossy, pinnately compound with linear divisions. Flowers solitary, saucer-shaped, white flushed green, 1.5–3 cm (⅗–1⅕ in) across, with five to eight oval sepals, the male with a boss of yellow stamens, the female with a cluster of achenes, sometimes accompanied by a few staminodes; spring. Readily raised from seed but the offspring are variable, the better and larger flowered plants generally being male. Hybridizes readily with far more vigorous climbing New Zealand species, notably *C. paniculata* and *C. petriei*.

Clematis tenuiloba (sometimes included in
   C. alpina subsp. *columbiana*)

Northwestern United States, Rocky Mountains, where it is a plant of limestone barrens. A low, spreading, stoloniferous, deciduous subshrub to 20 cm (8 in) tall in flower, with biternate, parsley-like foliage, forming a lax mat. Flowers lantern-shaped, rather *Pulsatilla*-like, purple-pink to lilac-purple, rarely white, 20–35 mm (⅘–1⅖ in) across, with white staminodes, borne on elegant slender stalks above the leaves; spring.

....

Clematis marmoraria

Clematis tenuiloba

Cornus

An important garden genus with some 45 species, some nowadays assigned to other genera, scattered in the northern temperate zone, but extending down into South America. They are trees or shrubs, occasionally carpeting, with paired or whorled leaves. The flowers are borne in clusters or heads, four- or five-parted, often surrounded by large and conspicuous bracts. Fruits are berry-like. Many of the species are highly decorative in flower, while others have attractive colored stems that are very effective in the winter garden. The one listed here is a fine plant for the woodland garden, along with plants like trilliums, epimediums, cyclamen, and jeffersonias. Propagation is from seed sown in the winter or, more usually, by division in the autumn.

Cornus canadensis (syn. Chamaepericly-menum canadense)

North America and eastern Asia, including Japan. A carpeting woodland plant, to 1 m (3 ft) across or more, to about 25 cm (10 in) tall at the most. Leaves in whorls, crowded toward the shoot tips, ovate, 2.5–7.5 cm (1–3 in) long. Flower clusters dense, solitary and terminal, greenish or creamish, surrounded by four white, cream, or pink-flushed leaf-like bracts, to 2 cm (⅘ in) long. Fruit a cluster of berries, bright shiny red when ripe.

Corydalis

A large genus with some 400 species scattered throughout northern temperate regions and in the African mountains. They range from coarse herbs and woodland plants to discreet high-altitude alpines and can have a fibrous, rhi-

Cornus canadensis

zomatous, or tuberous rootstock. The leaves are often rather fleshy and juicy, with variously dissected foliage of a ferny appearance. The flowers are borne in racemes and are two lipped with a closed mouth, four-petaled with the upper petal extended backward into a spur, while the two inner petals are shorter and partly enclosed by the outer. The fruit is an explosive two-parted capsule.

The genus has become increasing popular in recent years and contains some of the most cherished rock garden plants for spring and early summer. They are readily propagated from fresh seed, although most of those listed here self-sow in average garden conditions. The rhizomatous ones can be divided after flowering or in early spring, while the tuberous species multiply slowly by natural division. Most of those listed here thrive in a moist humus-rich soil, while *C. cheilanthifolia* and *C. ochroleuca* prefer a grittier medium and make excellent crevice plants for semi-shaded walls or raised beds in the garden.

Corydalis cheilanthifolia

Western China. Plant to 20 cm (8 in) tall in flower, forming wide rosettes of finely dissected, fern-like foliage, gray-green at first but often taking on pink or bronze hues in the autumn. Flowers primrose yellow with a downward-pointing spur, borne in elegant tapering racemes to 15 cm (6 in) long; spring and early summer. Excellent in shady places but tolerant of a wide range of garden conditions.

Corydalis flexuosa

Western China. A woodland species in the wild reaching 30 cm (1 ft) tall in flower, with erect stems from a short-creeping rhizomatous base. The foliage is gray-green, sometimes flushed with pink or purple. The beautiful, graceful racemes of flowers are congested at first but soon elongate as the fruits start to develop; they vary from pure blue to purplish, greenish blue, or whitish, 28–35 mm (1⅛–1⅖ in) long, the spur straight to curved; late spring and early summer, sometimes with a few later racemes. The easiest of the blue species in general cultivation and one of the most charming introductions from the wild in recent years (it was brought to

. . . .

Corydalis flexuosa 'Purple Leaf'

Corydalis 'Kingfisher'

the West in 1986). 'Balang Mist' whitish flushed blue against gray-green foliage; 'Blue Panda' sky blue with pale blue-green unmarked foliage; 'China Blue' sky blue with a hint of green, with brownish green foliage, green at first, with red blotches at the lobe bases; 'Purple Leaf' deep blue, a neat clone with reddish purple stems and blood red marked leaves.

Corydalis 'Kingfisher'

A fine hybrid between *C. cashmeriana* and *C. flexuosa* growing to about 30 cm (12 in) tall, with rich blue racemes of flowers over an extended season from late spring to autumn. Thrives in a humus-rich soil in dappled shade. The delightful, yet often difficult to maintain, Himalayan *C. cashmeriana* has vexed gardeners over many years: 'Kingfisher' is a suitable and easy-to-grow substitute.

Corydalis malkensis (often wrongly listed as
C. *caucasica* var. *alba* or 'Alba')

Northern Caucasus. Similar in proportion and general characteristics to *C. solida*, to about 15 cm (6 in) tall in flower. Leaves pale green, with rounded divisions. Flowers white, borne in lax racemes, with an expanded lip and upward curved spur; spring. A prolific seeder.

Corydalis ochroleuca (syn. *Pseudofumaria*
ochroleuca)

Balkans and Italy. A neat, tufted plant to 30 cm (1 ft) tall, forming domes of gray-green biternately dissected foliage. Flowers white to pale cream, tipped yellow and borne among the upper leaves in short racemes up to 5 cm (2 in) long; spring and summer. Will succeed in sun

. . . .

Corydalis malkensis

Corydalis ochroleuca

or part shade in moist gritty soils or in paving or wall crevices. The closely related, more vigorous, *C. lutea* (syn. *Pseudofumaria lutea*), with bright yellow flowers, often arrives in the garden unintentionally and, although pretty and with a long flowering season, can prove to be a vigorous weed.

Corydalis solida

Europe, Turkey, Russia, and Lebanon. The finest of the tuberous species for the spring gar-

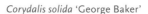

Corydalis 'Spinners'

A hybrid between the widely grown *C. flexuosa* and the taller Chinese *C. elata*, which is generally too large for the average rock garden. A recent excellent introduction with rich sky blue flowers on a plant to 25 cm (10 in) tall; late spring and summer.

Crepis

Dandelion relatives, with some 200 annual, biennial, or perennial species confined to the Northern Hemisphere. While most are rather weedy, several have a special charm. Many form basal leaf tufts or rosettes and bear flowerheads consisting entirely of strap-shaped ray florets, often yellow, but pink, red, and white also exist.

The two listed below are highly recommended and will thrive in most average garden soils in full sun. Propagation is best effected by spring-sown seed, although plants will often self-sow in the garden.

Crepis incana (syn. *C. rosea* of gardens)

Southern Greece. A biennial or short-lived perennial with rosettes of hoary, gray-green oblanceolate leaves to 12.5 cm (5 in) long, occasionally larger. Flower stems rising to 20 cm (8 in), usually with several branches. Flowerheads pink to purplish pink, about 3 cm (1⅕ in) across; summer and autumn. A very attractive and floriferous plant that inhabits rocky places in the wild above 1200 m (4000 ft).

Crepis rubra

Southern Italy to the Balkans, including Crete. Rather similar to *C. incana*, but an annual with

den, this quite variable species has a wide distribution in the wild. Plants grow up to 20 cm (8 in) tall in flower and have soft gray-green, biternate foliage, with blunt division. The racemes of up to 20 flowers, each 20–25 mm (⅘–1 in) long, vary in color from pink and purple to red; rather congested at first but elongating as the fruits develop, the spur downturned at the tip or more or less straight; spring. An excellent and floriferous species for the garden, most suitable for woodlands or among shrubs or other spring bulbs. Where several forms are grown in close proximity they will hybridize. There is a growing number of named cultivars, including 'Beth Evans' soft pink with white-flushed spur; 'Dieter Schacht' like a more vigorous 'Beth Evans'; 'George Baker' rich red; 'Highland Mist' smoky blue-pink; 'Lahovice' deep red; 'Munich Form' corolla red; 'Nettleton Pink' vigorous, rich pink; Prasil strain a seed selection varying from salmon-orange to scarlet-red or pink; 'Snowstorm' white.

Crepis incana
....

a simple rosette of dandelion-like leaves, to 15 cm (6 in) long. Flowerheads pink or white, 2–3 cm (⅘–1⅕ in) across, borne usually on unbranched stems to 40 cm (16 in) tall; summer.

Cyclamen

One of the most familiar and delightful genera of plants, which includes several very hardy subjects for the rock garden. The genus contains 24 species that are concentrated primarily in the Mediterranean region but spreading north into central Europe and east as far as northern Iran. All the species have a thick tuberous stock and basal, long-petioled leaves, these varying from rounded or kidney-shaped to heart-shaped or variously lobed. The leaves often have attractive patterning on the upper surface. The solitary, five-parted, pink, red, or white flowers are borne on long stalks and typically nod at the top of the stalk with the petals characteristically bent backward and varyingly twisted. Many have a delightful scent. The fruit is a fleshy, many-seeded capsule borne usually on a spirally twisted stalk (although not coiling in the familiar florist's cyclamen, *C. persicum*).

Five of the hardiest species are listed here. All thrive in dappled shade in a leafy, moist, yet well-drained soil and are best planted in drifts rather than as individuals. Cyclamen respond well to an annual top-dressing of sieved leafmold and bonemeal. Plants are readily raised from seed, which should be sown fresh or as soon as possible. The sugary-coated seeds are attractive to both ants and wasps and can be quickly carted away before the seed is harvested. Plants will often self-sow profusely in the garden.

Cyclamen cilicium

Southern Turkey. A small species with oval leaves to 6 cm (2⅖ in) long, deep green patterned with gray-green or creamy white, the margin slightly scalloped. Flowers elegant, honey-scented, pale to medium pink, 14–19 mm (½–¾ in) long, with narrow, twisted petals, appearing with the young leaves; spring. Forma *album* white, comes true from seed.

Cyclamen coum

Southeastern Europe, Turkey, the Caucasus. One of the true delights for the rock or woodland garden and an excellent harbinger of spring. Quite variable species with unlobed, rounded to kidney-shaped leaves to about 7.5 cm (3 in) across, plain deep green or variously patterned with cream, gray, or silver. Flowers appearing with the mature leaves, rather dumpy, 12–14 mm (½ in) long, pink to magenta, with rounded petals marked around the nose with a dark crimson-magenta M-shaped blotch; winter and early spring. Together with *C. hederifolium*, the most reliable of the hardy cyclamen in the open garden. Subsp. *caucasi-*

crimson flowers and plain green leaves; 'Rose-um' rose pink, large flowers and marbled leaves; 'Tilebarn Elizabeth' white or very pale pink, flushed rose-pink at the petal margins, contrasting with silvery leaves. In addition, both Silver and Pewter Leaf Groups are available, the leaves generally varying in the intensity of silver or pewter on the upper surface.

Cyclamen hederifolium

Southern and southeastern Europe, western Turkey. The ivy-leaved sowbread is an extremely variable species with often ivy-like, somewhat lobed leaves, but sometimes oval to oblong or lyre-shaped and unlobed. The leaf blade can be 15 cm (6 in) long, gray-green, with a heart-shaped pattern in a paler or darker shade, or silvery or pewter, the margin often shallowly lobed or angled and toothed. Flowers appearing with, or in advance of, the young leaves, pale to deep pink, with a double V-shaped purple-magenta mark at the base of each petal, 14–22 mm (½–⅞ in) long, with a broad auricled mouth; late summer and autumn. Scented and unscented forms are cultivated. 'Album' white; 'Perlenteppich' white, often with pink in the throat; 'Rosenteppich' deep pink to red-magenta, with rather dully marked foliage; 'Ruby Glow' (Ruby strain) rich magenta-purple; 'Silver Cloud' leaves silver overall, flowers pink; 'White Cloud' like 'Silver Cloud' but flowers white.

Cyclamen purpurascens

Central Europe south to northern Italy and Slovenia. Leaves practically evergreen, leathery, rounded to kidney-shaped, unlobed, to 7.5

cum from the eastern end of the range of the species has more heart-shaped leaves and larger flowers to 25 mm (1 in) long; forma *albissimum* pure white, unmarked. Many cultivars and selections exist: 'Album' white with magenta markings and plain leaves; 'Marbled Moon' white flowers with magenta markings and patterned leaves; 'Maurice Dryden' white, magenta-marked flowers and silver leaves thinly margined green; 'Meaden's Crimson' small

Cyclamen purpurascens

Cyclamen repandum

cm (3 in), plain shiny deep green or with a cream pattern. Flowers wonderfully and sweetly scented, pale rose-pink to purple or rosy-carmine, 17–25 mm (⅔–1 in) long, with elliptical, twisted, unmarked petals; summer and early autumn. Forma *album* white. Less easy to establish than the other listed here but seems best when placed beneath conifers or in a rocky, partly shaded spot in the garden and left undisturbed. 'Lake Garda' silvery leaves and pink flowers. Plants sold as "silver-leaved form" or "pewter-leaved form" are also available.

Cyclamen repandum

Southeastern France, Corsica, Sardinia, Italy, Sicily, Slovenia. A woodland species with deep green, ivy-like leaves to 15 cm (6 in) long, usually attractively marked with a gray-green or silvery heart-shaped pattern above. Flowers elegant, powerfully scented, deep carmine-pink or carmine-magenta, 15–21 mm (⅗–⅘ in) long, with narrow twisted petals; spring. An excellent plant. Forma *album* white.

Daphne

The genus contains about 50 species distributed in Europe and Asia. The smaller ones and numerous hybrids are first-rate dwarf shrubs for the rock garden, indeed few are able to rival them for their floriferousness and fragrance. Daphnes are deciduous or evergreen, often very twiggy plants with simple alternate or opposite, entire leaves. The flowers are borne in terminal or lateral clusters and are tubular, without petals but with a colored hypanthium with four, rarely five, short spreading lobes.

The fruit is berry-like usually, black, orange, or red when ripe and highly poisonous, but sometimes they are nonfleshy and enclosed in the base of the flower tube.

Daphnes range from easy to difficult in cultivation, but are also fine plants for pot culture in the alpine house or cold frame. They require a moisture-retentive yet well-drained soil, preferably neutral to somewhat alkaline, and a sunny or slightly shaded aspect. Propagation is

from seed, ideally sown the moment ripe or as soon as obtained, by cuttings in mid to late summer, or by layering in spring. Many of the cultivars are grafted plants.

Daphnes have a reputation of being short-lived or for suddenly dying away in part or whole for no apparent reason. Despite this, they are a group of plants to cherish and have few rivals in the rock garden. They deteriorate in response to pruning, and this is best only under-taken to remove dying or diseased growth.

Daphne alpina

Central and southern Europe. A rather upright deciduous shrub to 60 cm (2 ft) tall with oblan-ceolate leaves 1–4 cm (²⁄₅–1²⁄₅ in) long, often rather gray-green. Flowers in terminal clusters of up to 10, white or cream, usually fragrant, 8–10 mm (⅓–²⁄₅ in) across; late spring and early summer. One of the most reliable and longer-lived daphnes in the garden.

Daphne arbuscula

Carpathian Mountains. A small, low, mounded evergreen shrub to 20 cm (8 in) tall, with linear-oblong, deep shiny green leaves with revolute margins, to 5 cm (2 in) long. Flowers in terminal clusters of up to 30, deep rose-pink, 10–16 mm (²⁄₅–⅔ in) across; late spring and early summer. An excellent raised bed or trough plant. Forma *albiflora* pure white.

Daphne cneorum

Northwestern Spain eastward to the Alps, Carpathians, and Ukraine. A matted prostrate or semi-prostrate evergreen shrub to 30 cm (12 in) tall at the most, spreading to 1 m (3 ft)

Top left: *Daphne arbuscula*

Top right: *Daphne cneorum* 'Eximea'

Right: *Daphne ×hendersonii* 'Ernst Hauser'

across. Leaves narrow-oblanceolate, to 18 mm (¾ in) long, deep green above, grayish beneath. Flowers pink, in terminal clusters of up to 12, sometimes more, to 14 mm (⅖ in) across, intensely fragrant; late spring and early summer. 'Argenteum' silvery white margined leaves and rose flowers; 'Eximea' fine vigorous form with rather dense growth and extremely floriferous, the flowers a good deep rose, carmine in bud; 'Ruby Glow' compact plant with rich pinkish red flowers; 'Variegata' (syn. forma *variegata*) yellow-margined leaves and rose flowers; var. *pygmaea* excellent, yet variable, dwarf form, slow-growing but eventually 50 cm (20 in) across with pink flowers, while 'Alba' is a pure white version.

Daphne ×hendersonii

A fine hybrid between *D. petraea* and *D. cneorum* that produces small domed plants 10–30 cm (4–12 in) tall and up to twice as wide. Leaves vary from elliptic to oblanceolate, often very narrowly so. The clones produce terminal clusters of very fragrant flowers; spring to early summer, with a few flowers later in the season. 'Appleblossom' open plant to just 15 cm (6 in) wide, with glossy deep green leaves that curve downward, flowers pale pink from deep pink buds; 'Aymon Correvon' compact and semi-prostrate, not more than 15 cm (6 in) tall, much wider, with deep green foliage and shell pink flowers opening from deeper buds, but fading to near white; 'Ernst Hauser' rather open plant to 30 cm (12 in) high eventually, with dark green, bronze-flushed foliage and pale pink flowers that are purplish red in bud, the lobes notched at the apex; 'Fritz Kummert' flat-growing plant to 10 cm (4 in) high but 60 cm (2 ft) across, with matte green leaves and pink flowers opening from reddish buds; 'Rosebud' com-

pact, to 20 cm (8 in) high, twice as wide, with dark, matte green leaves and pale pink flowers, bright reddish purple in bud.

Daphne petraea

Northern Italy. A delightful little shrublet eventually to 15 cm (6 in) tall and 30 cm (12 in) across, with deep glossy green oblanceolate leaves to 15 mm (⅗ in) long, clustered at the shoot tips. Flowers in clusters of up to six, pale to bright pink, 6–10 mm (¼–⅖ in) across; late spring and early summer. A super little plant for trough or a block of tufa. 'Grandiflora' larger and more sumptuous, deeper colored flowers.

Daphne retusa

Eastern Himalaya to western China. Rather dense, rounded evergreen shrub to 60 cm (2 ft) tall eventually. Leaves deep green and shiny, elliptic to oblanceolate, to 5 cm (2 in) long, notched at the apex. Flowers purple, rose in bud, 14–20 mm (⅗–⅘ in) across, very fragrant, borne in terminal clusters; spring and early summer, sometimes a few later. Berries glossy red when ripe. White forms are known but are rare in cultivation.

Daphne ×susannae

A hybrid between *D. collina* of gardens and *D. arbuscula*, which produces evergreen, domed shrubs to 40 cm (16 in) tall and twice as wide, bearing matte to glossy green leaves. Flowers in terminal clusters of up to 12; late spring on the previous year's shoots, then in summer more on the current shoots. 'Anton Fahndrick' flowers rose-pink, about 13 mm (½ in) across,

....

Daphne petraea

Daphne retusa

Daphne ×susannae 'Cheriton'
Degenia velebitica

with somewhat hairy foliage; 'Cheriton' deep rose-purple, fading gradually after a few days, dark glossy green foliage; 'Tichborne' more compact than 'Cheriton', to only 25 cm (10 in) high with pale rose-purple, slightly larger flowers.

Degenia

A single species of crucifer suitable for raised beds, troughs, or scree, where it will on occasions self-sow. Best propagated from seed sown in late winter or early spring.

Degenia velebitica

Velebit Mountains, Croatia. A delightful and cheerful crucifer inhabiting limestone rocks in the wild. Plants form a lax silvery gray hum-

mock to 15 cm (6 in) tall in flower, the leaves in rosettes, linear lanceolate, 2–4 cm (⅘–1⅗ in) long. The racemes of relatively large bright yellow flowers, each 10–12 mm (⅖–½ in) across, are carried in short racemes above the foliage;

late spring to summer. An excellent raised bed or trough plant readily raised from seed.

Delosperma

Drought-resistant plants primarily from South Africa, with cactus-like flowers, ideal for hot dry situations where water is scarce, but also excellent plants for troughs and other containers. Closely related to *Mesembryanthemum*.

Delospermas come in a range of bright colors and often smother themselves in bloom. Cuttings or divisions taken in the summer afford the most ready means of propagation.

Delosperma congestum
South Africa. A flat, mat-forming plant to 30 cm (1 ft) across, or more, but not more than 5 cm (2 in) tall, with tightly packed, deep green elliptical to linear leaves, 14–18 mm (³⁄₅–²⁄₃ in) long. Flowers lemon yellow, about 20 mm (⁴⁄₅ in) across, with numerous spreading, linear petals, opening in sunshine; late spring and summer.

Delosperma cooperi
South Africa. A mat-forming subshrub spreading to 60 cm (2 ft) or more, with gray-green subcylindrical, pointed leaves to 5 cm (2 in) long, covered in gray papillae. Flowers purple, 4–5 cm (1³⁄₅–2 in) across; summer.

Dianthus

The pinks are a popular genus with many cultivars, prized for the beauty of their blooms as much as the scent of their flowers. The genus has about 300 species in Europe, Asia, and Africa, with a concentration in the mountains close to the Mediterranean. The species include shrubs and subshrubs as well as cushion- and mat-forming perennials and some annuals. They mostly have paired linear leaves and branched or unbranched inflorescences, the flowers solitary in some high-altitude species. The flowers have a tubular calyx that is clasped at its base by two or more pairs of scale-like

. . . .

Delosperma congestum

Dianthus alpinus

bracts, while the clawed petals have a broad limb that is often toothed or fringed on the margin. The fruit is a multiseeded capsule.

The high alpine species mostly require a well drained gritty compost and full sunshine, with some of the discreet, tight cushion-forming plants making ideal trough and tufa plants. Propagation is from seed sown in late winter and early spring or cuttings or layerings in late summer. Some of the tufted ones can be effectively divided in the spring as growth commences. In addition to those listed below, there are numerous other small *Dianthus* cultivars suitable for the rock garden, the smallest also excellent for troughs and raised beds.

Dianthus alpinus

Eastern Alps. A mat-forming evergreen perennial not more than 10 cm (4 in) tall, with deep green, narrow-oblong, blunt leaves. Solitary flowers, 3–4 cm (1⅕–1⅗ in) across, rich pink to cerise or purplish pink, petals speckled with small white dots, toothed at the margin; late spring and summer. Grows best in a gritty, leafy soil. 'Adonis' salmon-pink; 'Joan's Blood' deep red.

Dianthus deltoides

Europe and western Asia. The maiden pink is a charming mat-forming plant to 30 cm (1 ft) across, sometimes more, with spreading, branched slender stems and small narrow oblanceolate leaves to 2.5 cm (1 in) long. Flowers solitary or several, about 18 mm (¾ in) across, pale pink to cerise or crimson-red, the petals with a toothed margin; summer. 'Albus' white, pale foliage; 'Brilliant' carmine,

with purple-red-flushed leaves; 'Flashing Light' true red.

Dianthus erinaceus

Turkey. A tough, prickly, cushion-forming plant to 50 cm (20 in) across eventually, with narrow-triangular, spine-tipped, glaucous leaves, 15–20 mm (⅗–⅘ in) long. Flowers solitary or paired, held shortly above the cushion on stems to 5 cm (2 in) long, purple-pink, about 12 mm

Dianthus deltoides 'Brilliant'

Dianthus erinaceus

(½ in) across, petals slightly toothed; summer. Requires a sheltered, warm, sunny position. Some seed selections are more floriferous than others and are worth seeking out. Despite its spiny nature, this is a first-class cushion plant.

Dianthus 'La Bourboule' (syn. 'La Bour-brille')

A fine plant of hybrid origin forming low silvery gray tufts not more than 10 cm (4 in) tall in flower, with linear leaves. Flowers freely produced, solitary, bright pink, 20 mm (⅘ in) across, with nicely fringed petals; late spring and summer. A first-rate plant for paving, walls, and raised beds.

Dianthus 'Nyewood's Cream'

A dainty little pink forming mats of gray-green leaves to 20 cm (8 in) across with small cream flowers borne on stems to 8 cm (3⅕ in) tall. An excellent plant for the edge of raised beds or retaining walls.

Dianthus pavonius (syn. *D. neglectus*)

Southwestern Alps mainly. A cushion-forming plant to 20 cm (8 in) tall in flower, with linear, glaucous, three-veined leaves that taper to a fine point. Flowers one to three per stem, relatively large, 2–2.5 mm (⅘–1 in) across, pale to deep purplish pink, bearded in the center of the petals, with a buff reverse and toothed margin, the bracts as long as the calyx; early summer. One of the best rock garden pinks.

Dodecatheon

A primarily American genus with some 15 species, one restricted to eastern Siberia. They are closely related to *Primula*, but have characteristic dart-shaped flowers in which the petals are bent back through 180° and the stamens protrude as a cone from the mouth of the flower. The leaves are all in a basal tuft, while the flowers are borne several to a common scape, as in many primulas.

Dodecatheons or shooting stars are a delightful group of plants requiring cool, moist, humus-rich soils in sun or part shade. Propagation by seed sown the moment ripe or in late winter and early spring affords the best means of increase. Some species produce rice-like bulblets at the root bases, and these can be detached and grown on, treating them just like seeds.

Dodecatheon meadia (syn. *D. pauciflorum*)

Eastern North America from Manitoba to Pennsylvania and Georgia. Plant to 50 cm (20 in) tall in flower, often less, with ovate to oblong, medium green leaves to 30 cm (1 ft) long, with an entire or toothed margin. Umbels of five-petaled flowers, 20–50 normally, rich rose-purple to lilac or pink, each 2–3 cm (⅘–1⅕ in) long, with yellow stamens tipped maroon; late spring and early summer. Forma *album* white; 'Queen Victoria' rich rose-purple; 'Splendidum' crimson. Plants sold under the name *D. meadia* are often found to be *D. pulchellum*.

Dodecatheon pulchellum

Western North America from Canada to California and Mexico. Rather similar to *D. meadia*, but leaves often wavy or toothed on the margin and umbels with fewer (normally not more than 25) rather smaller flowers, magenta to lavender, purple, pink, or white, the tube yellow with maroon lines; late spring and early summer. Forma *album* white; 'Red Wings' deep crimson; 'Sooke's Variety' a smaller, neater form not more than 20 cm (8 in) tall usually.

Draba

Whitlow grasses are scattered across the tem perate Northern Hemisphere and in South America, a genus of some 300 species of annual and perennial herbs, the choicest being high-alpine mat- or cushion-forming plants. Like all crucifers, drabas have four-parted, yellow or white flowers, normally six stamens, and a two-parted, generally dehiscent, fruit capsule.

Drabas are readily raised from seed or from late summer cuttings of single-rosette shoots. Most of the higher alpine species thrive in a gritty, well-drained compost and, while the choicest are subjects for alpine house treatment, a number are fine outdoors, particularly for raised beds and troughs.

Draba aizoides
Europe. The yellow Whitlow grass is a small tufted plant not more than 15 cm (6 in) tall in flower with deep green rosettes of bristle-margined, linear-lanceolate leaves, 10–15 mm (2/5–3/5 in) long. The racemes of yellow flowers, each 6–8 mm (1/4–1/3 in) across, are congested at first but soon elongate as successive flowers open; spring. A widespread species in the European mountains, where it inhabits limestone rocks, crevices, and screes. Easy and reliable, often self-sowing in the garden.

Draba bryoides
Armenia, Caucasus. Plant forming neat, rather moss-like, low, bright green cushions to 20 cm (8 in) across, sometimes larger, with numerous crammed leaf rosettes of linear-elliptic,

petaled, solitary flowers. These are followed by attractive fluffy fruitheads. They thrive in a gritty, humus-rich soil in full sunshine. Propagation is effected by seed the moment ripe or from late summer cuttings.

Dryas octopetala

Arctic Northern Hemisphere, except North America. The mountain avens is a mat-forming, subshrubby plant to 60 cm (2 ft) across. The small leaves, 1–3 cm (²/₅–1¹/₅ in) long, are oblong-elliptic with a scalloped margin, deep green above, white-downy beneath. The solitary flowers are held above the foliage on slender stalks, white, 3–4 cm (1¹/₅–1³/₅ in) across, each with eight, occasionally more, petals; spring and early summer. 'Grandiflora' extra-large flowers, more free-blooming than the typical plant in cultivation; 'Minor' a smaller, neater, free-flowering version. Best grown in a calcareous soil.

Edraianthus

Colorful relations of the bellflowers (*Campanula*), differing in the irregular way the fruit valves separate, rather than by neat apical pores. The genus contains about 20 species found from the Balkans eastward to Turkey and the Caucasus. They are tufted or cushion-forming plants with linear leaves and solitary or clustered campanulate flowers in shades of blue and violet, occasionally white.

Edraianthus are excellent plants for raised beds, screes, and troughs in full sun, where a well-drained soil is an essential requirement. Fresh seed sown in late winter germinates

incurved leaves with a ciliate margin. Flowers pale yellow, 4–5 mm (¹/₆–¹/₅ in) across, in head-like racemes; spring, occasionally a few later flowers.

Dryas

Three or four species of carpeting subshrubs restricted to the cool temperate Northern Hemisphere, with leathery leaves and eight-

freely in pots in a cold frame, and this affords the best means of increase. Some success with spring cuttings is possible if enough material is available.

Edraianthus graminifolius

Balkans and Italy. Very like a small *Campanula*, this plant, not more than 10 cm (4 in) tall in flower, inhabits limestone rocks in the wild. Forms basal tufts of deep green, linear, grassy leaves 5–15 mm (⅕–⅗ in) long, ciliate at the base. From these arise several ascending stems bearing a tight cluster of up to six blue or violet bells, each 15–30 mm (⅗–1⅓ in) long; summer.

Edraianthus pumilio

Bosnia, Croatia, and Herzegovina. A flat, dense cushion plant to 30 cm (1 ft) across, often less, not more than 5 cm (2 in) high in flower, with linear, ciliate, silvery leaves to 20 mm (⅘ in) long. Flowers solitary, with short subtending

. . . .

Bottom left: *Edraianthus graminifolius*

Right: *Edraianthus pumilio*

Bottom right: *Edraianthus serpyllifolius*

bracts, violet-blue, occasionally white, erect bells 14–20 mm (⅗–⅘ in) long; summer. A limestone rock species in the wild and arguably the finest to cultivate.

Edraianthus serpyllifolius

Very similar to *E. pumilio* and from the same part of the world, although extending down into Albania. This species is another gem for the garden; it differs primarily in its more

spatula-shaped leaves up to 30 mm (1⅕ in) long, and in the larger deep violet flowers, 15–25 mm (⅗–1 in) long; summer.

Eranthis

A small genus with probably seven species scattered in the Northern Hemisphere from Europe to Japan. They resemble buttercups with a tuberous rootstock and one or two long-stalked basal leaves that are rounded in outline and deeply, palmately divided. Flowers are solitary, cup-shaped, surrounded by a ruff of sessile leaf-like bracts; sepals five or six, petal-like, yellow or white. The numerous stamens form a central boss surrounded by a ring of tubular nectaries, actually modified petals. Fruit a head of multiseeded follicles.

Those listed here can be readily grown in a moist leafy soil. Although mostly seen in a woodland setting, they make excellent plants for pockets in the rock garden or for containers. The species often self-sow in the garden. Propagation is by seed or careful division once the plants have died down.

Eranthis cilicica

Turkey eastward to Iraq and Iran. Very like *E. hyemalis* and sometimes included within it (as Cilicica Group). A bolder and rather stockier plant with more finely divided foliage, which is sometimes bronze-flushed when young, and with larger, deep golden flowers; spring.

Eranthis hyemalis

Europe, naturalized in much of the west. The winter aconite is a small, tufted, herbaceous perennial to 15 cm (6 in) tall, with deep, shiny green foliage, often only partly developed at flowering time, with five or seven lobed segments. Flowers yellow, 20–30 mm (⅘–1⅕ in) across, deeply cupped at first, later opening widely; late winter and spring. 'Pauline' pale yellow. Orange-flowered and double-flowered forms are known and occasionally available.

Eranthis ×tubergenii (Tubergenii Group)

A sterile hybrid between *E. cilicica* and *E. hyemalis*, more or less of intermediate character. 'Guinea Gold', the finest selection, has wonderfully bronze-flushed young foliage and deep golden flowers to 4 cm (1⅗ in) across when fully expanded. A fine plant for a semi-shaded niche in the rock garden. Needs to be increased by division of the parent tuber; these can be carefully broken apart by hand or by using a sharp clean knife, treating the cut surfaces with a fungicide before they are replanted.

Erigeron

Fleabanes are a genus of some 200 species with a cosmopolitan distribution but particularly

Eranthis ×tubergenii 'Guinea Gold'

rich in North America. They are related to the more familiar *Aster*, with daisy-like flowerheads bearing numerous linear rays in several rows. Most are tufted or clump-forming perennials, although a few are annuals or even subshrubs, with simple or occasionally lobed leaves, often congested into basal rosettes. Those included here are plants for sunny well-drained sites in the rock garden or for raised beds and troughs. Propagation is by division or cuttings in late summer or by seed sown in late winter and spring. Most species are very attractive to butterflies and bees.

Erigeron aureus

Northwestern United States; Oregon and Washington. One of the mountain gems of North America, thriving particularly on rather dry volcanic slopes in low sward in the wild. Plants form small clumps to 15 cm (6 in) tall in flower. Leaves gray-green, basal petiolate, elliptic to obovate, to 5 cm (2 in) long. Flowerheads solitary, rich yellow, about 2.5 cm (1 in) across; late spring and summer. 'Canarybird' larger creamy yellow flowers.

Erigeron compositus

Western North America, including Canada, Greenland. A neat, laxly tufted plant to 20 cm (8 in) tall. Leaves fan-shaped, several times ternately divided, rather crowded. Flowerheads solitary, 13–24 mm (½–1 in) across, white or pink, occasionally bluish, with a yellow disk; summer. Var. *glabratus* is smaller and more compact. A fine plant for a raised bed or trough.

....

Erigeron aureus

Erigeron compositus

Erigeron glaucus

California. A vigorous, handsome coastal subshrub to 90 cm (3 ft) across, forming lax domes or mats of relatively large blue-green leaf rosettes, leaves obovate, 6–12.5 cm (2⅖–5 in) long, toothed or entire on the margin. Stems bearing several flowerheads, 3.5–6.5 cm (1⅖–2⅗ in) across, with pale violet or lavender rays surrounding a golden disk; spring and early

long, the lowermost generally three-lobed. Flowerheads white or pale lilac with purple underneath, 2–3 cm (⅘–1⅕ in) across; late spring to autumn. Often self-sowing in the garden, this little gem is excellent for wall crevices—hence its common name, wall daisy.

Erinacea

This genus contains just two species of spiny subshrubs from southern France, Spain, and North Africa, of which only one is in general cultivation. *Erinacea* is a member of the pea family (Leguminosae or Fabaceae), with the branches terminating in a sharp spine. Leaves are small and rather inconspicuous. The typical pea flowers are solitary or in small terminal clusters. The fruit is a small few-seeded pod.

The species below requires a warm, sheltered, sunny place in the garden if plants are to thrive and flower well, and a gritty, very well-drained soil. Propagation is from seed when available, and best sown under glass in the spring. However, late summer cuttings of one-year shoots is probably the main means of increase. Once established plants should not be disturbed, otherwise they will almost certainly die.

summer, occasionally later. 'Elstead Pink' clear lilac-pink; 'Roseus' pink.

Erigeron karvinskyanus (syn. *E. mucronatus*)

Mexico. This delightful little daisy has become thoroughly naturalized in the milder parts of Europe and elsewhere. Plants form lax mounds of numerous slender stems bearing gray-green, obovate to elliptic leaves, 1–3.5 cm (⅕–1⅖ in)

Erinacea anthyllis

Southern France, Spain, and Morocco. Dense, very spiny, hedgehog-like plant forming mounds to 60 cm (2 ft) across, but only half that in height, with downy young, spine-tipped, gray-green, forking stems. Leaves small, 4–5 mm (⅕ in) long, narrow-oblanceolate. Flowers violet-blue, occasionally white, 16–18 mm

(⅔–¾ in) long, generally in clusters of two or three, calyces somewhat inflated, pale green; early summer.

Erinus

One of the very easiest of rock garden plants and a great delight in flower, it will happily colonize parts of the rock garden, as well as old walls and crevices. The genus contains a single species that is distantly related to other familiar genera in the foxglove family (Scrophulariaceae), most notably *Chaenorhinum* and *Linaria*. In *Erinus* the small flowers are slightly two-lipped, with spreading, notched lobes that unite below into a very short tubular base. The small seed capsules contain numerous seeds. It requires no special treatment and will thrive in any well-drained compost. Readily raised from seed, indeed plants usually self-sow in the garden and seedlings are easy to move around.

Erinus alpinus

Spain eastward to Italy and the eastern Alps. Known as the fairy foxglove, this little evergreen gem forms lax, deep green rosettes of hairy, obovate, slightly toothed leaves, to 4 cm (1⅗ in) long. From the rosettes arise leafy flowering stems to 15 cm (6 in) long, bearing racemes of rose-purple flowers, each 5–10 mm (⅕–⅖ in) across; spring and intermittently through summer. Var. *albus* white; 'Carmineus' carmine-pink; 'Doktor Hähnle' ('Hanaele')

....

Erinacea anthyllis

Erinus alpinus

carmine; 'Mrs Charles Boyle' soft pink. Intermediate colors will occur spontaneously in the garden where several cultivars are grown close together.

Eriogonum

A North American genus concentrated in the western and southern United States containing about 150 species commonly referred to as buckwheats. They are members of the Polygonaceae, which contains familiar garden genera such as *Bistorta*, *Polygonum*, and the rhubarbs, *Rheum*. Eriogonums are annuals, perennials, or subshrubs. In the most desirable, the leaves form mainly basal rosettes that are often downy or woolly. The small flowers have parts in combinations of three and are generally borne in

umbels of heads close to, or well above, the foliage. The fruit is a small triangular achene.

Some of the choicest species are challenging plants for the rock gardener, but there are, nonetheless, several that are attractive and accommodating plants for the rock garden, raised bed, or trough, requiring a sunny well-drained site in the open garden, but one that is never allowed to desiccate. Propagation from seed sown in late winter and early spring provides the best means of increase, although semi-ripe cuttings taken in the summer can also be very effective.

Eriogonum ovalifolium

Western North America; British Columbia to California and Montana. Another mat-forming species, not more than 20 cm (8 in) tall in flower and with dense rosettes of white-woolly obovate leaves to 12 mm (½ in) long. Flowers in heads on long slender stems, rather crowded, bright primrose yellow; summer. The plant usually offered by nurseries is var. *nivale*, restricted to the Sierra Nevada of California in the wild, which has a denser, more compact, habit with small leaves not more than 5 mm (⅕ in) long. The white, red-veined flowers become suffused with rose as they age.

Eriogonum umbellatum

North America; British Columbia to California, Wyoming, and Arizona. A plant of sagebrush and rocky alpine slopes in the wild. A quite variable species forming a mat to 30 cm (1 ft) tall in flower. Leaves gray-green or green above, white-felted beneath, elliptic to obovate, to 2.5 cm (1 in) long. Inflorescence a

Eriogonum umbellatum

compound umbel to 10 cm (4 in) across, cream to yellow; summer. Var. *polyanthum* (syn. var. *haussknechtii*) is smaller than the type in all its parts with elliptic-oblong, grayish leaves and simple umbels of yellow flowers; var. *torreyanum* (syn. var. *glaberrimum*) has glabrous leaves and bracted inflorescences.

Eriophyllum

A western North American genus with about a dozen species that range from annuals and perennials to subshrubs, one of which makes an excellent and bright addition to the rock garden. Eriophyllums bear woolly, often lobed, leaves and daisy-like flowerheads that usually have yellow rays.

The species below flourishes in any well-drained average garden soil, providing it is given a good sunny position. Propagation is easily effected by division of the parent plant in early spring just before growth commences.

Eriophyllum lanatum

Western North America; British Columbia to California, the Rockies in particular. A variable silvery gray, clump forming perennial to 90 cm (36 in) tall in flower. Leaves gray-woolly, especially beneath, entire to pinnately lobed, 1–4 cm (²⁄₅–1³⁄₅ in) long. Flowerheads bright yellow, to 4 cm (1³⁄₅ in) across, borne on stems that are leafless in the upper half; late spring and summer. The dwarfer, higher altitude forms, often only 20 cm (8 in) tall in flower, are well worth seeking out: these include var. *monoense* (syn. *E. lutescens*) and var. *integrifolium*.

. . . .

Eriophyllum lanatum

Erodium glandulosum

Erodium

A genus of some 60 species, commonly referred to as stork's-bills, closely related to *Geranium*, widely distributed in the Mediterranean region, especially North Africa, but with some weedier annual and biennial species distributed as far afield as the Americas, India, and Australasia. Erodiums were at one time included in *Geranium* but are distinguished by

having only five fertile stamens (the other five are modified into staminodes) and in the spiral twisting of the fruit awns.

The smaller species make desirable plants for the rock garden and raised bed, requiring a sunny position and well-drained compost, preferably alkaline, although this is not essential. They can be propagated from seed sown in late winter or early spring or from basal cuttings struck in spring and summer. Plants tend to hybridize in the garden environment so that seed may not come true to type.

Erodium chrysanthum

Greece. A tufted evergreen perennial with separate male and female plants, to about 25 cm (10 in) tall in flower, with silky gray, binnately lobed leaves to 20 cm (8 in) long. Flowers two to seven per umbel, each about 2 cm (⅘ in) across, white to cream in male plants, sulfur yellow in female, usually with pink anthers; summer. Hybridizes readily with other species in the garden.

. . . .

Erodium pelargoniflorum

Erodium glandulosum (syn. *E. petraeum*)

Southern France and Spain. A complex species with numerous variants recognized, some the finest storksbills for the average rock garden, being both dependable and colorful. Forms rounded clumps to 40 cm (16 in) across and half that in height. Leaves oblong, bipinnately lobed, with both large and small leaflets intermixed. Flowers up to five per umbel, each 2.5 cm (1 in) across, white to lilac, with deep blotching on the upper two petals and a five-branched purple style; summer.

Erodium pelargoniflorum

Turkey. A short-lived tufted perennial to 30 cm (1 ft) tall in flower with a woody, branching base. Leaves mostly basal, ovate, shallowly lobed, with a heart-shaped base, soft-hairy. Flowers up to 10 per umbel, about 2.5 cm (1 in) across, white with reddish purple veining, upper two petals with large basal blotch; borne throughout most of the year except in severe weather. Although not reliably hardy in many gardens, it does redeem itself by self-sowing, especially close to a warm sheltering wall.

Erodium reichardii (syn. *E. chamaedryoides)*

Balearic Islands. A dense, hummock-forming gray-green plant to 25 cm (10 in) across, with rounded to oblong, crenate-margined leaves to 15 mm (⅗ in) long. Flowers solitary, 15–20 mm (⅗–⅘ in) across, white veined and suffused with pinkish purple, borne on short thread-like stems just above the foliage; spring to autumn. 'Album' white; 'Rubrum' red.

Eryngium

The so-called sea hollies comprise a genus of over 200 species with a worldwide distribution

Eryngium bourgatii

except for central and southern Africa. Most are too gross for the rock garden. They are thistle-like plants with smooth or spiny, sometimes deeply lobed, leaves. Inflorescences are comprised of numerous tiny florets, in dense rounded to conical heads, surrounded at the base by a ruff of spiny, often delightfully colored, bracts.

Plants are readily grown from seed sown in late winter or early spring. The one species included here thrives in a sunny well-drained site and will seed around modestly in some gardens. It is a fine plant, as are the other species, for attracting insects into the garden, especially bees and butterflies.

Eryngium bourgatii

Southern France and northern Spain. The Pyrenean sea holly is a herbaceous perennial to 40 cm (16 in) tall in flower, with mostly basal leaves, these rounded and long-stalked, three-parted, with each segment further lobed and with spiny teeth. Flowerheads globose, about 15 mm (⅗ in) across, bluish, surrounded by up to eight metallic blue flushed, shiny, linear bracts; summer. Several cultivars are readily available: 'Oxford Blue', 'Picos Amethyst', and 'Picos Blue'.

Euphorbia

A very large and impressive genus with some 1600 species scattered throughout the world, including annuals, perennials, shrubs, trees, and succulents, especially concentrated in tropical regions. All euphorbias or spurges have a white gummy sap when cut. The curious petalless flowers (botanically called cyathea)

consist of several single-stemmed male flowers and a single female reduced to a three-lobed ovary. The attractiveness of the spurge inflorescences, which can be very large, is in the conspicuous bracts and bractlets, which are often yellow or yellow-green, sometimes white, orange, red, or pink. The fruit capsule contains three seeds normally.

Most euphorbias are too large for the smaller rock garden. The one listed here is a perfect rock garden plant, seeding itself quietly around. Being Mediterranean in origin, it requires a sunny, well-drained site in the garden and makes a fine raised bed or paving plant.

Euphorbia myrsinites

Southern Europe and western Asia. A robust, spreading, evergreen perennial with all the stems radiating over the ground from a single point, to 30 cm (12 in). Stems thick, bearing numerous glaucous, sometimes purple-flushed, fleshy, obovate leaves, 2.5–5 cm (1–2 in) long.

Flowers in umbel-like heads to 10 cm (4 in) across, surrounded by chrome yellow bracts; late spring and early summer. Readily raised from seed sown in late winter and early spring.

Euryops

An African genus of some 100 species, also found on the island of Socotra and in Arabia. They are evergreen shrubs with simple or variously dissected leaves and yellow daisy-like flowerheads.

Only one species is generally grown in the rock garden. It requires a sheltered position and abundant sunshine. Propagation is easiest from cuttings, both semi-mature and hardwood, taken in late summer and autumn.

Euryops acraeus

Basutoland. A hummock-forming silvery gray shrub to 60 cm (2 ft) tall, twice as much across,

Euphorbia myrsinites

Euryops acraeus

with rather waxy, sessile, linear, grooved leaves to 3 cm (1¼ in) long. Several daisy-like flowerheads are produced from each shoot tip, lemon yellow, about 2.5 cm (1 in) across; late spring and early summer.

Genista

A genus of legumes (Leguminosae), with about 90 species of trees and shrubs similar in appearance to, and closely relate to, the brooms (*Cytisus*), although a number of genistas are very spiny. They have small simple leaves and clusters or racemes of relatively small, yellow peaflowers.

The smaller species are excellent little shrubs for the rock garden, giving both height and form. Any well-drained sunny site will suit them. They can be propagated from seed sown in late winter and early spring or from late summer cuttings. Plants deteriorate if disturbed once established and seedlings should be pricked out and moved on from pots with great care.

Genista lydia

Eastern Balkans. In the wild, this species is found on limestone rocks. One of the finest rock garden shrubs, it makes an intricately branched green bush, with arching, ridged, green stems bearing small, rather inconspicuous, linear-oblong leaves, 3–10 mm (⅛–⅖ in) long, but soon falling. Flowers bright yellow,

. . . .

Genista lydia (far right) on a scree in the author's garden.

10–13 mm (⅖–½ in) long, in small clusters of two to four, borne profusely; late spring and early summer. An excellent plant for draping over rocks or low walls. Plants can become infested with aphids in the spring when they come into growth.

Genista sagittalis (syn. *Chamaespartium sagittale*)

Central and southern Europe. A mat-forming plant with winged prostrate stems forming patches up to 1 m (3 ft) across, sometimes more. Flowering stems ascending to erect, winged, green, to 25 cm (10 in) long, bearing a few alternate, elliptic leaves, to 20 mm (⅘ in) long. Flowers pea-shaped, bright yellow, about 15 mm (⅗ in) long, borne in short dense racemes; late spring and summer. A good carpeter for the larger rock garden, in sun or part shade.

Gentiana

A large and beautiful genus with some 350 species in temperate and arctic regions of the world, primarily in the mountains, but excluding Africa. The species, many noted for their intense blue flowers, are among the most important rock plants favored by growers and include some of the most glorious sights to be seen in high mountains around the world. The genus consists primarily of both evergreen and herbaceous perennials, many small and tufted, but also a number of annual and biennial species that are scarcely grown. Gentians have simple, paired, sometimes whorled, untoothed leaves and solitary or clustered flowers, these sometimes arranged in racemes. The calyx is usually green, sometimes purple or blackish, and five-toothed, while the corolla is either trumpet- or salver-shaped, with a pronounced tube, inside which is housed the five stamens, ovary, and style. The fruit is a two-parted, dehiscent capsule containing numerous tiny seeds.

The more widely available species make excellent subjects for the rock garden, raised beds, troughs, and containers. While most thrive in a gritty, calcareous compost, some (especially the *G. sino-ornata* group) require an acid, humus-rich compost and cooler conditions if they are to succeed. Propagation is from seed, by division, or from cuttings taken in the spring.

Gentiana acaulis (syn. *G. kochiana*)

Alps, Carpathians, and Pyrenees. The trumpet gentian is one of the most spectacular rock garden plants in general cultivation and requires a

· ·
Gentiana acaulis

sunny situation in the garden. Plants form broad mats up to 30 cm (1 ft) wide eventually of deep green elliptical leaves. Solitary, trumpet-shaped flowers, 6–7 cm (1⅖–2⅖ in) long, intense kingfisher blue with some green spotting within, borne above the foliage on short stems to 7.5 cm (3 in) long; spring. Forma *alba* ('Alba') white; 'Coelestina' Cambridge blue. Other freely available cultivars include 'Belvedere', 'Rannoch', and 'Trotter's Variety'. The species is the emblem of the Alpine Garden Society and is one of the most stunningly attractive rock plants when seen in the wild, inhabiting alpine meadows at the higher elevations.

Gentiana asclepiadea

Central Europe eastward to the Caucasus and northern Iran. A clump-forming herbaceous perennial with erect to arching, slender stems to 60 cm (2 ft) tall. Leaves lanceolate to ovate, pointed, to 4 cm (1⅗ in) long. Flowers in pairs or threes from all the upper leaves, blue

to purple-blue or white (var. *alba*), trumpet-shaped, to 5 cm (2 in) long; late summer and autumn. The larger forms of willow-leaved gentian are too gross for the smaller rock garden, but the dwarfer ones are perfect, especially as they are late flowering. Good for dappled shade in a leafy, moist soil. 'Knightshayes' deep blue, white in throat; 'Nana' not more than 30 cm (12 in) tall; 'Pink Swallow' white tipped pink; 'Rosea' pink.

Gentiana cruciata

Central Europe to Turkey and western Siberia. A rather coarse, leafy, tufted perennial, with a wide range in the wild, where it is a plant of meadows and woodland fringes. Basal leaves oblong or oval, to 10 cm (4 in) long, deep green and three-veined; stem leaves smaller. Stiff stems bear whorls of small trumpet-shaped

....

Gentiana asclepiadea 'Nana'

Gentiana cruciata

flowers, 2–2.5 cm (⅘–1 in) long, blue or purplish with a pale, often whitish throat: unusually the flowers have only four, instead of the normal five to seven, lobes; late summer to autumn.

Gentiana paradoxa

Western Caucasus. Plants form discreet tufts with all stems radiating from a central rosette of leaves, stems spreading to erect, 15–23 cm (6–9 in) tall. Leaves characteristically arranged

in whorls of four or five, rather pale bright green, linear-lanceolate, long-pointed. Solitary, terminal, trumpet-shaped flowers, 4–5.5 cm (1⅗–2⅕ in) long, rich kingfisher blue in the best forms, with delicate fringing in mouth and deep spotting in tube; borne from late summer to autumn.

Gentiana saxosa

New Zealand. Short-lived perennial forming tufts rarely more than 20 cm (8 in) across, of deep glossy green, spoon-shaped to oval leaves. The purplish, sparsely leafy stems carry a solitary or several pure white, pencil-lined flowers, each about 20 mm (⅘ in) across, with spreading petals fused together only near the base; late spring and early summer. It thrives best in a humus-rich, free-draining compost and will self-sow in favored situations in the garden.

Gentiana scabra

Northwestern China, Korea, and Japan. A clump-forming species, 15–30 cm (6–12 in) tall in flower. Leaves gray-green, lanceolate to oval-triangular, with a long pointed tip. Leafy purplish or reddish stems bear clusters of trumpet or rather bell-shaped flowers, 3.5–5 cm (1⅖–2 in) long, blue or purple-blue, sometimes rather pale, with white spotting on the lobes; late summer to autumn. Sometimes sold as a potted plant often under the name 'Sensation', a well-flowered selection. White forms are sometimes available.

Gentiana septemfida

Turkey, Iran, and the Caucasus. One of the easiest and most reliable species in the garden,

. . . .

Gentiana paradoxa

Gentiana saxosa

forming discreet tufts with prostrate to spreading stems, 15–30 cm (6–12 in) long, bearing numerous oval to lanceolate deep green leaves. The solitary, or more normally clustered, trumpet-shaped flowers, 3.5–4 cm (1⅖–1⅗ in) long, vary from rich blue to purple-blue, each with five to seven white-spotted lobes; midsummer to autumn. Seedlings can be quite variable and only the best colored forms should be retained, otherwise the stock will diminish in quality.

Gentiana sino-ornata

Western China; Sichuan, Tibet, and northwestern Yunnan. The autumn gentian is a plant of marshy mountain meadows. Plants form small tufts with one or a cluster of basal rosettes of narrow, grassy, pointed leaves. Solitary erect flowers borne on slender wide-spreading stems up 20 cm (8 in), trumpet-shaped, 5–6 cm (2–2⅖ in), rich blue with pale yellowish green tube strongly striped with deep

purple-blue outside; autumn. Requires acid, cool conditions and regular splitting (at least every three years) if it is to thrive. 'Alba' white, a less vigorous form; 'Brin Form' rich blue, extra-long trailing stems; 'Edith Sarah' very deep blue with white stripes; 'Mary Lyle' deep green foliage, white flowers with blue streaks in folds; 'White Wings' pale blue and white. *Gentiana sino-ornata* is a parent of a range of fine hybrids with allied species. The plant is sometimes sold as a cut flower.

Right: *Gentiana scabra*

Bottom left: *Gentiana septemfida*

Bottom right: *Gentiana sino-ornata*

Gentiana veitchiorum

Western China. A fine species, superficially resembling *G. sino-ornata*, but with shorter, blunter, deep green, crowded leaves. Flowers solitary, narrow-funnel-shaped, rich deep blue, bearing whitish or greenish bands on the outside of the tube; autumn. Requires a rather drier acid soil than *G. sino-ornata*. Occasionally available, but well-worth seeking out as it is one of the finest autumn-flowering rock garden plants.

Gentiana verna

European mountains eastward to Turkey and the Caucasus. The spring gentian is a familiar little rock garden plant forming neat tufts, 5–7.5 cm (2–3 in) tall in flower, with grayish green lanceolate to elliptic leaves, mostly basal. Solitary, salver-shaped flowers, 1.5–2.5 cm (⅗–1 in) long, intense blue with white center and neat little folds between the five main lobes; spring. Subsp. *tergestina* (syn. *G. angulosa*, 'Angulosa') with deep sky blue flowers is the form most commonly seen in cultivation. White forms are occasionally available. Generally short-lived in cultivation, but readily replenished from cuttings or seed. One of the most sought after rock garden plants and a must in any collection, looking especially effective with other rock garden plants when grown in an old stone trough.

Geranium

A large genus with some 300 annual, biennial, and perennial species with a worldwide distribution. They mostly have long-stalked, rounded, palmately lobed leaves, the lobes subsequently further lobed and toothed. The flowers are often in pairs and are rather flat to saucer- or bowl-shaped with five small, often green, sepals and five prominent petals and 10 stamens. The five-seeded fruit is beaked, hence the common names of crane's-bill, each seed portion and a section of beak peeling away to release the seeds.

One of the most popular genera of hardy herbaceous and evergreen perennials in the garden, with a number of excellent ones for

. . . .

Gentiana veitchiorum

Gentiana verna

the rock garden. Geraniums are easy to grow on most well-drained, yet moisture-retentive soils in sun or part shade. Propagation is effected easily from seed sown when ripe or in early spring, or by division of the parent clump as growth commences in the spring or after flowering. Species hybridize readily in the garden and the offspring can, as a consequence, be quite variable.

Geranium cinereum

Southern France and northern Spain. A rather compact plant making rounded mounds of foliage to 40 cm (16 in) across, occasionally more. Leaves bluish green, rounded, deeply five-segmented, the segments further divided and with overlapping lobes. Flowers saucer-shaped, 2.5–3 cm (1–1⅕ in) across, pale pink with a fine network of purple veins; late spring and summer. 'Album' white.

Geranium cinereum × subcaulescens
   hybrids

These are intermediate in character between the parent species: 'Artistry' veiny flowers with a clear pink ground color; 'Ballerina' pink with a filigree of deep purple veins and a dark blotch at the base of each petal; 'Laurence Flatman' like 'Ballerina', but a more vigorous plant with slightly frilly petals with a darker inverted triangle at the apex of each petal.

Geranium dalmaticum

Montenegro and Albania. Closely related to *G. macrorrhizum* and a more refined and less vigorous, fragrant, plant for the rock garden, not more than 15 cm (6 in) tall in flower. Leaves

glossy and glabrous, not more than 4 cm (1⅗ in) wide, with five to seven segments. Flowers in small clusters, about 30 mm (1⅕ in) across, bright pink; early summer. 'Album' slightly less vigorous, white.

Geranium farreri

Western China; high mountains of northern Sichuan and southern Gansu. A little gem of a plant forming neat little clumps not more

....

Geranium 'Laurence Flatman'

Geranium dalmaticum

than 15 cm (6 in) tall in flower. Leaves semi-glossy, green, to 5 cm (2 in) wide, with seven segments, each further divided into three or more lobes. Flowers solitary or paired, saucer-shaped, about 3 cm (1⅕ in) across, soft pink with deep veining and blue-black anthers; late spring and early summer. Needs a rich scree in the garden but even then tends to be rather short-lived. Readily raised from seed and worth

every effort. Sometimes sold under the incorrect and misapplied name *G. napuligerum*.

Geranium macrorrhizum

Southern Alps and Italy eastward to the Balkans and Carpathians. A colonizing, rhizomatous perennial to 1 m (3 ft) or more across, with thick, slightly sticky stems. Leaves 10–20 cm (4–8 in) across, with five to seven diamond-shaped segments, these further lobed and toothed, slightly sticky, strongly pungent when bruised. Flowers in compact clusters on a stalk just clear of the foliage, 2.5–3 cm (1– 1⅕ in) across, purplish pink, with markedly protruding orange-red stamens; late spring and summer, sometimes later. 'Album' white petals contrasting with red sepals; 'Bevan's Variety' a compact form with smallish, deep magenta-purple flowers with red sepals; 'Ingwersen's Variety' a vigorous selection with extra-large flowers of soft pink, contrasting with pale green,

....

Left: *Geranium farreri*

Bottom left: *Geranium macrorrhizum*

Bottom right: *Geranium macrorrhizum* 'Ingwersen's Variety'

slightly glossy foliage; 'Variegatum' leaves variegated with cream and purple-pink flowers; 'White-Ness' white flowers with green sepals, leaves rather small, glossy pale green.

Geranium subcaulescens (syn. *G. cinereum* subsp. *subcaulescens*)

Balkans. Very similar to *G. cinereum*, but flowers magenta with a deep base to each petal, late spring and summer. 'Guiseppii' rich magenta-pink; 'Splendens' vigorous selection with intense magenta flowers.

Geum

A genus of some 65 species restricted primarily to the Northern Hemisphere, especially in the cooler regions. They are closely related to *Potentilla*, both possessing divided leaves and epicalyx segments, but in *Geum* the achenal fruits are adorned with a feather appendage that sometimes is hooked at the tip.

Both those described here thrive in a gritty neutral or alkaline soil in full sun. Propagation is from seed sown in late winter or early spring or by division in late winter, before growth recommences. Runners can be separated from stoloniferous forms and grown on separately.

Geum reptans

Central Europe. Plants form mounded clumps to 20 cm (8 in) tall in flower but more in fruit, spreading by means of red, strawberry-like runners. Leaves in tufts, to 7.5 cm (3 in) long, evenly pinnate, with up to 10 pairs of oval or obovate, toothed segments. Flowers solitary, butter yellow, 3–5 cm (1⅕–2 in) across, with

five to eight somewhat overlapping, notched petals; late spring and early summer. Fruit erect with feathery persistent styles. The closely similar *G. montanum*, which has a wider distribution in central and southern Europe, is readily distinguished by its nonstoloniferous habit, more unevenly lobed leaves, and golden flowers.

....

Geranium subcaulescens 'Splendens'

Geum reptans

Globularia

A charming genus of rather more than 20 species of evergreen shrubs and shrublets with entire, often leathery, leaves. Flowers small but in dense globular heads, the corollas somewhat two-lipped, five-lobed overall.

Globularias make fine rock garden plants, the smaller ones perfect for raised beds and troughs, where they will often creep down over the sides. Propagation is by seed sown in the spring or by division at the same time. Alternatively, cuttings of mature vegetative shoots can be taken in late summer and placed in a cold frame to root.

Globularia cordifolia
Central and southern Europe to Turkey. A mat-forming plant to 40 cm (16 in) across, with woody main stems and evergreen leaves, glossy deep green, oblanceolate to spathulate, up to 20 mm (⅘ in) long, with a notched tip. Flower-heads held above the mat on stems to 10 cm (4 in) long, blue, 10–20 mm (⅖–⅘ in) across; summer.

Globularia meridionalis
Mountains of southeastern Alps, Italy, and the Balkans. A mat-forming species similar to *G. cordifolia*, but rather more robust, the leaves lanceolate to oblanceolate, to 5 cm (2 in) long, deep green, generally without a notched tip. Flowerheads rich blue, about 20 mm (⅘ in) across; summer. 'Alba' white; 'Hort's Variety' a free-flowering form.

Gypsophila

A genus of some 125 species found in the Mediterranean region and western and central Asia. Species range from large coarse perennials and subshrubs to delightful little tufted and cushion-forming rock plants. They have simple opposite leaves and small flowers borne in airy panicles, these with a tubular or campanulate calyx and five separate, usually notched, spreading petals. The small capsules contain numerous seeds.

The smaller ones are excellent plants for the rock garden, raised bed, or trough, most thriving in a calcareous, gritty compost and a sunny aspect in the garden. Readily raised from seed sown when ripe or in early spring or, alternatively, from late summer cuttings.

Gypsophila briquetiana
Eastern Turkey. A fairly dense symmetrical cushion to only 7.5 cm (3 in) high, intricately branched, with green, three-edged linear leaves to 10 mm (⅖ in) long. Flowers white or pink,

Globularia meridionalis

about 16 mm (¾ in) across, up to eight borne on a wiry stem shortly above the foliage, the petals purple-veined; late summer. A fine trough plant or secured in a block of tufa.

Gypsophila cerastioides

Himalaya. Plants form low mats not more than 10 cm (4 in) tall in flower, gray-green oval to obovate leaves, 6–10 mm (¼–⅖ in) long. The flowers are borne in small terminal clusters that are congested at first, each bloom about 10 mm (⅖ in) across, white with purple pencil-lines radiating from the base of each petal; spring and early summer. Requires a well-drained humus-rich soil.

Gypsophila repens

Central and southern Europe. The most popular and widely grown rock garden gypsophila, which inhabits rocky meadows and open shrubberies in the wild. A mat-forming peren-

. . . .

Right: *Gypsophila briquetiana*

Bottom left: *Gypsophila cerastioides*

Bottom right: *Gypsophila repens*

nial to 60 cm (2 ft) across, with gray-green linear-lanceolate or somewhat scimitar-shaped leaves. Flowers 10 mm (⅖ in) across, white or palest pink, borne in spreading cymose clusters; summer. 'Dorothy Teacher' neat habit and blue-green foliage, with pale pink flowers darkening with age; 'Dubia' white; 'Rosea' medium rose-pink; 'Rosenschleier' (ROSY VEIL) neat habit and masses of rose-pink flowers darkening with age.

Gypsophila tenuifolia

Caucasus. A plant of rocky and grassy meadows in the wild. Forms low, rather dense mounds of bright green, linear leaves, 10–18 mm (⅖–⅔ in) long. The white flowers, 10–15 mm (2–5–⅗ in) across, are borne in lax cymose masses well above the cushion, on slender, few-leaved stems to 20 cm (8 in) long; summer. An excellent plant for raised beds and containers.

Haberlea

A single species from the Balkans, closely related to *Ramonda*, but readily distinguished on account of the tubular rather than flat flowers.

Haberleas are rock crevice dwellers in the wild, requiring a shaded or partly shaded site in the garden, in a moist, humus-rich soil, or a sunny site that does not dry out. Propagation is

from seed sown in the spring: seedlings are slow to develop and need to be nurtured carefully, taking care that liverworts and mosses do not overwhelm them in their infant stage. A moist propagating frame is desirable for the first year or so until the young plants have become established. Alternatively, plants can be divided after flowering into single rosette portions or, as with most gesneriads, leaf cuttings taken in summer provide a ready means of increase.

Haberlea rhodopensis

Bulgaria and northern Greece. A rosette-forming evergreen perennial forming substantial clumps in time up to 50 cm (20 in) across. Leaves deep green, leathery, rough, hairy, oblong-ovate, to 18 cm (7 in) long, with a finely toothed margin. Flowers up to seven in a cluster on a stalk as long as, or slightly longer than, the leaves, lilac to violet-blue, with a yellow, violet freckled throat, tubular, about 25 mm

Gypsophila tenuifolia

Haberlea rhodopensis 'Virginalis'

(1 in) long, flared at the mouth into five some-what toothed lobes; late spring and early summer. 'Virginalis' pure white.

Hacquetia

An unusual member of the carrot family (Umbelliferae or Apiaceae) containing a single species from central Europe. A charming and rather subtle plant for semi-shaded places in the rock garden or for woodland settings, where it will often seed around in a noninvasive manner. Propagation is from seed sown in late winter and early spring or by division of the parent clump in autumn or late spring.

Hacquetia epipactis
Central Europe. A neat little woodland plant making clumps up to 40 cm (20 in) across in time. It is an herbaceous perennial with five-lobed, toothed, palmate leaves, which develop primarily after the flowers. The yellow, five-petaled flowers are very small and borne in

. . . .
Hacquetia epipactis

tight pin cushion clusters, but set off by the presence of five to seven oval, slightly toothed and lobed, bright yellow-green, leaf-like bracts 1–2 cm (²/₅–⁴/₅ in) long; late winter and spring. Requires dappled shade and a moist humus-rich soil. Readily raised from seed (it will self-sow in favored gardens) or by division in the autumn. 'Thor' attractive cream-variegated foliage and bracts.

Helianthemum

The rockroses are excellent and often very floriferous plants for the rock garden or path edges, thriving in well-drained soils in sunny, warm sites. The genus contains more than 100 species scattered primarily in Europe, North Africa, and western and central Asia, but with representatives in the Americas as well. Those cultivated are essentially subshrubs with a woody base and simple to moderately branched stems bearing opposite, simple leaves with stipular bases. The flowers are cupped or flat with five uneven sepals and five broad petals, borne in one-sided cymes; stamens numerous.

Rockroses are easily grown in most well-drained garden soils in a warm sunny position in the garden. They are superb plants for banks, the tops of retaining walls, or path and driveway edges. The more vigorous ones can be trimmed back after flowering to keep the plants in shape. They are readily grown from spring-sown seed, but named forms are best multiplied from late summer cuttings placed in a cold frame.

Helianthemum apenninum
Western and southern Europe. Very similar to *H. nummularium*, but leaves often narrower, gray, or whitish with the margins rolled under,

while the flowers are white, often with yellow at the base of each petal, or rose-pink; summer.

Helianthemum nummularium

Widespread in Europe. The common rockrose is a vigorous and variable mat- to hummock-forming subshrub to 1 m (3 ft) across, although often less. Leaves lanceolate to ovate, to 5 cm (2 in) long, generally white-downy beneath. Flowers up to 12 in a cyme, usually golden yellow, sometimes with an orange spot at the petal base, or white, cream, orange, or occasionally rose, to 35 mm (1⅖ in) across; late spring and summer.

Cultivars

There are numerous named *Helianthemum* cultivars available, in a range of bright and cheerful colors. These have been derived mainly as

Helianthemum cultivars

hybrids from the above two species, although other species have also almost certainly been involved. 'Amy Baring' deep yellow with orange center; 'Ben Afflick' deep orange suffused with buff, with an orange eye; 'Ben Dearg' flame orange; 'Ben Fhada' golden with an orange center; 'Ben Hope' carmine with an orange eye; 'Ben More' bright orange with a deep center; 'Ben Vane' terracotta; 'Big Ben' yellow with orange center; 'Broughton' double, soft primrose yellow; 'Cerise Queen' double, cerise-red; 'Double Cream' double, cream; 'Fire Dragon' bright orange-scarlet; 'Jubilee' double, primrose yellow; 'Mrs C. W. Earle' double, red; 'Old Gold' soft golden yellow; 'Raspberry Ripple' reddish pink, tipped white; 'Rhodanthe Carneum' ('Wisley Pink') carmine-pink with an

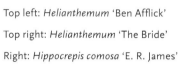

Top left: *Helianthemum* 'Ben Afflick'

Top right: *Helianthemum* 'The Bride'

Right: *Hippocrepis comosa* 'E. R. James'

. . . .

orange eye; 'Salmon Queen' bright salmon-pink; 'The Bride' creamy white with a yellow center contrasting with silvery gray foliage; 'Wisley White' pure white.

Hippocrepis

The horseshoe vetches represent a small genus of about 20 species from Europe, North Africa, and western Asia of yellow peaflowers with pinnate leaves and segmented pods that break up into one-seeded pieces. Good for sunny, rather dry places on alkaline soils. Propagation is by seed in early spring. Basal cuttings taken in summer also give some degree of success.

Hippocrepis comosa

Europe and western Asia. A mat-forming perennial with a rather woody base, to 60 cm (2 ft) across, with gray green pinnate leaves with up to nine oval to obovate, notched leaf-

lets. Flowers bright golden yellow, typical pea flowers, about 1 cm (⅖ in) long, borne in clusters of up to 12 on slender stalks above the foliage; summer. 'E. R. James' free-flowering selection with somewhat paler flowers.

Horminum

A solitary species found growing among rocks and on meadows in the wild. It is readily cultivated in any well-drained soil, especially favoring the base of a wall or a substantial rock crevice in sun or part shade. Plants are readily propagated from seed sown in late winter and early spring or by careful division in late summer.

Horminum pyrenaicum

Alps and Pyrenees. A clump-forming perennial, 30 cm (1 ft) tall in flower, with most leaves in flattish basal rosettes, thick and leathery, deep green, oval to ovate, 3–7.5 cm (1⅖–3 in) long, with a coarsely crenated margin, wrinkled above. Flowers borne in one-sided spikes, deep violet-blue, tubular, two-lipped, 18–20 mm (⅔–⅘ in) long; summer. 'Roseum' mauve-pink. Excellent rock ledge or crevice plant for well-drained calcareous soils.

Houstonia

A genus of some 50 species of both annuals and perennials from the United States and Mexico, sometimes included in the genus *Hedy-*

otis by botanists. The two listed below are hardy mat-forming perennials with very small leaves. The solitary flowers, borne on slender stalks above the mat, have four spreading lobes.

Houstonias are delightful, little, free-flowering plants for a shaded moist site in the rock garden or in a secluded corner of the garden, thriving best in a humus-rich soil. Propagated from seed sown in late winter or early spring or, more simply, by pulling off ready rooted portions from the parent plant.

Houstonia caerulea

Eastern North America. A mat- or hummock-forming plant not more than 15 cm (6 in) tall in flower, with oblanceolate leaves, 10–15 mm (⅖–⅗ in) long. Flowers violet, blue, or lilac, occasionally white, with a yellow eye, about 12 mm (½ in) long; spring to autumn.

Houstonia michauxii

United States; Pennsylvania to Tennessee and Georgia. Plants form creeping mats with the stems rooting down freely. Leaves ovate to rounded, about 10 mm (⅖ in) long. Flowers deep blue to purple or violet, about 12 mm (½ in) long; spring and summer. 'Alba' pure white; 'Fred Mullard' ('Mullard's Variety') clear blue.

Hutchinsia

A single species restricted to Europe, often known as the chamois cress. It is an easy and accommodating little cress, thriving in rather poor, gritty, alkaline soils, in sun or part shade. Plants tend to be short-lived but often seed around in the garden.

. . . .
Horminum pyrenaicum

Hutchinsia alpina

Mountains of central and southern Europe. A charming plant to about 10 cm (4 in) tall, forming lax hummocks to 20 cm (8 in) across, with deep green, pinnately lobed leaves to 2.5 cm (1 in) long. Flowers pure white, 5 mm (⅕ in) across, in congested racemes that elongate as the fruits develop; spring.

Hylomecon

Several similar species of poppy relatives native to eastern Asia. They are rhizomatous, patch-forming perennials suitable for moist, humus-rich soils and dappled shade, being woodland species in the wild. Propagation is easiest by division of the parent clump after flowering or in early spring as growth commences.

Hylomecon japonica (syn. *Chelidonium japonicum, Hylomecon vernalis*)

Northwestern China, Korea, Japan. A cheerful, early flowering herbaceous perennial to 30 cm (12 in) tall. Foliage rather bright green, mostly basal, divided into five or seven ovate, toothed leaflets, to 25 cm (10 in) long overall. Flowers solitary, bright yellow, cupped, about 5 cm (2 in) across, poppy-like, with four petals, held above the foliage; spring. Var. *dissectum* has more finely divided foliage.

Hypericum

A large and complicated genus with more than 400 species concentrated in temperate regions of the world. The species include herbs, shrubs, and trees with opposite, sometimes whorled leaves that are variously dotted with glands. Flowers five-parted with numerous stamens in distinctive bundles, the sepals and petals also often dotted with glands. Fruit a multiseeded capsule opening by pores at the apex.

The small species make first-rate plants for the rock garden, and both those listed below are fine for a beginner's collection. They will thrive in most ordinary well-drained soils in a sunny position. Propagation is by seed sown in

Hutchinsia alpina

Hylomecon japonica

early spring or cuttings in late summer. Division is also possible, and this is best undertaken in the spring just before growth commences.

Hypericum cerastoides

Southeastern Balkans and northwestern Turkey. A mat-forming perennial spreading to 50 cm (20 in) across with slender stems bearing oblong-ovate, gray-hairy leaves, to 3 cm (1⅕

in) long. Flowers yellow, 2–4 cm (⅘–1⅗ in) across, often borne in profusion; summer.

Hypericum olympicum

Balkans and Turkey. A patch-forming, woody-based perennial or subshrub to 50 cm (20 in) tall, with narrow-oblong to elliptic or lanceolate leaves, to 5 cm (2 in) long, edged with tiny black glands. Flowers bright yellow, to 6 cm (2⅖ in) across, solitary or few in a cluster; summer. 'Citrinum' lemon yellow; forma *minus* a more prostrate plant with narrow, smaller leaves; forma *uniflorum* broad-elliptic to obovate leaves and pointed sepals; 'Sulphureum' pale yellow; 'Variegatum' leaves with creamy variegations.

Iberis

The candytufts are familiar, if not slightly unusual, members of the crucifer family (Cruciferae or Brassicaceae), in which two petals in each flower are larger than the other two. There are about 30 species, distributed from Europe to western Asia, the majority perennials or subshrubs, a few annuals. The flowers are borne in flattish or elongated racemes, often densely so. The fruit is a heart-shaped, two-parted capsule.

These are excellent rock garden plants, the smaller ones for a large trough or raised bed. They thrive best in a sunny position in a well-drained alkaline compost. Propagation is from seed sown in late winter or early spring or from late summer cuttings.

Top: *Hypericum olympicum* 'Citrinum'

Bottom: *Iberis pruitii* Candolleana Group

Opposite: *Iberis sempervirens*

Iberis pruitii (syn. *I. candolleana, I. petraea, I. spruneri*)

Southern Europe. A tufted perennial, sometimes short-lived, to 20 cm (8 in) tall with spreading to ascending stems and obovate to oblanceolate, rather fleshy leaves to 3 cm (1⅕ in) long, slightly toothed. Flowers white to lilac, in compact cluster that gradually elongate as the fruits develop; summer. Plants sold as Candolleana Group originated from Mount Ventoux in France and have flowers that start white but flush with lilac on aging.

Iberis sempervirens

Mediterranean region. A spreading, mat-forming, evergreen shrublet to 20 cm (8 in) tall, but to 70 cm (28 in) across, with deep green, oblong or spathulate, rather leathery leaves to 2.5 cm (1 in) long. Flowers pure white in congested heads (corymbs) to 5 cm (2 in) across; spring and summer. 'Golden Candy' yellow-leaved variant; 'Snowflake' (syn. 'Schneeflocke') a vigorous plant to 22 cm (9 in) with large pure white flowers, in cylindrical racemes; 'Weisser Zwerg' (LITTLE GEM) a compact plant ideal for smaller rock gardens.

Incarvillea

A genus of about 18 species in central and eastern Asia and the Himalaya, especially in western China. They are eye-catching subshrubs and tuberous perennials in the same family (Bignoniaceae) as the jacaranda, mostly with pinnately divided foliage. The trumpet-shaped, brightly colored flowers are solitary or borne in racemes. The fruit is a long, two-parted capsule containing numerous winged seeds.

Plants require a humus-rich, well-drained but not dry soil and sun or part shade. They are

readily raised from seed sown the moment ripe or in early spring, pricking out seedlings once they have produced their first true leaf.

Incarvillea grandiflora

Southwestern China. Similar to *I. himalayensis*, but leaves deep shiny green, generally without lateral leaflets, and flowers crimson- or magenta-purple, solitary or two to three; late spring and early summer. Both species are fine

plants for pockets in the rock garden or for raised beds.

Incarvillea himalayensis

Western Nepal and southern Tibet. A rosetted herbaceous perennial to 10 cm (4 in) in flower but taller in fruit. Leaves in rather flat rosettes, metallic gray-green, sometimes with a purplish flush, pinnate, with a large terminal leaflet and up to four pairs of much smaller laterals. Flowers solitary, pink, with a whitish, yellow-marked throat, 5–6 cm (2–2⅖ in) across, with five wide-spreading lobes; early summer. 'Frank Ludlow' crimson-pink; 'Nyoto Sama' bright pink.

Jeffersonia

Two species of woodland plants related to the epimediums, one from North America and the other from Asia, sometimes put in the genus *Plagiorhegma*. Seed is best sown as soon as possible after the fruits ripen. Alternately, plants can be propagated by careful division of established clumps in late summer, but this is by no means a certain success.

Jeffersonia dubia

Northeastern China and Korea. A clump-forming, glabrous, herbaceous perennial to 35 cm (10 in) tall in flower, with long-stalked, all-basal leaves that are almost circular in outline, with a scalloped margin, often flushed violet when young and only partly developed at flowering time. Flowers erect on long leafless stalks, pale lavender-pink, cupped, 2–3 cm (⅘–1⅕ in) across, with five to seven oval petals and cream

Incarvillea himalayensis 'Nyoto Sama'

Jeffersonia dubia

anthers; spring. A beautiful little plant requir
ing a cool, moist leafy soil and dappled shade
in the garden. 'Alba' pure white. The related
eastern North American *J. diphylla* is less satisfactory with more meager white flowers and
bilobed leaves with two fan-shaped segments.

Lathyrus

About 150 species of annuals and herbaceous
and evergreen perennials, many climbing by
means of leaf tendrils. The genus is distributed
in northern temperate regions, on the higher
African mountains, and in temperate South
America. The stems are often winged, and the
leaves bear up to six pairs of leaflets. The typical peaflowers are sometimes solitary, but
mostly borne in lateral racemes. The fruit is a
pod, splitting lengthwise into two when ripe.

Most species are readily grown in humus-
rich garden soils but are generally unsuitable
for all but the largest of rock gardens. However,
several of the smaller, nonclimbing species are
worthy of consideration. Propagation is from
seed sown in the spring or by division of the
parent clump in late winter or after flowering.

Lathyrus laxiflorus
Southeastern Europe eastward to the Caucasus
and Iran. A spreading, lax, mound-forming tuberous perennial to 80 cm (32 in) across, often
less, with angled stems. Leaves gray-green,
with a pair of elliptic to ovate, simple, downy
leaflets, 1–4 cm (⅖–1⅗ in) long, sometimes
with a simple tendril; leaf-like stipules present
at the leaf base. Peaflowers in small lateral
racemes of up to five, lavender to lilac with a
whitish keel, 15–20 mm (⅗–⅘ in) long, late
spring and early summer. Will self sow in the
garden to some extent.

Lathyrus vernus
Europe and western Asia. One of the loveliest
of spring flowers for the rock garden, making
clumps to about 30 cm (1 ft) in height. Leaves
rather bright green with prominent leaf-like
stipules and two to four pairs of ovate to lanceolate leaflets. Reddish purple flowers, 13–20
mm (½–⅘ in) long, borne in racemes of up to
10, age gradually to blue; spring. Good in sun
or partial shade. 'Alboroseus' bicolored pink
and white flowers; 'Albus' white; 'Cyaneus' rich
blue; 'Roseus' pink.

Lathyrus vernus

Leontopodium

A complicated genus with possibly 40 species scattered in the mountains of Europe and Asia. They are generally small plants with simple leaves and small flowerheads that are surrounded by prominent white-woolly or yellowish bracts, so that they resemble large daisy heads. The genus contains the famous edelweiss of the Alps, an intriguing if not particularly beautiful alpine plant, but one with romantic connotations.

Those leontopodiums available are generally good plants for raised beds or troughs in a well-drained gritty compost and sunny open site. Propagation is best effected by division in late winter shortly before plants come into growth or from seed sown during the winter.

Leontopodium alpinum
Mountains of central and southern Europe. The edelweiss is a small tufted plant to 20 cm (8 in) tall in flower, with linear to narrow-oblong leaves to 5 cm (2 in) long, gray-green and slightly hairy above, white-woolly beneath.

Brownish flowerheads are surrounded by narrow oblong to elliptic white-woolly bracts, the whole up to 10 cm (4 in) across, though often less; late spring and summer. Dwarf, more compact forms with relatively large inflorescences with the leaves white-woolly above and beneath are usually referred to as subsp. *nivale* or *L. nivale*. 'Mignon' a more delicate plant, making more substantial clumps to 20 cm (8 in) across, with numerous linear-oblong, bright green leaves and rather smaller inflorescences.

Lewisia

An important and popular North American genus of some 20 species that includes both evergreen and herbaceous species. They are perennial herbs with a fleshy thickened stock or caudex. The leaves vary a lot in shape but are undivided, flat, or cylindrical, sometimes with an undulate or somewhat toothed margin. The cactus-like flowers (the genus is not in the cactus family but in the Portulacaceae) open in bright light and have 5 to 19 silky petals, which are often brightly colored, with a boss of numerous stamens within. The fruit is a multi-seeded capsule.

The herbaceous species die down quickly after flowering, leaving their fruit capsule to mature. At this stage the plants need to be kept dry through the summer months. Lewisias make first-class plants for pot culture in an alpine house or cold frame, although some can be grown with success in a well-drained scree mixture in raised beds and troughs. The evergreen species are less demanding, although they dislike overwatering, even during the summer. They also make good and colorful

Leontopodium alpinum

subjects for wall crevices and raised beds. Propagation is from seed sown when ripe or in early spring: deciduous kinds should not be pricked out but kept in their seed container until at least the second year, while the evergreen ones, especially *L. cotyledon*, can be pricked out at the two true leaf stage. The evergreen selections can also be propagated from offsets rooted in pure sharp sand, taking great care not to overwater them; this is the only way to maintain named clones in cultivation.

Lewisia Ashwood Carousel Hybrids

An interesting development from Ashwood Nursery in England are these delightful little hybrids resulting from crosses between *L. pygmaea* and *L. cotyledon*. These form neat rosettes of shiny, deep green linear to narrow oblanceolate leaves from the center of which arise numerous small flowers, 15–25 mm (⅗–1 in) across in a wide range of colors, including pink, red, apricot, orange, tangerine, purple, and white; late spring and summer. They make ideal little trough plants but are, unfortunately, sterile.

Lewisia cotyledon

Northern California and southern Oregon. Plants forming substantial, symmetrical rosettes of deep green, leathery, succulent leaves, spatula-shaped and up to 10 cm (4 in) long, larger in some vigorous forms in cultivation, often crisped at the margin. Flowers in cymes of up to 10, opening in succession, 2.5–4 cm (1–1⅗ in) across, with 7 to 10 pink petals with a deeper or purple central stripe, or white or cream with an orange stripe, rarely pure white (forma *alba*); late spring and summer, occasion-

ally later. This species inhabits non-limestone rock formations and crevices in the wild. It has been extensively hybridized in cultivation to give a wide range of very colorful plants that are freely available: some of these are self-colored named cultivars, others are selections or strains such as Ashwood strain, Rainbow mixed (Regenbogen mixed), and Sunset mixed (shades of yellow to deep orange-reds). 'Ashwood Ruby', 'Kline's Red', 'Rose Splendour', 'Siskiyou White', and 'White Splendour' are self-explanatory. Others include 'Carroll Watson' white; 'Harold Judd' yellow; 'Jean Turner' soft pink; 'Kathy Kline' good white; 'Late Orange' soft orange; 'Weald Gold' golden yellow.

Lewisia rediviva

Western North America from British Columbia to California, inhabiting open rocky places. A little gem forming deciduous tufts of deep green, fleshy, linear-cylindrical leaves to about 5 cm (2 in) long. Flowers remarkably cactus-like, solitary, 5–6 cm (2–2⅖ in) across, with 11–19 glistening, elliptic, white, pink, or carmine petals; spring and early summer. Re-

Lewisia cotyledon hybrids

4.5–6 cm (1⅘–2⅖ in) across, with generally eight glistening petals in soft peach or yellow; summer. 'Alba' white; 'Rosea' medium rose-pink. It inhabits acid pockets over granite formations in the wild and will succeed outdoors if winter wet is kept out of the center of rosettes. A wall crevice is an excellent niche for it, although plants can be successfully grown in raised beds and troughs, as well as in pots in an alpine house.

Limnanthes

A genus of seven species from North America with pinnately divided leaves and generally showy, bowl- to cup-shaped, five-petaled flowers.

Annuals are rarely seen in the rock garden, indeed their presence there is often frowned upon. However, there are several fine, colorful, and easy annuals that are excellent space-fillers, providing color in late spring and summer (see also *Omphalodes linifolia*). They thrive in any well-drained soil in full sun or part shade. Plants are readily grown from seed sown where the plants are to flower; thin sowing is essential. They generally self-sow in the garden and may overwinter as small seedlings. If they become too invasive, the excess seedlings are readily removed.

quires a summer-dry position if it is to be grown outside in the garden, otherwise a raised bed or pot under glass is a good option.

Lewisia tweedyi

British Columbia and Washington State. An exquisite plant forming large succulent rosettes to 25 cm (10 in) across; leaves green, generally purple-flushed, broad-elliptic to oblanceolate, 10 cm (4 in) long, occasionally larger, with a flat, entire margin. Flowers several per cyme,

Limnanthes douglasii

Western United States; California and Oregon. A spreading, bright green annual to 15 cm (6 in) tall in flower, twice as broad, with pinnately lobed, rather fleshy leaves. Flowers bowl-shaped, 2.5–3 cm (1–1⅕ in) across, the petals

Limnanthes douglasii var. *sulphurea*

yellow with white, notched tips; late spring and summer. The yellow and white flowers give the plant its common name, poached egg plant. Various color forms are recognized and are sometimes available: var. *nivea*, white overall, often with faint purple veins; var. *rosea*, white with pink veins, aging to rose, or rose overall; var. *sulphurea*, yellow overall.

Limonium

The sea lavenders comprise a genus of some 150 species of annual, biennials, perennials, and subshrubs with a cosmopolitan distribution, the species particularly associated with coastal habitats, often on saline soils, or in dry inland regions. They often have thick leathery leaves that can be simple of variously lobed, but untoothed. The small salver-shaped, five-lobed flowers are borne in stiff, erect panicles composed of short to long spikelets. They have a persistent calyx, which is often a different color than the corolla and becomes papery and parachute-like in the fruiting stage. The everlasting quality of the flowers in some species lend themselves to dried flower arrangements.

The smaller hardy species make interesting subjects for the rock garden or raised bed, thriving in most ordinary, well-drained soils in full sun. Propagation is by spring sown seed or by division at the same time. Many were formerly included in a separate genus, *Statice*.

Limonium bellidifolium

Europe and western Russia, Crimea. A clump-forming plant to 20 cm (8 in) tall in flower, with leathery deep green, stiff obovate to spathulate leaves to 10 cm (4 in) long. Inflorescences

stiffly erect, with numerous nonflowering branches, the flowers pale violet, about 5 mm (⅕ in) long; summer. 'Dazzling Blue' blue flowers.

Linaria

The toadflaxes are closely related to the snapdragons (*Antirrhinum*) but have generally smaller, distinctly spurred flowers. The genus has about 100 species that are confined to the northern temperate region, particularly around the Mediterranean, and range from annuals to perennials. As in *Antirrhinum*, the corollas are two-lipped and bear a distinct raised area or palate on the lower lip. The fruit is a small two-parted capsule containing numerous seeds.

Although some species are too large for the average rock garden, several are super little gems well worthy of a place. They excel especially in scree conditions and will seed around. Beware though, most will hybridize readily and the resultant offspring are likely to be quite variable if, nonetheless, delightful. Propagation is from seed sown in late winter or early spring or from root cuttings taken in late winter.

Linaria aeruginea

Portugal, Spain, and the Balearic Islands. A small decumbent perennial not more than 20 cm (8 in) tall, with linear, glaucous leaves to 20 mm (⅘ in) long, borne mostly in whorls of three or four. Racemes rather dense, with up to 35 flowers, these yellowish tinted and veined with purple-brown, occasionally more violet or cream, 15–25 mm (⅗–1 in) long, with a spur to 10 mm (⅖ in) long; summer. Yellow-flowered forms are generally referred to subsp. *nevadensis* and are sometimes seen in gardens.

Linaria alpina

Central and southern Europe. A rock- and scree-dweller in the wild, this short-lived perennial sometimes behaves as a biennial. It forms decumbent tufts to 15 cm (6 in) tall, with slender spreading stems that arch up at the tips, especially in flower. The fleshy glaucous leaves are linear or linear-lanceolate, to 15 mm (⅗ in) long, mostly borne in whorls of three or four. The racemes of up to 15 flowers are violet with a yellow palate, occasionally all yellow, or pink or whitish, 13–20 mm (½–⅘ in) long, with a

slender downcurved spur to 12 mm (½ in) long; summer.

Linaria supina

Southwestern Europe to Italy. Rather like *L. alpina*, but often behaving as an annual or biennial with flowers in racemes of up to 20, pale yellow with an orange palate and with a somewhat longer spur; summer.

Linum

A genus of some 200 species commonly referred to as the flaxes, distributed in many parts of the world but especially prominent in the Mediterranean region. The common flax, *Linum usitatissimum*, is widely grown for its fiber (flax) and seed (linseed). The species generally have simple stems with entire linear to lanceolate leaves. The flowers, which are borne in one-sided racemes, have funnel-shaped flowers often with a silky sheen, with five sepals and petals. The fruit is a small many-seeded capsule.

Flaxes are generally relatively easy to grow, the perennial species finding greatest favor among rock gardeners. Most thrive in average well-drained garden soils, preferring those with calcium, and a good sunny position; the flowers will not open in dull conditions. The smaller species are excellent trough and raised bed plants. Propagation is from seed sown in late winter and early spring or cuttings struck in late summer in a cold frame.

Linum arboreum

Crete, Aegean islands, and Turkey. A small evergreen shrublet to 50 cm (20 in) tall, with

Linum arboreum

Linum monogynum

spathulate to obovate, entire, bluish green leaves, 10–20 mm (⅖–⅘ in) long. Flowers yellow, 20–30 mm (⅘–1⅕ in) across, borne in rather dense clusters; summer. A good plant for rock crevices, requiring some protection in severe weather.

Linum flavum

Central Europe northeastward to Russia, south to northern Italy. A woody-based perennial to 30 cm (1 ft) tall in flower, sometimes more, with lanceolate to spathulate, deep green leaves, 2–3.5 cm (⅘–1⅖ in) long. Flowers bright yellow, about 2.5 cm (1 in) across, in few-flowered racemes; summer. 'Compactum' a fine dwarf form to 20 cm (8 in) tall with especially large flowers.

Linum 'Gemmel's Hybrid'

This exceptional hybrid is a cross between *L. elegans* and another southern European species, *L. campanulatum*, less often seen in cultivation. It forms attractive compact plants with glaucous leaves and butter yellow flowers, often borne in profusion; summer. Needs to be propagated from cuttings in order to maintain stock.

Linum monogynum

New Zealand and Chatham Island. Tufted woody-based perennial to 40 cm (16 in) tall in flower, with ascending to erect stems clothed with bluish green, linear to narrow-lanceolate leaves, to 2.5 cm (1 in) long. Flowers pale bluish white, 20–30 mm (⅘–1⅕ in) across; summer. A subtly attractive plant.

Linum perenne subsp. alpinum (syn. *L. alpinum*)

Southern Europe. A tufted perennial with ascending to arching slender stems to 50 cm (20 in) tall, often less, with glaucous narrow-lanceolate, alternate leaves to 2 cm (⅘ in) long. Flowers clear deep sky blue, to 3 cm (1⅕ in) across, borne in racemes that droop at the tip in bud; summer. One of the loveliest blue flowers for the rock garden. Several blue selections

the base. Leaves linear, rather rough, glaucous, to 15 mm (⅗ in) long, with the margins rolled under. Flowers few per cluster, white with a conspicuous purple or violet eye, 3–4 cm (1⅕–1⅗ in) across; summer. 'Nanum' a particularly dwarf selection ideal for trough culture. The typical plant, subsp. *suffruticosa*, is altogether larger and more obviously woody at the base, to 50 cm (20 in) tall in flower. It is less often seen in cultivation.

Lithodora

A genus of just seven species of dwarf ever-green shrubs once included in the genus *Litho-spermum*. They are characterized, apart from their woody habit, by simple, generally rough, and bristly leaves and by their small cymes of tubular to funnel-shaped flowers, with five spreading lobes at the end.

In cultivation they require full sun and a sheltered warm site along with a gritty well-drained compost. Seed can be sown in early spring or cuttings of leafy, mature, current year's shoots in late summer. The species are excellent for attracting bees.

Lithodora diffusa (syn. Lithospermum diffusum)

Spain and Portugal. A mat- or hummock-forming dark green shrublet, to 60 cm (2 ft) across. Leaves elliptic to narrow-oblong, bris-tly, rather crowded. Flowers in small cymes, pure deep blue, to 20 mm (⅘ in) long; late spring and summer. The species requires an acid soil: on alkaline soils it will grow but the leaves will turn yellowish and the flowers will

have been made including 'Alice Blue' and 'Blau Saphir'.

Linum suffruticosum subsp. *salsoloides*
Spain, southern France, and Italy. A super little flax to 25 cm (10 in) tall forming small, neat, somewhat decumbent tufts, slightly woody at

be more mauve or purple than blue. 'Heavenly Blue', 'Grace Ward', and 'Picos' are all fine named forms, the last particularly compact and richly colored.

Lithodora oleifolia

Eastern Pyrenees. Plants form lax hummocks to 30 cm (1 ft) across, with oblong to obovate leaves to 4 cm (1⅗ in) long, silky white with hairs beneath, greener and only slightly hairy above. Flowers pale pink at first, aging to blue, 8–12 mm (⅓–½ in) long, borne in small cymes; late spring and summer.

Luetkea

A single species from rocky meadows and screes in North America, belonging to the rose family (Rosaceae) and closely related to both *Spiraea* and *Petrophytum*. This is a fine, if somewhat demure, rock plant for sunny or

....

Right: *Lithodora diffusa*

Bottom left: *Lithodora oleifolia*

Bottom right: *Luetkea pectinata*

partly shaded aspects, preferring a gritty, humus-rich soil in the rock garden or raised bed. Seed, if available, is best sown the moment it is ripe or as soon after as possible, otherwise cuttings taken in late summer afford a suitable means of increase.

Luetkea pectinata

Western North America from Alaska to California, east to Montana. A mat-forming ever-

green perennial with a woody base, to 40 cm (16 in) across, but only 15 cm (6 in) tall in flower. Leaves fan-shaped, to 15 mm (⅗ in) long, dissected into linear lobes. Flowers creamy white, small, five-petaled, condensed into cylindrical, *Spiraea*-like racemes to 5 cm (2 in) long; summer.

Lychnis

A small genus with about 35 species scattered in Europe and Asia. It is closely related to the true catchflies (*Silene*), differing most obviously in the fruit capsule that dehisces with just four or five teeth, equaling the number of petals; in *Silene* the capsule dehisces with six

. . . .

Lychnis alpina

or ten teeth. They are tufted perennials mostly too large for the rock garden.

Lychnis alpina

Northern Europe and higher mountains further south. A small, rather sticky, tufted plant to 15 cm (6 in) tall in flower, with erect, often purplish stems. Leaves paired, mostly crowded at the base of the plant, linear to narrow-obovate, to 7.5 cm (3 in) long, deep green, often suffused bronze or purple. Flowers in narrow, branched cymes, rose-purple, to 12 mm (½ in) wide, the smaller flowers in the inflorescence generally female, the others hermaphrodite; spring and early summer. An easy and colorful little plant suitable for most sunny positions in the rock garden or on raised beds, tolerating average, moist, well-drained soils. 'Rosea' rose-pink; white selections include 'Alba', 'Snow Flurry', and 'Snowflake'.

Meconopsis

A genus of about 60 species primarily in the Himalaya and western China, but with a single species confined to western Europe. The two described here are fully perennial, although the genus does contain quite a few monocarpic species. They all have poppy-like flowers with often four, sometimes more, somewhat crimpled petals. The presence of a style distinguishes them from the true poppies (*Papaver*), along with other minutiae of their morphology. The fruit is a capsule dehiscing at the top by a number of short valves.

Meconopsis, which includes the fabled blue poppies, is a genus for cool moist climates: they will not survive in hot dry conditions, however much water they are given. Propagation is from seed sown the moment ripe or in late winter.

Seedlings are quite brittle and need to be handled with care.

Meconopsis cambrica

Western Europe; Britain to Spain. A tufted, fresh green, taprooted plant with stiffly erect, somewhat bristly, somewhat branched stems to 60 cm (2 ft) tall in flower. Leaves mostly toward the base of the plant, pinnately lobed, long-stalked, to 20 cm (8 in) long. Flowers solitary, four-petaled, yellow or orange (var. *aurantiaca*), erect to ascending, 4–5 cm (1⅗–2 in) across; borne from late spring to autumn. A very attractive plant much underrated in gardens but with a reputation for seeding around everywhere. However, there are few better and more colorful plants for the shadier areas of the garden or a cleft in the rock garden. It looks very fine planted in association with ferns of a similar size. 'Flore Pleno' double yellow; 'Francis Perry' ('Rubra') deep orange-crimson; 'Muriel Brown' semi-double, red.

Meconopsis quintuplinervia

Western China. A slow-spreading, mat-forming herbaceous perennial, to 40 cm (16 in) tall in flower. Leaves all in small basal rosettes, elliptic to oblanceolate, to 20 cm (8 in) long, covered with pale bristles, usually five-veined. Flowers borne on long, slender, somewhat bristly scapes, nodding, campanulate to narrow bowl-shaped, to 4 cm (1⅗ in) long, pale lavender-blue to purple, darker at the petal bases; summer, occasionally in autumn. 'Kaye's Compact' dwarfer plant with rather pale flowers but

....

Meconopsis cambrica

Meconopsis quintuplinervia

nonetheless elegant. This species requires a moist humus-rich soil in which to thrive, deteriorating under hot conditions; however, when suited it makes a very fine plant for a semi-shaded niche in the rock garden.

Mimulus

The monkeyflowers are popular flowers in the garden, especially in summer beds and as water margin plants, but several are excellent rock garden subjects. The genus contains about 150 species, primarily in the Americas but extending into eastern Asia. They have opposite leaves set on square or rounded stems. The tubular to trumpet-shaped flowers are borne in the upper leaf axils, varying in color from yellow to pinks and reds or white, the corolla two-lipped, sometimes inconspicuously so. There are often insect guides in the form of ridges in the throat of the corolla. The fruit is a two-parted, many-seeded capsule.

The small species are showy plants for moist soils in sun or part shade. They can be propagated from seed sown in early spring or from midsummer root cuttings; some will root down naturally, making the taking of cuttings a simple procedure.

Mimulus cupreus

Southern Chile. A short-lived perennial, sometimes acting as an annual, to 30 cm (1 ft) tall at the most. Leaves ovate, 2–3 cm (⅘–1⅕ in) long, remotely toothed with three or five prime veins. Flowers coppery orange or coppery red, with yellow in the throat, 3.5–4 cm (1⅖–1⅗ in) long; late spring and summer. There are a number of readily available cultivars, all varying in the intensity of their red, scarlet, or orange-red flowers: 'Fire Dragon', 'Fire King', 'Highland Red', 'Inshriach Crimson', 'Plymtree', 'Rota Kaiser' (Red Emperor), 'Scarlet Bee', 'Scarlet Bay', 'Wisley Red'. 'Whitecroft Scarlet' is the finest and most widely available.

Mimulus cupreus 'Whitecroft Scarlet' (Photo courtesy of Alpine Garden Society)

Mimulus naiandinus

Mimulus naiandinus (syn. 'Andean Nymph')
Chile. A bushy perennial to 25 cm (10 in) tall,
spreading to 50 cm (20 in). Leaves rather gray-
green, ovate to triangular-ovate, to 2.5 cm (1
in) long, toothed. Flowers white to cream suffused with pink or reddish purple, the lower lip
often pale yellow with red spots in the throat,
3–4 cm (1⅕–1⅗ in) long; summer. Short-lived
but readily raised from seed. Beware, it will
cross with other monkeyflowers in the garden
giving varied offspring, some of which may
well be delightful.

Mimulus primuloides

Western United States. A mat-forming plant
no more than 10 cm (4 in) tall in flower, with
thread-like, whitish stolons that rot down
readily. Leaves bright lettuce green, in small
rosettes, oblong to obovate, to 4 cm (1⅗ in)
long. Flowers solitary, yellow, 15–20 mm (⅗–
⅘ in) long, deeper in the throat and with some
reddish brown spotting, borne on slender, erect
stalks to 10 cm (4 in) long; late spring and
summer. Requires regular dividing to maintain vigor.

Moltkia

A genus of just six species of borage relations
confined to the central Mediterranean region
and western Asia. They are rough-hairy evergreen shrublets or woody-based perennials
with small tubular flowers borne in dense,
somewhat spiraled, terminal cymes.

The single species included here is a sun-
lover for a gritty well-drained soil, looking especially effective sandwiched between rocks. It
can be propagated from late summer cuttings

Moltkia suffruticosa

overwintered in a cold frame or from seed
sown in early spring. Plants should be clipped
back moderately after flowering unless, that is,
the seed is required.

Moltkia suffruticosa

Northern Italy. A shrublet to 25 cm (10 in) tall,
with a tufted habit comprising short nonflowering and longer flowering shoots. Leaves gray-
green, linear, to 15 mm (⅗ in) long, white-hairy
beneath. Flowers deep blue, 13–16 mm (½–⅔
in) long, in dense cymes that slowly unravel;
late spring and summer.

Morisia

A single species of rosette-forming crucifer
(Cruciferae) from sandy habitats in the wild. In
cultivation it makes an excellent pan plant for
the alpine house, but it will also succeed outdoors on a raised bed or a block of tufa, if protected from excessive winter wet. Propagation
is from side rosette cuttings taken in late summer and rooted in a fine gritty sand or, more
successfully, from root cuttings taken in spring

and inserted in a similar compost. Seed, if available, can be sown in early spring. Plants can be subjected to aphid damage, especially when growth starts in the spring.

Morisia monantha

Corsica and Sardinia. Rosettes bright green, rather flat, forming evergreen hummocks in time to 20 cm (8 in) across; leaves lanceolate, pinnately lobed, to 7.5 cm (3 in) long, with tri-angular lobes. Flowers bright yellow, typical four-petaled crucifers, about 15 mm ($\frac{3}{5}$ in) across, borne on short stalks from the middle of a rosette; spring to early summer. 'Fred Hemingway' a selected form with extra-large flowers.

Nierembergia

A member of the potato family (Solanaceae) with 25 species scattered in Mexico and South America, although the majority are not hardy. They are perennial herbs and subshrubs with alternate leaves and funnel-shaped, petunia-like flowers.

The species included below is the hardiest, requiring a moist, yet well-drained, soil or raised bed and a sunny position. Propagation is best effected by division in the spring just as plants come into growth. Another species, *N. hippomanica*, with blue flowers is often treated as a half-hardy bedding plant and can look effective as a summer addition to dull corners in the rock garden.

Nierembergia repens (syn. *N. rivularis*)

Argentina, Chile, and Uruguay. A mat-forming, rhizomatous, herbaceous perennial spreading to 50 cm (20 in) or more across, the rhizomes located just beneath the soil surface. Leaves ascending, oblong to spathulate, to 3 cm ($1\frac{1}{5}$ in) long, with an entire margin. Flowers white with a yellow eye, solitary in the leaf axils, broad funnel-shaped, 30–50 mm ($1\frac{1}{5}$–2 in) across, with five shallow triangular lobes to the corolla; summer.

Morisia monantha 'Fred Hemingway' (Photo courtesy of Alpine Garden Society)

Nierembergia repens

Oenothera

A well-known genus of the Americas containing about 80 species popularly called evening primroses because most open their flowers fully in the evenings, thereby attracting night-flying moths and other nocturnal creatures. They are members of the willowherb family (Onagraceae), consisting of annual, biennial, and perennial species that generally form basal rosettes, at least to begin with. The flowers characteristically have four sepals and petals borne on an apparent, sometimes exceedingly long, stalk, which is in reality the ovary. The fruit is a capsule that splits lengthways into five parts to release numerous seeds.

The two included here are both excellent and colorful additions to the rock garden, requiring a gritty, well-drained compost and plenty of sunshine, although they will cope with partial shade. They can be propagated from seed sown in early spring or from basal leafy cuttings taken in early summer.

Oenothera acaulis

Chile. A short-lived perennial to 40 cm (16 in) tall, with decumbent leafy stems. Leaves oblanceolate, to 20 cm (8 in) long, pinnately lobed, rather dandelion-like. Flowers borne from the upper leaf axils, white soon flushing with pink or purple, to 7.5 cm (3 in) across; summer. The flowers open in late afternoon, earlier on dull days. In areas where this plant fails to overwinter it can be treated as an annual, sowing the seed in very early spring to flower from midsummer onward. The mature fruits only open when wetted to release their seeds. Var. *alba* pure white.

· ·

Oenothera macrocarpa

Oenothera macrocarpa (syn. O. missouriensis)

Central and southern United States. A stout tufted perennial to 1 m (3 ft) across, although often less, with decumbent leafy stems, about 50 cm (20 in) tall in bloom. Leaves oblong-lanceolate, sometimes narrowly so, untoothed, to 10 cm (4 in) long, thick and somewhat fleshy. Flowers bright yellow, deep chalices to 8 cm (3⅕ in) across, the petals often reddening with age, generally opening in the midafternoon; summer and autumn. 'Greencourt Lemon' primrose yellow.

Omphalodes

A colorful genus of forget-me-not (*Myosotis*) relatives, with almost 30 species scattered in Europe, western Asia, North Africa, and Mexico, ranging from pretty annuals to tufted perennials. The leaves are simple and untoothed, while the flowers are borne in lax somewhat spiraled cymes, the corolla forget-me-not-like, with a flat five-lobed limb with a small pore in the center leading to a short tube.

The fruit is composed of one to four nutlets located at the base of the persistent calyx.

The perennial species thrive in most good, humus-rich soils in sun or part shade, the three described below being indispensable rock garden plants for spring and early summer. They respond quite poorly to scorching conditions so that a position protected from the midday sun is advisable. Propagation is best effected by division of the parent clumps in late summer

or early spring, before growth commences or from seed.

Omphalodes cappadocica

Turkey and the Caucasus. A rather robust clump-forming evergreen perennial with long-stalked, ovate leaves with a somewhat heart-shaped base, to 10 cm (4 in) long, deep green, paler beneath. Flowers deep blue with a pale eye, 10–13 mm (⅖–½ in) across, borne in ascending cymes to 25 cm (10 in) long; late spring and early summer. 'Alba' pure white; 'Anthea Bloom' grayish leaves and sky blue flowers; 'Starry Eyes' chalk blue with a deep blue stripe down each petal.

Omphalodes linifolia

Southwestern Europe. A delightful annual with stiffly erect stems to 30 cm (12 in) tall. Leaves alternate, markedly glaucous, the basal oblong to spathulate, to 7.5 cm (3 in) long, the stem leaves small, linear to lanceolate. Flowers borne in airy sprays, white, rarely very pale blue, about 10 mm (⅖ in) across; late spring and summer. Best grown as a patch or drift. Plants will often self-seed, the young plants appearing in the autumn and overwintering, otherwise spring-sown seed will flourish just as well, although flowering several weeks later.

Omphalodes luciliae

Greece. A tufted perennial with a basal rosette of leaves and spreading, rather slender flowering stems. Leaves glaucous, oblong to ovate, stalked, to 5 cm (2 in) long. Flowers borne in bracted cymes, pale sky blue, about 8 mm (⅓ in) across; summer. A charming plant that is

Omphalodes luciliae (Photo courtesy of Alpine Garden Society)

Omphalodes verna

not always easy to please in the garden but well worth a try: a position in sun or part shade is best, otherwise plants tend to be shy flowering. A position sandwiched between rocks or tufa is ideal; it is a gem for a large trough or raised bed. Subsp. *cilicica,* from Turkey, is similar but with greener leaves.

Omphalodes verna

Southeastern and eastern Europe. A spreading, stoloniferous, herbaceous perennial making patches to 70 cm (28 in) across, or more, with short stolons. Leaves rather bright green, ovate to heart-shaped, to 18 cm (7 in) long. Flowers bright blue, 8–10 mm (⅓–⅖ in) across, borne in cymes of up to 12; spring. 'Alba' white. A fine woodland plant requiring dappled shade in the rock garden.

Onosma

A genus with some 60 species in Europe and Asia, particularly the Mediterranean region. Generally known as golden drops, these members of the borage family (Boraginaceae) have flowers in various colors, although yellow predominates. They are biennial, perennial, or subshrubby, with bristly stems and leaves. The tubular, nodding or half-nodding flowers are borne in simple or branched, somewhat spiraled cymes.

Onosmas are excellent bee plants in the garden and, despite their bristly nature, are handsome plants for dry sunny places in a well-drained gritty compost. Propagation is from seed sown in early spring or from cuttings taken in mid to late summer.

Onosma alborosea

Eastern Turkey, Syria, and Iraq. A rough, bristly, subshrubby perennial to 20 cm (8 in) tall with gray-green oblong to obovate leaves, 2.5–6 cm (1–2⅖ in) long, covered with stiff white hairs. Flowers white at first but soon turning pink, then bluish violet, pendent tubular bells, 1.8–3 cm (⅔–2⅕ in) long, borne in spiraled clusters at the shoot tips; summer. In the wild it is a plant of limestone rocks and cliffs.

untoothed leaves are borne in pairs along square-sectioned stems. The small flowers are in whorls one above the other, or in heads, the corolla two-lipped (typical of most labiates) and with a short to long tube. Typical of most species are the large, showy, overlapping bracts that enclose the base of the flowers.

The rock garden species are readily grown in a gritty well-drained compost in warm sunny situations. Propagation is from cuttings taken of elongating young vegetative shoots in the spring, especially of the named hybrids, or from seed.

Origanum amanum

A delightful plant from the Amanus Mountains of southern Turkey, where it is a rock crevice dweller. Plants form rather dense hummocky subshrubs no more than 20 cm (8 in) tall, the short wiry stems beset with small gray-green heart-shaped leaves, 10–15 mm (²⁄₅–³⁄₅ in) long. The terminal clusters of flowers are surrounded by leaf-like, purplish bracts, the flowers deep pink with a slender protruding tube 3–4 cm (1¹⁄₅–1³⁄₅ in) long, flaring at the tip into a small five-lobed limb; summer. Var. *album* white.

Origanum 'Barbara Tingey'

A hybrid between *O. rotundifolia* and the little-grown *O. tournefortii*, which forms spreading, subshrubby mounds to 20 cm (8 in) tall, but up to 60 cm (2 ft) across. The arching shoots bear bluish green, somewhat hairy leaves with a purple reverse. The terminal, drooping, hop-like flower clusters are enveloped in green bracts heavily flushed with purple that progressively darkens with age. The pinkish flow-

It requires a sunny well-drained gritty soil in the garden.

Origanum

The marjorams represent a European and western Asian genus with about 40 species of aromatic perennial herbs and subshrubs, which includes several important culinary herbs such as dittany, marjoram, and oregano. The small

Origanum 'Kent Beauty'

Origanum rotundifolium

ers just protrude beyond the rim of the bracts; summer into early autumn. An excellent raised bed or rock garden plant.

Origanum 'Kent Beauty'

Very similar to *O.* 'Barbara Tingey' (but a cross between *O. rotundifolium* and *O. scabrum*) noted for its even larger and more strongly colored bracts; summer.

Origanum rotundifolium

Turkey. A spreading subshrub to 23 cm (9 in) tall with arching, wiry branches clothed in rounded, rather pale gray-green leaves to 25 mm (1 in) long. Flowers borne in drooping, hop-like clusters dominated by closely overlapping, broad-rounded, pale apple green bracts, which partially obscure the whitish or pale pink flowers; summer to early autumn. An easy plant and an important parent of some fine garden hybrids.

Oxalis

A large genus with about 500 species of annuals, perennials, and shrubs with a cosmopolitan distribution. While many species are weedy—indeed several are noxious weeds in the garden—others have considerable ornamental appeal and make first-rate plants for the rock garden and containers of various sorts. Most are rather fleshy plants with a fibrous, scaly, rhizomatous or bulbous rootstock. The leaves are typically trefoil like, although some species have more than three leaflets. The five-parted flowers are basically funnel-shaped and have separate sepals and petals. The fruit is

a five-parted, explosive capsule, containing few to many seeds.

Although many of the species are not fully hardy, others are and make very good rock garden plants, requiring any good, well-drained loamy soil in which to thrive. Sunshine is a necessity for the majority, otherwise the flowers will fail to open properly. Propagation is by seed sown in the spring or by division or separation of the bulbs when the plants are dormant.

Oxalis adenophylla

Argentina and Chile. A neat, tufted, bulbous species forming rather dense clumps to 12.5 cm (5 in) tall in flower. Leaves glaucous, parasol-like, with up to 12, sometimes more, heart-shaped leaflets, folded along the center. Flowers solitary, wide funnel-shaped, 2.5–3 cm (1–1⅕ in) across, white flushed with purple toward the petal margins and adorned with lilac or purple veins; late spring and early sum-

mer. 'Rosea' pink flowers with purple veins. In addition, white-flowered forms are sometimes seen in cultivation. The bulbs should not be deep planted but placed with their noses at ground level.

Oxalis articulata (syn. *O. floribunda*)

South America; Brazil to Argentina. Like *O. corymbosa*, but with thick, branching, tuber-like rhizomes, often rather taller, the leaflets not more than 3 cm (1⅕ in) long. Flowers somewhat larger, bright deep pink, in sizeable umbels, nodding in bud; late spring to autumn.

Oxalis corymbosa

South America. A clump-forming bulbous perennial to 15 cm (6 in) tall in flower. Bright green trefoil-like leaves, the leaflets heart-shaped, to 5 cm (2 in) long. Flowers in cymes of up to eight, above the leaves, rose-purple, funnel-shaped, about 20 mm (⅘ in) across; summer and autumn.

Oxalis enneaphylla

Patagonia and Falkland Islands. A rhizomatous, patch-forming plant forming clumps or laxer mats, with scaly rhizomes, up to 10 cm (4 in) tall in flower. Leaves neat and tight, glaucous and fleshy, with nine or more deeply notched leaflets. Flowers solitary, white to pale rose-purple, with deeper veining, broad funnel-shaped, about 2.5 cm (1 in) across, fragrant; late spring and summer. Individual plants are sterile but multiply by the production of bulbils, which can be removed and grown on, an especially effective way of increasing the best clones. 'Alba' pure white; 'Minuti-

Oxalis adenophylla

Oxalis articulata

folia' an especially compact form with very small leaves and pale rose-purple flowers; 'Rosea' purple-pink; 'Rubra' purplish red; 'Ruth Tweedie' shell pink; 'Sheffield Swan' white with yellowish green veins.

Oxalis 'Ione Hecker'

A hybrid between two Patagonian species, *O. enneaphylla* and *O. laciniata*, forming a clump to 7.5 cm (3 in) tall in flower. Leaves bear about 10 leaflets, each strongly folded along the center and wavy along the margin. Wide funnel-shaped flowers dark purple merging into blue at petal margins, with deeper veining overall; late spring and early summer.

Papaver

Poppies need little introduction, for they have been long-cherished in the garden. Most of those commonly grown are annuals or perennials that are too coarse for the average rock garden; however, there are some delightful little alpine species worthy of a space, being excellent in the rock garden, but also very effective for gravel or scree conditions and raised beds. The rock garden species are tuft-forming biennials or short-lived perennials with only basal leaves and solitary flowers borne on basal scapes above the foliage. They thrive in sunny aspects in most well drained gritty composts and will self-seed to some extent in most gardens.

Papaver alpinum

Mountains of central and southern Europe east to the Carpathians. The name *alpinum*,

Papaver burseri

which is widely used in horticulture, is ambiguous and covers a series of closely related species of which the most important are *P. burseri* (white), *P. corona-sancti-stephani* (pale yellow), *P. kerneri* (yellow), *P. rhaeticum* (bright yellow), *P. sendtneri* (white), and *P. suaveolens* (yellow, orange, or red). Seed or plants may be found under any of these names or as simply *P. alpinum*, with many of the plants in cultivation in fact being hybrids between two or more of them. All make small tufted plants to 25 cm (10 in) tall in flower, with green or gray-green, neatly dissected, pinnately lobed, somewhat hairy leaves. Flowers deeply cupped, 3–5 cm (1⅕–2 in) across, borne on slender bristly scapes well above the foliage, petals range in color from white to yellow, orange, and red; summer. 'Summer Breeze' a fine selection with good-sized flowers in the full range of colors.

Papaver miyabeanum

Kurile Islands, north of Japan. A neat little poppy to 15 cm (6 in) tall in flower with tufts of gray-green, bristly, pinnately lobed leaves. Flowers solitary on erect, bristly basal scapes

above the foliage, pale primrose yellow, 3–4 cm (1⅕–1⅗ in) across, followed by small bristly globose capsules; late spring and summer. Plant will succumb to excessive winter wet: if plants fail during the winter, then usually new seedlings will appear in the spring. The Japanese *P. fauriei*, which is sometimes listed by nurseries, is very similar and comes from the Rishiri Islands to the northwest of Hokkaido.

Papaver nudicaule

Siberia to Mongolia. This is the so-called Iceland poppy, widely sold by nurseries and garden centers as flowering plants or as packeted seed. Plants form tufts 30–50 cm (12–20 in) tall in flower, with rather bright green or gray-green, pinnately lobed leaves, basically elliptical in outline. Large, rather blowsy flowers, up to 7.5 cm (3 in) across, sometimes larger, borne on bristly scapes well above the foliage, primarily in shades of yellow, red, orange, and vermilion, as well as white and pink on occasions; late spring and summer. Although most poppies deteriorate in response to disturbance and pricking out at the seedling stage, *P. nudicaule* will respond well, as it is a short-lived

Papaver miyabeanum

Papaver nudicaule

perennial. Regular sowing will ensure its permanence in the garden. Seed houses sell various strains in a wide range of bright, sometime gaudy colors that can look out of place in the rock garden. The most well known of these include 'Aurora Borealis', 'Champagne Bubbles', 'Gartenzwerg' (GARDEN GNOME), 'Oregon Rainbows', 'San Remo', and 'Wonder Hybrids'.

Penstemon

An important and varied genus with some 270 species, primarily in North America but stretching south as far as Guatemala. They are members of the figwort family (Scrophulariaceae) along with other familiar genera, such as *Antirrhinum, Digitalis, Verbascum*, and *Veronica*. The species include evergreen and herbaceous perennials and evergreen shrubs and subshrubs, many excellent garden plants but often too gross for the average rock garden. Penstemons have paired, simple leaves and terminal, branched or unbranched cymose panicles of flowers; the corolla is tubular, flaring at the mouth into a two-lobed upper and a three-lobed lower lip, often ridged in the mouth. The fruit is a two-parted capsule containing numerous seeds.

Penstemons are not particularly difficult to cultivate and the smaller alpine species make excellent rock garden plants for scree conditions or raised beds; however, they deteriorate in aspects that are too windy in the garden and may succumb in part in particularly cold or wet winters: a sheltered sunny aspect and a well-drained gritty compost will help them survive such periods. Propagation is from seed sown in late winter or early spring or from late summer cuttings overwintered in a cold frame.

Penstemon fruticosus

British Columbia south to Oregon, Montana, and Wyoming. A bushy subshrub to 40 cm (16 in) tall, generally not more than 25 cm (10 in), with elliptic-lanceolate, almost entire leaves to 6 cm (2⅖ in) long. Flowers lavender-blue to pale purple, up to 4 cm (1⅗ in) long, borne in glandular-hairy inflorescences; summer. A quite variable species in which several variants are recognized, the most widely grown being var. *scouleri* (syn. *P. scouleri*), which has smaller, somewhat toothed leaves, to only 2.5 cm (1 in) long, rather larger flowers to 5 cm (2 in) long; forma *albus* and *rubra* have white or red flowers, respectively; 'Amethyst' good amethyst lavender.

Penstemon hirsutus

Central and eastern United States north to Quebec. A tufted perennial to 60 cm (2 ft) tall, with lanceolate to elliptic or ovate-elliptic leaves to 7.5 cm (3 in) long. Flowers in cymose panicles, pale violet with a white throat, about 2.5 cm (1

Penstemon hirsutus var. *pygmaeus*

in) long; late spring and summer. Var. *pygmaeus* (syn. 'Pygmaeus') the best form for the alpine garden, being dwarfer, not more than 15 cm (6 in) tall in flower; forma *albus* white.

Penstemon pinifolius

Southwestern United States. A low spreading, rather wispy subshrub to 30 cm (1 ft) tall, but at least twice as wide. Leaves bright green, glabrous, linear, to 2.5 cm (1 in) long, with revolute margins. Flowers in lax cymose racemes,

3–4 cm (1⅕–1⅗ in) long; late spring to autumn. 'Mersea Yellow' mustard yellow; 'Wisley Flame' maroon-red.

Penstemon rupicola

Western United States; Washington to California. A spreading subshrub to 60 cm (2 ft) across but only 10 cm (4 in) tall in flower. Leaves rather leathery, glaucous, elliptic to obovate, to 17.5 cm (7 in) long, mostly smaller, finely and irregularly serrate. Flowers in small cymose racemes, pink to pinkish lavender, to 35 mm (1⅖ in) long; summer. An excellent cool crevice plant. 'Albus', 'Conwy Lilac', and 'Conwy Rose' are all fine cultivars.

Persicaria

Formerly included in the genus *Polygonum*, *Persicaria* contains the plants generally referred to as bistorts, which have cylindrical spikes of flowers borne terminally on the shoots. The genus has some 40 species, primarily in northern temperate regions.

They are readily grown in sun or part shade on most ordinary garden soils. Many are either too weedy or too vigorous for all but the largest rock gardens. However, the following is well worth consideration. Propagation is readily effected by division in the spring just prior to plants coming into growth.

Persicaria affinis (syn. *Bistorta affinis*, *Polygonum affine*)

Eastern Afghanistan to Nepal. A woody-based, matted perennial to 80 cm (32 in) across, about 20 cm (8 in) tall in flower. Leaves narrow-

....

Penstemon rupicola

Persicaria affinis 'Donald Lowndes'

elliptic to oblanceolate, to 10 cm (4 in) long, deep green with a glaucous reverse, dying to bronze in the autumn. Flower spikes dense, cylindrical, to 7.5 cm (3 in) long, pink; summer and autumn. 'Darjeeling Red' dark crimson; 'Donald Lowndes' rose-pink; 'Superba' soft pink.

Petrocallis

An unusual genus of two species, one in the European mountains, the other marooned in northern Iran. They are members of the Cruciferae with four-petaled flowers. A little gem for a gritty, well-drained compost in sun or part shade. Propagation is from seed sown in late winter.

Petrocallis pyrenaica
Pyrenees, Alps, Carpathians. A small tufted plant often cushion-forming, rather *Draba*-like. Leaves in rosettes, three-lobed, about 6 mm (¼ in) long. Flowers lilac to pale pink, 5–8 mm (⅕–⅓ in) across, borne in racemes; summer. A fine little rock plant for scree, raised beds, or troughs.

Petrophyton

A western North American genus with three species of cushion-forming or matted evergreen shrublets in the rose family (Rosaceae), but very different in appearance than most other members of that important family. They have crowded, simple leaves and dense racemes of small five-petaled flowers.

Excellent rock garden plants, especially fine for troughs and large blocks of tufa. Petrophytons require a neutral to slightly acid compost and partial shade, and they will self-sow in some gardens. Propagation is from seed sown in early spring or cuttings in midsummer.

Petrophyton hendersonii
Northwestern United States; Washington State. Plant forming low hummocks to 10 cm (4 in) high, three times as much across. Leaves bluish

Petrocallis pyrenaica

Petrophyton hendersonii
(Photo courtesy of Alpine Garden Society)

green, oblanceolate, to 20 mm (⅘ in) long, borne in crowded rosettes. Racemes creamy white, to 7.5 cm (3 in) long, with numerous protruding stamens; early summer.

Phlox

A genus of about 70 species nearly all confined to North America, with one isolated in Siberia. This popular genus of mountain and high

alpine plants and stout herbaceous perennials bears opposite, often rather narrow leaves. The flowers are borne in small clusters or more substantial cymose inflorescences, the corolla salver-shaped with a long narrow tube and a spreading five-lobed limb.

The smaller species are indispensable in the rock garden, coming as they do in a wide variety of colors and form. They are best grown in scree conditions in full sun, although several prefer moist and cooler woodland conditions, particularly *P. adsurgens* and *P. divaricata* and their derivatives. Propagation is by seed when ripe or sown in early spring or by cuttings taken in late summer and overwintered under cover. Phloxes are great plants for attracting insects into the garden, especially bees and butterflies. Both *P. douglasii* and *P. subulata* are best trimmed back lightly after flowering to keep them in good form.

Phlox adsurgens

Oregon. A mat-forming species to 50 cm (20 in) wide, producing ascending flowering shoots to 30 cm (1 ft). Leaves ovate to elliptic, to 3 cm (1⅕ in) long. Flowers pink, lilac, or purple, 2–2.5 cm (⅘–1 in) across, with a pale eye and a dark basal streak to each petal, borne in airy cymes; late spring to early autumn. 'Amazing Grace' white flushed pink with a darker eye; 'Red Buttes' rose-pink; 'Wagon Wheel' medium pink with a white eye, narrow lobed.

Phlox bifida

Northern and central United States. A tufted to lax, mat-forming plant to 60 cm (2 ft) across, about 20 cm (8 in) tall in flower, with linear to

Phlox bifida 'Thefi'

Phlox divaricata 'Blue Dreams'

lanceolate, downy leaves, to 6 cm (2⅖ in) long. Flowers in small cluster of up to nine, lavender, pink, or white, about 2 cm (⅘ in) across, slightly perfumed, the petals very deeply notched; spring and early summer. 'Alba' white; 'Petticoat' lilac-pink with deeper markings in center; 'Ralph Heywood' powder blue with a yellow eye; 'Thefi' very pale blue with a deeper eye.

Phlox divaricata

Eastern United States. A lax, matted perennial with decumbent stems, which often root at the nodes, giving rise to erect flowering shoots to 40 cm (16 in) tall. Leaves deep glossy green, elliptic to lanceolate, occasionally ovate, to 5 cm (2 in) long, sometimes glandular-downy. Flowers often fragrant, violet-blue, about 2.5 cm (1 in) across, with a darker eye, borne in lax cymes of up to 25, the petals with a broad notch normally; late spring and summer. 'Blue Dreams'; 'Blue Perfume'; 'Chattahoochee' rather larger lavender, crimson-eyed flowers (plants sold as 'Charles Ricardo' are scarcely different); 'Clouds of Perfume' powder blue; 'Eco Texas Purple'; 'Fuller's White'; 'Plum Perfect'; 'White Perfume'.

Phlox douglasii

Western United States; Oregon to Montana, south to California. Plants form deep green mats or low cushions not more than 10 cm (4 in) tall in flower but spreading to 50 cm (20 in). Flowers pungent, in small lax clusters, pink, lavender, or white, about 15 mm (⅗ in) across; spring and early summer. Many cultivars are available; some may be of hybrid origin, particularly with *P. subulata*. 'Boothman's Variety'

. . . .

Phlox douglasii 'Boothman's Variety'

Phlox mesoleuca 'Mary Maslin'

rounded flowers of pink with a deeper eye; 'Crackerjack' bright pink; 'Eva' mauve with a deeper eye; 'Iceberg' pure white; 'Ochsenblut' (OXBLOOD) rich red; 'Red Admiral' rose, with a deeper eye; 'White Admiral' white with a tiny yellowish eye.

Phlox mesoleuca (including *P. lutea*, *P. purpurea*)

Texas south to New Mexico. A small tufted

plant with slender spreading stems, to 20 cm (8 in) tall in flower, with gray-green, linear leaves to 7.5 cm (3 in) long. Flowers in lax clusters, variable in color from purple with a pale eye to pink, white, or yellow, about 3 cm (1⅕ in) across; late spring and summer. Not particularly easy to grow but it is such a striking plant that it is well worth the effort. 'Mary Maslin' signal red, more vigorous than the others; 'Paul Maslin' canary yellow, marked with a purple V at the base of each petal.

Phlox subulata

Northeastern United States. A mat-forming plant to 60 cm (2 ft) across but only 10 cm (4 in) tall, densely branched, with linear to awl-shaped leaves to 2 cm (⅘ in) long, finely hairy. Flowers varying from purple-violet to pink, lilac, or red, 13–25 mm (½–1 in) across; late spring and early summer. Generally referred to as a moss phlox, this species is the most popular among rock garden plant growers and has given rise to some first-class selections. 'Amazing Grace' white with a pink eye; 'Bonita' mauve; 'Candy Stripe' white with a broad lilac-pink stripe down each petal; 'Coral Eye' white flushed pink, deep pink eye; 'Emerald Cushion' lilac-pink; 'Emerald Cushion Blue' pale mauve-blue; 'Maischnee' (MAY SNOW, SNOW QUEEN) white; 'Marjorie' pink with deep eyelash markings in the center; 'McDaniel's Cushion' deep green foliage and extra-large deep pink flowers; 'Red Wings' rose red with deeper eye; 'Scarlet Flame' scarlet-red; 'Tamaongalei' white, carmine-streaked in center; 'Temiskaming' magenta, slow-growing; 'White Delight' pure white.

Phuopsis

A single species originating in western Asia, prized for its prolific bloom over an extended season. The species is perhaps too vigorous for the small rock garden but it certainly has a place in the garden especially as a path or driveway edging in sun or part shade. In addition, the flowers, which have a slightly unpleasant smell, attract butterflies into the garden. It is related to the bedstraws (*Galium*) in the family Rubiaceae.

Plants will succeed readily on most ordinary garden soil, provided they are well drained. Propagation is easy by division undertaken in early spring or after flowering. If plants are clipped back after their first flush of bloom, they will produce another crop later in the year.

Phuopsis stylosa

Eastern Turkey, the Caucasus, and northern Iran. A vigorous stoloniferous, patch-forming plant often exceeding 1 m across. Stems thin and somewhat square, bearing whorls of six or

Phuopsis stylosa 'Purpurea'

seven narrow-elliptic leaves, to ⅖ cm (1 in) long, strong-smelling when crushed. Flowers pink, slender-tubular, to 20 m (⅘ in) long, with five short, spreading lobes and a long-protruded style; summer and autumn. 'Purpurea' purple.

Physoplexis

A single species long associated with the genus *Phyteuma*. This curious member of the bell-flower family (Campanulaceae) is one of the most fascinating of rock garden gems. Fairy readily grown in a trough, raised bed, or a block of tufa, it is prone to the depredations of slugs and snails. If these can be kept at bay, then this is a rock garden plant for every collection. It needs a very well-drained alkaline compost and a reasonably sunny position in which to succeed. Propagation is by seed when ripe or sown in early spring. Basal cuttings can be taken in the spring or summer, but are not always easy to root.

Physoplexis comosa (syn. *Phyteuma comosum*)
Southeast Alps and Dolomites. The devil's-claw is a small tufted plant not more than 10 cm (4 in) tall in flower. The leaves vary from kidney-shaped to oblong-elliptic, to 5 cm (2 in) long, green or gray-green, toothed or somewhat lobed, long-stalked. Flowers clustered into tight heads of up to 20, flask-shaped, pinkish lilac tapering upward to a deep blackish violet tip, to 2 cm (⅘ in) long overall, with a long protruded style; summer. A perfect trough plant or as a specimen in a block of tufa.

. . . .

Physoplexis comosa

Platycodon

Popularly known as the balloon flower because of its inflated flower buds, this Asian genus consists of just a single, though somewhat variable species, related to the better-known bell-flowers (*Campanula*). Although the normal plant is generally too large for the rock garden, there are smaller variants available, some of which have found favor as potted plants in recent years.

They thrive in most ordinary, well-drained garden soils. Propagation from seed sown in early spring affords the readiest means of increase, although the offspring can be quite variable. Established plants can be divided, but this is quite tricky owing to the nature of the fleshy rootstock.

Platycodon grandiflorus
Japan, northern and northeastern China, eastern Siberia (Ussuri). An erect herbaceous perennial to 60 cm (2 ft) tall in flower. Leaves ovate, 4–7 cm (1⅗–2⅘ in) long, toothed, green above, slightly glaucous beneath. Flowers large

Platycodon grandiflorus var. *apoyama*

Platycodon grandiflorus 'Astra Blue'

'Hakone Double Blue' has semi-double blue flowers on a medium-sized plant; 'Hakone White' white, dwarf; 'Mariesii' to 45 cm (18 in) tall, has deeply colored, somewhat earlier flowers; 'Mariesii Album' the white version of 'Mariesii'; 'Semiplenus' semi-double flowers in pink, white, or blue. Other cultivars are available from a few suppliers. These will all come reasonably true from seed; however, if grown in close proximity in the garden they will hybridize all too readily.

Polemonium

A smallish genus with about 30 species, scattered right across temperate and boreal regions of the Northern Hemisphere. While most are too tall or weedy for the rock garden, several of the smaller are real gems, although some of the finest require rather exacting conditions in cultivation. They are commonly known as Jacob's ladder because of their neat, step-like, pinnate foliage. The flowers, which are borne in cymes or racemes, are five-parted, the corolla with a short tube uniting the petals toward the base.

Those listed here will succeed in a well-drained or gritty soil in sun or part shade. They can be propagated from seed sown in late winter or early spring,

Polemonium 'Apricot Delight'
A cultivar of *P. carneum* from the northwestern United States. Similar in stature to 'Lambrook Mauve' but with bronze-flushed leaves and rather larger pink, more open, flowers with an apricot center; spring and early summer.

and balloon-like in bud, opening to wide bowl-shaped bells, to 5 cm (2 in) across, borne in few-flowered racemes or solitary, blue or purple; mid to late summer. Var. *apoyama* (syn. 'Apoyama') from Japan's Mount Apoi, is dwarfer, to 25 cm (10 in) tall, and more suitable for rock garden culture; 'Astra Blue' dwarf plant with rich blue flowers; 'Blue Pygmy' the dwarfest of all, with relatively large good blue flowers; 'Fuji Pink' like var. *apoyama* but pink;

Polemonium 'Lambrook Mauve'

Polemonium pulcherrimum
. . . .

Polemonium 'Lambrook Mauve'

A mound-forming evergreen perennial to 45 cm (18 in) tall. Leaves medium green with five to nine leaflets. The branched stems bear clusters of pale mauve, yellow centered, cupped flowers, 10–15 mm (⅖–⅗ in) across, in profusion over an extended season; spring and summer. Will repeat flower if trimmed back after the first flush of bloom has faded. The plant is sterile and needs to be increased by division.

Polemonium pauciflorum

Southwestern United States. A rather elegant tufted plant 30–50 cm (12–20 in) tall, with sparsely leafy, erect stems that are sticky in the upper part. Leaves pinnate, adorned with silvery hairs. Flowers in lax terminal clusters, half-nodding, pale yellow, sometimes blue-flushed outside, narrow trumpets to 4 cm (1½ in) long; summer and early autumn. Short-lived in cultivation, but readily raised from seed, although it will sometimes self-sow in the garden. Thrives best in dappled shade. 'Sulphur Trumpets' well-colored sulfur flowers set against silvery foliage.

Polemonium 'Pink Beauty'

A compact plant like a dwarfer version of *Polemonium* 'Lambrook Mauve', but flowers pale mauve; late spring and early summer.

Polemonium pulcherrimum

Western United States; Washington to Colorado. A clump-forming perennial to 40 cm (16 in) tall, often half that height. Leaves to 5 cm (2 in) long, with up to 25 neat, elliptic leaflets. Flowers in small terminal cymes, blue or mauve

with a white or yellow eye, campanulate, 10–13 mm (⅖–½ in) long; late spring and early summer. A good plant for scree conditions, not as much grown as it deserves; although short-lived, it does produce abundant seed.

Polygala

A large genus with about 500 species with a cosmopolitan distribution. Commonly called milkworts, the flowers of *Polygala* are almost legume-like, except that three of the sepals are very small while the other two form prominent, often colored, wings. The petals are also modified with only three apparent; the lowermost are folded, and usually fringed at the tip, to form a keel. Milkworts range from annuals and perennials to dwarf and quite substantial shrubs, and even small trees. They are especially prized for their blue flowers, although other colors do occur.

Those listed here are relatively easy to grow and decorative, requiring a gritty, well-drained compost and full or part shade. Propagation is by seed sown in early spring, by division at the same time, or by cuttings taken during the summer and overwintered in a cold frame.

Polygala calcarea

Western and southwestern Europe. A charming little stoloniferous plant forming a close mat to 30 cm (1 ft) across in time. Leaves mostly in lax rosettes, deep green, obovate, to 20 mm (⅘ in) long. Flowers in terminal racemes to 3 cm (1⅕ in) long, gentian blue, about 8 mm (⅓ in) long; spring and early summer. An excellent scree or raised bed plant for full sun. 'Lillet' very compact and especially free-flowering.

Polygala chamaebuxus

Southern and southeastern Europe. A stoloniferous, evergreen shrublet forming low mounds or mats to 40 cm (16 in) across, not more than 15 cm (6 in) tall. Leaves leathery, deep glossy green, lanceolate to ovate, 15–30 mm (⅗–1⅕ in) long. Flowers solitary or paired, 10–15 mm (⅖–⅗ in) long, wings yellow or white, keel golden at first changing to purple or brownish crimson; spring and summer or a few in the autumn. Requires a leafy compost and dappled shade on a neutral or somewhat acid soil. Var. *grandiflora* (syn. 'Atropurpurea', 'Grandiflora', 'Purpurea') a fine variant with larger flowers with rose-purple wings.

Polygala vayredae

Eastern Pyrenees. Much like *P. chamaebuxus* var. *grandiflora*, but with linear to narrow-

....

Polygala calcarea 'Lillet'

Polygala vayredae

lanceolate, rather duller foliage; flowers in late spring and summer.

Potentilla

A large genus with about 500 species distributed in most parts of the world, especially the temperate Northern Hemisphere. The genus is noted for its colorful evergreen and deciduous perennials and for a number of twiggy shrubs much grown in gardens, particularly the various forms of *P. fruticosa*. *Potentilla* is a member of the rose family (Rosaceae), with compound, digitately or pinnately lobed leaves. The flowers are disk-like or bowl-shaped, often yellow, although other colors are present, and have five petals. An interesting feature of the flower is the presence of an epicalyx (literally a calyx outside the prime calyx), in which smaller sepals alternate with the five main ones. This feature clearly distinguishes the flower from the unrelated buttercups with which they are sometimes confused, but it does occur in other genera in the rose family, notably in the strawberry (*Fragaria*). The fruit is a collection of small single-seeded achenes.

The genus has a large number of potentially good rock garden plants, although relatively few are generally available at the present time. They thrive in a well-drained, yet moisture-retentive soil in full sun or part shade. Propagation is by seed sown in late winter or early spring or by division in the spring as the plants come into growth. The following all make good rock garden or raised bed subjects, although they can be quite invasive; however, they are generally easily grown and flower profusely.

Potentilla aurea

Central and southern Europe. A tufted perennial forming mats, to 50 cm (20 in) across and to 20 cm (8 in) tall in flower. Leaves digitate,

. . . .
Potentilla aurea

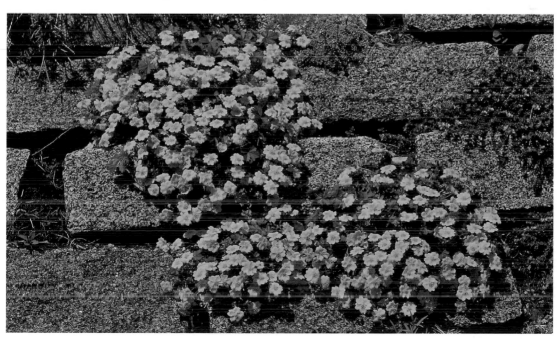

with five obovate, silky-haired leaflets. Flowers bright yellow, generally with an orange eye, 13–25 mm (½–1 in) across, borne in small clusters; late spring to early autumn. 'Aurantiaca' orange; 'Goldlumpen' golden yellow; 'Plena' double, yellow.

Potentilla crantzii (syn. *P. alpestris*)

Widespread in arctic and subarctic regions and higher mountains in the Northern Hemi-sphere. A rather vigorous mat- or mound-forming plant with arching stems, woody at the base. Leaves deep green, digitate, with five obovate to oblanceolate, toothed leaflets, sparingly hairy. Flowers in lax clusters, golden yellow, often orange in the center, 15–25 mm (⅗–1 in) across, the petals notched at the top. The larger-flowered forms are worth seeking out and only the best-flowered forms kept for sowing. Surprisingly, this species thrives best in rather poor stony ground.

Potentilla cuneata

Himalaya to western China. A mat-forming perennial to 30 cm (1 ft) across or more but only a few centimeters tall in flower, spreading by underground stolons. Leaves bluish green, ternate, with obovate leaflets to 13 mm (½ in) long, three-toothed at the apex. Flowers bright yellow, 15–25 mm (⅗–1 in) across, solitary, the petals rounded and somewhat overlapping, slightly notched at the top; summer. A bright and cheerful plant that can at times prove rather invasive, especially in a trough or raised bed.

Potentilla nitida

Southern Alps and northern Apennines. A true alpine gem, this delightful tufted or low cushion plant will in time eventually spread to 30 cm (1 ft) across, but no more than 5 cm (2 in) tall in flower. The ternate leaves are silky with silvery hairs, the leaflets obovate to oblanceolate, generally slightly toothed at the apex, no more than 10 mm (⅖ in) long. Flowers pale pink to rose red, solitary or paired, 20–25 mm (⅘–1 in) across, with neatly notched petals; mid to late summer. An excellent trough or

Potentilla cuneata

Potentilla nitida

raised bed plant, which will also grow well on tufa. It requires ample sunshine to flower at its best. 'Alba' white; 'Rubra' rich rose red.

Pratia

A small Australasian genus sometimes included in the more familiar genus *Lobelia*. The species described here is an excellent little plant for carpeting ground in shade or part shade along pathways or on gravel, between troughs or in quiet corners in the rock garden. It is easily propagated by removing ready rooted portions from the parent plant.

Pratia pedunculata

Southeastern Australia and Tasmania. A very low mat-forming plant that spreads above and below ground level and roots down readily as it spreads. Leaves ovate to rounded, slightly toothed, 5–20 mm (⅕–⅘ in) long. Flowers solitary, on slender stalks, about 10 mm (⅖ in) across, blue to purplish blue; summer and autumn. 'County Park' rich violet-blue; 'Tom Stone' variable pale blue. The species is often confused with *Houstonia caerulea* but is easily distinguished on account of its two-lipped, five-lobed flowers; *Houstonia* has four even lobes.

Primula

Few genera are more important in the rock garden, or indeed the garden as a whole, than *Primula*. With over 400 species, primarily restricted to the temperate Northern Hemisphere, but with a few scattered on the mountains of Southeast Asia, Africa, and South America, the genus has plenty to offer the gar-

· ·
Pratia pedunculata

dener, from excellent woodland and border plants, to those for boggy conditions and poolside plantings, to crevice and rock dwellers. They are suitable for the rock garden, raised beds, and troughs, as well as more specialized, often high-alpine species, needing more exacting conditions.

Primulas have basal rosettes of leaves that are with or without white or yellowish farina. The flowers are solitary or in umbels or tiers, held erect to horizontal or nodding. The corolla is essentially salver- or bell-shaped with the stamens included in the tube, while the calyx is tubular with five teeth. In *Primula* there are generally two types of flower, short- or long-styled, with plants having either one or the other type. This condition, known as heterostyly, essentially ensures cross-pollination, with stamens and style held at different levels within the flower. In addition, there is usually a self incompatibility system working within the plant that generally inhibits self-pollination. This all sounds very technical, and it is, but from the gardener's point of view seed will only be produced if both forms of plant are

present, while hybridization between different species or clones is very likely in the garden environment.

The primulas listed below are all excellent rock garden plants, requiring a moist, humus-rich soil and sunny or partly shaded conditions. They can be divided after flowering, and this is essential every three or four years for many to ensure that they stay vigorous and flower well in the garden. Root aphids can be a potential problem and need to be guarded against.

Primula auricula

Alps and Carpathians. The auricula is a tufted evergreen plant with one or several, rather fleshy, mealy or plain leaf rosettes, to 15 cm (6 in) tall in flower. Leaves obovate, green or gray-green, to 12.5 cm (5 in) long, toothed or not along the margin. Flowers nodding to half-nodding, borne in umbels of up to 30 at the height of the leaves or somewhat above, pale to deep yellow, 15–25 mm (⅗–1 in) across, with a mealy white ring in the center; spring. The wild type is rarely seen in gardens today: the garden auricula has been cultivated and developed

over five centuries and today includes numerous named cultivars, many of which involve *P. hirsuta* (*P. ×pubescens*). While many of these are so-called Show Auriculas requiring specialist growing conditions, other selections make excellent garden plants for the rock garden or elsewhere. They come in a wide range of colors apart from yellow, including red, purple, mauve, bluish or greenish, often with attractive zoning or patterning and with or without a mealy white ring in the center. There are single, semi-double, and fully double types available.

Primula denticulata

Sino-Himalaya (where China, Tibet, and India meet). The drumstick primula is an easy and accommodating plant with large, coarse rosettes of oblong or oval, finely toothed leaves, which enlarge considerably after flowering. The purple to mauve flowers are crammed together in globose heads atop stout mealy scapes, 10–25 cm (4–10 in) long; spring. 'Glenroy Crim-

. . . .

Primula auricula cultivars

Primula auricula

son' crimson-red; 'Pritchard's Ruby' glowing purple, 'Rubin' red, var. *alba*, pure white with a yellow eye. Blue, lilac, and red selections are also offered in the trade.

Primula elatior

Europe including southeastern England, western Asia. The oxlip is a delightful plant closely related to the primrose. It is a woodland dweller in many areas, although some forms ascend to high alpine meadows. Plants form clumps to 25 cm (10 in) tall in flower, with rosettes of broad paddle-shaped leaves. Fragrant primrose yellow flowers borne in one-sided umbels are half-nodding, funnel-shaped, 18–25 mm (¾–1 in) across; spring. Excellent for naturalizing in partially shaded, moist places in the garden or cool pockets in the rock garden. Hybridizes readily with the primrose (*P. vulgaris*).

. . . .

Bottom left: *Primula denticulata*

Right: *Primula elatior*

Bottom right: *Primula frondosa*

Primula frondosa

Bulgaria. A rather delicate-looking primula to 12.5 cm (5 in) tall in flower, with obovate leaves to 9 cm (3⅗ in) long, deep green above but mealy white beneath. Flowers in umbels of up to 30 on a common scape above the foliage, pinkish lilac to reddish purple with a darker eye, to 16 mm (⅔ in) across; early spring. Good in semi-shade or in a trough, where it will seed around on occasions. The widespread *P. fari-*

nosa (the bird's-eye primrose), distributed from Britain to China, is very similar but generally with paler, yellow-eyed flowers. It is a less satisfactory garden plant.

Primula marginata

French and Italian Alps. A tufted evergreen plant to 15 cm (6 in) tall in flower, characterized by its stem-like aboveground rhizomes and rosettes of obovate to lanceolate, leathery, and somewhat fleshy leaves that are distinctly toothed and mealy at the margins, the meal sometimes extending over most of the leaf surface. Flowers bluish lavender, occasionally pink, with a white mealy eye, half-nodding, borne in umbels of up to 20, each 15–30 mm (⅗–1⅕ in) across; late spring and early summer. A limestone dweller in the wild. Several cultivars are available, some are *P. marginata* crosses with related species, including 'Caerulea' blue; 'Holden Variety' dark blue, compact; 'Kesselring's Variety' mauve-lilac; 'Linda Pope' large rounded pale mauve-blue flowers; 'Prichard's Variety' purple flowers and gray leaves; 'White Lady' (syn. 'White Linda Pope') creamy white.

Primula ×pruhoniciana

Excellent garden hybrids resulting from crosses between the common primrose, *P. vulgaris*, and the purple or magenta-flowered Caucasian *P. juliae*. Plants form neat, slow-spreading clumps of oblong to rounded, toothed leaves, in various shades of green, sometimes flushed with bronze or purple. The erect flowers, essentially like those of the common primrose, come in a range of colors from white and yellow to purple, violet, magenta, and red; late winter and spring. 'Kinlough Beauty' pink-mauve; 'Lady Greer' cream; 'Wanda' bright magenta-purple.

Primula ×pubescens

This fine hybrid encompasses all the crosses between two European species, *P. auricula* and *P. hirsuta*. Included here are some readily available cultivars: 'Beverley White'; 'Boothman's Variety' red; 'Faldonside' bright crimson; 'Freedom' lilac-pink; 'Harlow Carr' white; 'Mrs J. H. Wilson' luminous violet; 'Rufus' red.

. . . .

Primula marginata (Photo by Robert Rolfe)

Primula ×pruhoniciana 'Lady Greer'

Primula rosea

Western Himalaya and eastern Hindu Kush. A small tufted, nonmealy, herbaceous, plant to 20 cm (8 in) tall, with overwintering resting buds. Leaves deep green, oblanceolate, to 20 cm (8 in) long eventually, neatly toothed at the margin. Flowers rose red with a small yellow eye, in umbels of up to 12, only 10–15 cm (4–6 in) tall in flower but the scapes greatly elongate as the fruits develop; spring.

Primula veris

The cowslip is a familiar European plant of grassy meadows and banks, but it is widely distributed elsewhere in various forms from Turkey and the Caucasus to Russia and eastern Siberia. Plants form tufts, often with several leaf rosettes, to 30 cm (1 ft) tall in flower, often less. Gray-green leaves are ovate to oblong, up to 20 cm (8 in) long, abruptly narrowed at base into a widely winged petiole. Up to 16 nodding or half-nodding flowers borne in one-sided umbels, sweetly scented, relatively small, to 12 mm (½ in) across, deep yellow with an orange mark at base of each petal lobe; spring. Forms with orange or red flowers, referred to as Canadian cowslips and sometimes offered for sale, are of hybrid origin involving the common primrose. All make easy and accommodating and colorful garden plants.

Primula vulgaris

Europe and western Asia. The common primrose is a quite variable and widespread species and one of the most accommodating primulas in the garden, often seeding around freely in shaded and semi-shaded, moist places. Plants form tufts of rather dull green, somewhat wrinkly, elliptic to oblanceolate leaves, 5–25 cm (2–10 in) long. Solitary, fragrant flowers borne on slender, softly hairy stalks from the center of each rosette, often in large numbers; pale yellow with orange markings in the the center, up to 35 mm (1⅖ in) across; late winter and spring, intermittently at other times of the year. Subsp. *balearica*, from Majorca, has pure white flowers; subsp. *heterochroma*, from northern Iran,

Primula rosea

Primula vulgaris

has leaves white with hairs beneath and abruptly narrowed at the base, along with rose-pink to purple or occasionally white flowers; subsp. *sibthorpii* is like the last but without the white-hairy leaf undersurfaces, flowers various shades of soft pink normally. In the garden these all tend to hybridize, giving a medley of colorful offspring. As well as the singles there are also many double-flowered forms in a wide range of colors, Jack-in-the-green types in which the calyx lobes become enlarged and leafy, and hose-in-hose forms in which one corolla fits within another. In addition, crosses with *P. veris*, *P. ×polyantha*, which mostly have stout umbels of flowers in a very wide range of exciting colors, have given gardeners the modern polyanthus, sold in very large numbers at garden centers and other outlets.

Prunella

A small genus of seven species, commonly referred to as self-heals, restricted to the Northern Hemisphere. They are tufted perennials, sometimes mat-forming, spreading by short rhizomes, with erect, square stems bearing opposite leaves. The leaves are simple or lobed, mostly crowded at the base of the plant. Flowers two-lipped, tubular in the lower half, borne in dense, bracted spikes. The fruit, as in other labiates (Labiatae), consists of four nutlets located at the base of the persistent calyx.

The species listed here will thrive in any ordinary, well-drained garden soil. Prunellas are readily propagated from seed sown in late winter or by division after flowering or in the winter.

Prunella grandiflora

Central and southern Europe. A clump-forming plant to 30 cm (12 in) tall in flower with erect, hairy stems. Leaves deep green, ovate to elliptic, to 10 cm (4 in) long, the basal long-stalked, with an entire to toothed margin. Flowers deep violet, about 2.5 cm (1 in) long, in dense oblong spikes to 5 cm (2 in) long; summer. An easy plant, thriving on most well-drained soils in a sunny position, fine for a larger rock garden or the front of the flower border. Subsp. *pyrenaica* (syn. *P. hastiifolia*) has hastate (wide arrow-shaped) leaves and longer flower spikes. *P. ×webbiana* is a hybrid between *P. grandiflora* and its subspecies *pyrenaica*. 'Loveliness' pale violet; 'Pink Loveliness' clear pink; 'White Loveliness' pure white.

Pulsatilla

One of the loveliest plants for the rock garden, cherished for their silky chalices and feathery fruitheads. The genus contains 30 species scattered across the temperate Northern Hemisphere. *Pulsatilla* is included by some authori-

Prunella grandiflora

ties in the far larger genus *Anemone*; however, the combination of feathery fruits and the presence of nectariferous staminodes in the flowers serves to distinguish the genus quite clearly from *Anemone*.

Pulsatillas, or pasque flowers, are clump-forming perennials with feathery, often carrot-like foliage. The solitary flowers bear a ruff of leaf-like or dissected bracts immediately below, while the nodding to erect flowers generally have six tepals, which are silky-hairy on the exterior. Inside there is a boss of stamens, with some staminodes surrounding them, and a central core of carpels.

Those listed below will thrive on any well-drained soil and are ideal rock garden subjects. They tend to hybridize readily and will seed themselves around, especially on raised beds or scree gardens. Propagation from seed sown fresh or in late winter produces good results. Seedlings should be pricked off the moment the first true leaf appears. Established plants deteriorate in response to disturbance and will generally wilt or die if moved. Root cuttings of especially fine forms are possible, but this needs to be undertaken with care.

Pulsatilla grandis

North and central Europe. Rather similar to *P. vulgaris* but leaves scarcely developed at flowering time and with only five or seven prime divisions, with dense tawny or white hairs, especially when young. Flowers larger, to 9 cm (3⅗ in) across, purple to purplish blue or lilac purple; spring. 'Budapest Blue' (sometimes listed as 'Budapest Seedling') an exceptionally beautiful plant with large flowers in shades of lavender-blue; 'Papageno' large, campanulate

Pulsatilla grandis 'Budapest Blue'

to open cup-shaped flowers with deeply dissected tepals, sometimes semi-double, in a wide range of colors: pink, salmon, red, carmine, purple, lavender-purple, cream, and white predominating.

Pulsatilla halleri

A quite variable species with a number of subspecies found in isolated pockets in the Alps, Carpathians, Balkans, and Crimea. They often form substantial clumps to 20 cm (8 in) tall in flower, sometimes more. Leaves partly developed at flowering, pinnate with three or five prime segments, these pinnately lobed with oblong-lanceolate segments, densely hairy at first. Flowers large, erect, lavender to violet-purple, with golden anthers, to 10 cm (4 in) across; spring. Of the subspecies the finest are subsp. *halleri* from the southwestern and central Alps, with five primary leaf segments and dark violet flowers, and subsp. *slavica* from the Carpathians, which has leaves with three primary segments and substantial lavender-purple flowers.

Pulsatilla rubra

Central France and northern Spain. A small tufted plant to 15 cm (6 in) tall in flower with bipinnately lobed, deep green, somewhat hairy leaves, with short elliptic to lanceolate divisions. Flowers nodding to horizontal, campanulate, to 5 cm (2 in) long, deep reddish brown to reddish black or reddish purple; spring. 'Eva Constance' flowers velvety red; comes true from seed.

Pulsatilla rubra 'Eva Constance'

Pulsatilla vulgaris

Pulsatilla vulgaris

Western and central Europe. The common pasque flower is a variable plant to 15 cm (6 in) tall in flower, twice that height in fruit, forming a tuft of green or gray-green, feathery leaves with seven or nine main segments, these further divided into linear or linear-lanceolate divisions. Flowers appear with developed leaves, nodding to horizontal, narrow-campanulate, 4–9 cm (1⅗–3⅗ in) wide, pale to dark purple or reddish purple, occasionally white; spring. Many color variants are known in cultivation and some of these come true from seed. There is little doubt that some of these have arisen through hybridization with other species. 'Alba' white; 'Barlett's Pink' flesh pink; 'Röde Klokke' (RED CLOCK) rich red; 'Rubra' red (not to be confused with *P. rubra*); 'White Swan' white.

Ramonda

A member of the saintpaulia family (Gesneriaceae), the genus *Ramonda* contains just three species confined to southwestern Europe and the Balkans. Ramondas make spreading rosettes of deep green rather rough leaves. The flowers, borne on hairy scapes, are four- or five-parted and open out quite flat. The fruit pod is a slender capsule containing dust-like seed.

The prime species grown is *R. myconi*, one of the finest of all rock garden plants, excellent for rock crevices and ledges in the rock garden or trough, or grown on a large block of tufa. It requires a partly shaded, moist position in the garden but is surprisingly drought tolerant, plants shriveling severely in hot dry periods

Ramonda myconi

Ramonda myconi 'Alba'

but reviving like a resurrection plant on the application of water. Propagation is by division of the parent clump after flowering or leaf cuttings rooted during the summer. They can be grown from seed in an enclosed, moist environment and are very slow to develop at first. Care must be taken to avoid contamination during the first year or so, otherwise the tiny seedlings are easily swamped.

Ramonda myconi
Pyrenees. Leaf rosettes to 20 cm (8 in) across, solitary or a number clumped together, the leaves ovate to diamond-shaped, to 10 cm (4 in) long, deep green above, rusty with hairs beneath, margin irregularly toothed. Flowers on glandular-hairy stems to 12.5 cm (5 in) long, medium to deep violet, 3–4 cm (1⅕–1⅗ in) across, with yellow anthers, five-petaled; late spring and early summer. 'Alba' pure white; 'Rosea' rose-pink.

Ranunculus

The buttercups genus is large and cosmopolitan with some 400 species, some lowland but many confined to the higher mountains or to extreme latitudes. They have simple or various divided (often palmately dissected) leaves and solitary or clustered flowers that are most frequently yellow or white, although other colors do occur; flowers have both sepals and petals, the latter usually five, but more in some species. The fruit is a rounded or cylindrical head of achenes.

There are many rock garden gems in the genus, but most are quite or very difficult to

grow and maintain in cultivation. A sunny, well-drained site is essential for most. They are best grown from seed the moment it is ripe or soon afterward; older seed can give very poor results. Established clumps can be divided in the autumn or when growth commences in the spring.

Ranunculus calandrinioides

A North African species found on rocky slopes in the Atlas Mountains. It forms tufts to 30 cm (1 ft) tall in flower of primarily basal leaves, lanceolate to oval, blue-green, glabrous, with a wavy entire margin. Flowers several in lax cymes, occasionally solitary, white, often flushed mauve-pink that deepens with age, about 5 cm (2 in) across; late winter and spring. Although often grown under cover, this plant can respond extremely well to outside cultivation, especially in a raised bed in a protected site.

Ranunculus gramineus

Southern Europe and North Africa. A clump-forming herbaceous perennial to 45 cm (18 in) tall in flower, with mostly basal leaves, these glaucous, narrow-lanceolate to linear, to 15 cm (6 in) long. Flowers bright yellow, saucer-shaped, 20–30 mm (⅘–1⅕ in) across, several borne on slender, branched stems. In the wild this is a dry grassland species. It is one of the most accommodating buttercups for the garden.

Ranunculus montanus

Mountains of central and southern Europe. A clump-forming perennial to 30 cm (12 in) tall in flower, generally less. Leaves deep green, mostly basal, three- to five-lobed, with obovate, toothed, somewhat hairy segments. Flowers up to three per stem, rich yellow, 25–30 mm (1–1⅕ in) across, bowl-shaped, with overlapping petals; late spring and early summer. 'Molten Gold' a fine floriferous form with double, golden flowers.

. . . .

Ranunculus gramineus

Ranunculus montanus 'Molten Gold'

Rhodanthemum

A small genus most of whose species were at one time placed in the genus *Chrysanthemum* or *Leucanthemum*. Whatever their name, they are fine evergreen perennials and subshrubs, often with neatly dissected gray or silvery foliage and prominent, showy daisy flowers.

Two species are popularly cultivated in the open garden, thriving in sunny, sheltered sites in the rock garden or raised bed, in an open gritty soil. Propagation from cuttings taken during the summer affords the best means of increase.

Rhodanthemum catananche (syn. *Chrysanthemum catananche, Leucanthemum catananche*)

Morocco. A tufted perennial to 20 cm (8 in) tall in flower, with silvery gray, pinnately lobed leaves with narrow, pointed segments. Flowerheads solitary, cream to yellow with a dark red base to the rays, about 5 cm (2 in) across. Requires a warm, sunny, and sheltered site, otherwise it is a first-rate alpine house or container plant. 'African Eyes' creamy white daisies with a large brown eye; 'Tizi-n-Test' dwarf plant to 10 cm (4 in) with white daisies backed faint orange and with dark green foliage; 'Tizi-n-Tichka' white daisies with a blood red eye.

Rhodanthemum hosmariense (syn. *Chrysanthemopsis hosmariense, Chrysanthemum hosmariense, Leucanthemum hosmariense*)

Morocco. A hummock-forming subshrub to 60 cm (2 ft) across but not more than 25 cm (10 in) tall. Leaves silvery gray, to 4 cm (1⅗ in) long, three-segmented with the segments further lobed, giving a filigree effect. Flowerheads solitary, 4–5 cm (1⅗–2 in) across, with a broad yellow disk and white rays, the short surrounding bracts silvery with a black margin; late winter to early summer.

Rhodanthemum catananche 'Tizi-n-Tichka'

Rhodanthemum hosmariense

Rhodiola

A succulent genus closely related to the stone-crops (*Sedum*), differing primarily in having separate male and female plants (rather than hermaphrodite flowers) with four- rather than five-parted flowers. As with *Sedum* and the related *Sempervivum*, *Rhodiola* is an ideal genus for warm and hot dry areas and rock gardens subjected to summer drought. A planting of these succulent, drought-resistant plants can be highly effective and, even when many are not in flower, they can be nonetheless interesting and colorful. Propagation is by division or cuttings in the summer, after flowering affords a ready means of increase.

Rhodiola rosea (syn. *Sedum roseum*)

Temperate and boreal regions of the Northern Hemisphere. A clump- or mound-forming perennial commonly called roseroot, with thick succulent stems arising from a substantial caudex. Leaves glaucous, ovate to oblong, to 2.5 cm (1 in) long, with a serrated margin. Flowers greenish yellow, 6–7 mm (¼ in) across, borne in dense terminal clusters, each with four narrow petals and a ring of small orange nectaries; male flowers with eight stamens; summer. An excellent plant for rock crevices or retaining walls, as well as in the general rock garden. Some forms have purple-flushed stems and leaves as well as purple flowers.

Rhodohypoxis

A South African genus of six species of small rhizomatous perennials with tufts of grassy leaves. Flowers held at leaf height, solitary, with a short to long tube and six spreading to ascending elliptic to rounded tepals, often brightly colored. The fruit is a small three-parted capsule.

If they can be kept reasonably dry during the winter months, then these charming little plants, especially *R. baurii*, can be grown in troughs and raised beds outdoors: a cloche or glass placed overhead will probably be sufficient in all but the severest winters. They can be propagated from seed sown in early spring or by division of the corm-like rhizomes during the resting period. Rhodohypoxis are little jewels seen at their best in large patches or drifts.

Rhodohypoxis baurii

Lesotho and eastern South Africa. A patch-forming plant only 5–7.5 cm (2–3 in) tall in flower with erect to ascending narrow-elliptic, gray-green, hairy leaves not more than 10 mm (⅖ in) wide. Flowers solitary, 15–25 mm (⅗–1 in) across, with a short tube; white, pink, or red; late spring to autumn, often intermittently. A charming species that is popular among growers and, as a consequence, quite a large number of selections have been made, some

Rhodohypoxis baurii cultivars

resulting from crosses with other species. 'Albrighton' deep carmine-pink; 'Appleblossom' pink; 'Claret' wine red; 'Dawn' white flushed pink; 'Douglas' rose red; 'Fred Broome' pink, paler in center; 'Garnett' red; 'Great Scot' red; 'Helen' white; 'Margaret Rose' rose-pink; 'Perle' crisped white flowers; 'Picta' white flushed pink; 'Pink Candy' sugar pink with a white stripe down each tepal; 'Pinkeen' medium pink; 'Pink Pearl' pink; 'Pintado' white with a pink flush; 'Red King' carmine; 'Stella' clear pink; 'Tetra Red' deep red; 'Venetia' dark pink.

Salix

The willows represent a very large, important, and complicated genus with at least 350 species scattered throughout the world, with the exception of Australasia. They range from hefty trees to the smallest creeping and mat-forming shrublets. Willows tend to be rather twiggy plants with alternate, deciduous leaves that are entire to toothed, the buds with a single all-enveloping scale. The inflorescences are in the form of erect to ascending catkins, male and female separate and located on different plants, the male, generally the more attractive form with numerous yellow stamens (usually two per individual flower, accompanied by a pair of nectaries), the female with a flask-shaped ovary, generally rather dully colored. The catkins may appear in advance of the leaves or when they are partly or wholly developed. The fruiting catkins dehisce to reveal tiny seeds enveloped in cottony hairs that are wafted away in the slightest breeze.

The smallest willows are fine plants for the rock garden, raised beds, and troughs and are suitable for sunny or partly shaded situations with the proviso that they never dry out at the root. Cuttings provide the prime means of increase: these can be taken either semi-mature during the summer or hardwood in the autumn.

Salix ×boydii

Scotland, where it was found just once in the 1880s. This interesting hybrid willow, believed to be a cross between *S. lanata* and *S. reticulata*, has always been a favorite among rock garden plant growers, making in time an attractive feature. Plants are very slow-growing but eventually make an erect shrub 30 cm (1 ft) high, after many years perhaps reaching 1 m (3 ft), the branches rather thick, becoming gnarled in time. Leaves confined to the shoot tips, rounded, just 10–20 mm (²/₅–⁴/₅ in) long, almost clasping the stem with their heart-shaped base, rather rough, deep green, with a somewhat recurved and entire margin. The hybrid is female, with broad-cylindrical catkins to 2 cm (⁴/₅ in) long, which appear in advance of, or with, the emerging leaves; early spring.

Salix lanata

Arctic and subarctic Europe and northern Asia. A handsome well-branched shrub to 1 m (3 ft), often less, with fairly stout ascending branches, gray-felted at first. Leaves whitish or

gray with hairs, ovate to obovate, to 6 cm (2⅖ in) long, short-stalked. Catkins appearing in advance of the leaves, bursting through the large gray-felted buds, the male (the usual form offered) being cylindrical, to 5 cm (2 in) long, shrouded in golden anthers; spring. Although a somewhat large shrub eventually, this is one of the finest mountain willows for the larger rock garden, where it can make an effective feature. The related *S. lapponum* (northern Europe and western Russia, extending south onto the higher European mountains), which is equally fine, has reddish brown shoots and more elliptic-lanceolate leaves that are gray-green and eventually almost hairless above, while the male catkins can have yellow or reddish anthers.

Salix reticulata

Arctic and subarctic regions of the Northern Hemisphere, extending onto the higher mountains in southern Europe. A charming prostrate, matted shrublet spreading to 30 cm (12 in) sometimes more, the stems rooting down as they go. Leaves dull green, gray beneath, oval to rounded, 10–40 mm (⅖–1⅗ in) long, with an impressed netted pattern of veins. Catkins terminal, appearing with the leaves, narrow and spike-like, long-stalked, the male with reddish purple anthers; spring. One of the choicest willows for the rock garden, especially for troughs and raised beds.

Salvia

A large and diverse genus with perhaps some 900 species found in Europe, Asia, Africa, and

Salix lanata (Photo courtesy of Alpine Garden Society)

Salix reticulata (Photo courtesy of Alpine Garden Society)

Central America in particular. Many are very showy and prized for their long flowering season and wide range of colors; as a result a large number of species and their hybrid derivatives are grown in gardens. They are excellent plants for attracting insects, especially species of bee, into the garden. While some of the most familiar are not fully hardy or too gross for the rock garden, there are some gems worth considering, particularly the one described here.

Salvia jurisicii

Northern Balkans. A laxly branched tufted perennial to 40 cm (16 in) tall, with neatly dissected, pinnately lobed leaves with linear segments. Flowers borne in whorls, forming branched inflorescences, the two-lipped flowers violet-blue, about 12 mm (½ in) long; summer. A delightful plant that is also occasionally seen in a pink- or white-flowered form. Although the flowers are small they are borne in abundance, a great delight against the filigree of foliage. It requires a well-drained gritty compost and plenty of sunshine to succeed. 'Alba' pure white.

Sanguinaria

A North American genus with a single species, the bloodroot, which is an interesting plant for shaded places in the rock garden or for the woodland border, thriving in good deep, humus-rich, moist compost. Propagation is by division of the parent clump in the autumn or after flowering, but plants can be slow to establish and are best left undisturbed as much as possible.

. . . .

Salvia jurisicii 'Alba'

Sanguinaria canadensis

Sanguinaria canadensis

Eastern United States and Canada. A clump-forming herbaceous perennial to 20 cm (8 in) tall in flower. Rhizomes thick and fleshy, occasionally branching, with an orange red sap when cut, hence the common name of bloodroot. The attractive leaves are only partly developed at flowering time, at first folded along the middle but maturing to 15 cm (6 in) or more across, rounded with heart-shaped base

and scalloped margin, bluish gray at maturity. Flowers fleeting, glistening white, enclosed in bud in the young folded leaves, expanding to 3–4 cm (1⅓–1⅗ in) across, with 8 to 16 narrow-elliptic tepals; spring. Although seen in gardens, it is the far-longer-lasting double-flowered versions that are the more effective: forma *multiplex*, fully double, waterlily like, pure white blooms; 'Plena' fully double flowers; 'Amy' and 'Peter Harrison' both produce single, pink-flushed flowers.

Saponaria

The soapwort genus, closely related to the catchflies (*Silene*), includes about 30 species scattered in Europe and Asia, particularly the Mediterranean region, and includes both annual and perennial species. They have catchfly-like flowers with a tubular calyx and five clawed petals that have a characteristic pair of scales at the base of the limb.

The rock garden species requires scree conditions in the garden and plenty of sunshine. They are readily grown from seed sown in late winter or early spring or the moment it is ripe.

Saponaria ocymoides

Central and southern Europe. A low tufted, much-branched perennial forming a lax mat or mound to 60 cm (2 ft) across, with hairy, often purplish stems. The paired leaves are lanceolate to almost ovate, to 4 cm (1⅗ in) long, the upper smaller and narrower than the lower. Flowers in laxly branched cymes, pink to purple-pink, to 12 mm (½ in) across, with rather narrow petals and a purple flushed calyx; late spring and summer. Although small, the flowers are borne in abundance, giving very good effect. A good, easy rock garden plant for dry acid or alkaline banks and retaining walls. 'Alba' white; 'Rubra Compacta' smaller version

....
Saponaria ocymoides

Saponaria pumilio

with reddish purple flowers; 'Snowtip' reasonably compact, pure white.

Saponaria pumilio

Southeastern Europe eastward to Turkey and Lebanon. A dwarf tufted to hummock-forming plant to 40 cm (16 in) across, but only 10 cm (4 in) high at the most. Leaves bluish green, linear, to 8 mm (⅓ in) long, glandular hairy like the short stems. Flowers solitary or several in a cluster, pale purple to crimson, rarely white, to 15 mm (⅗ in) across. An excellent trough or raised bed plant preferring slightly acid soils.

Saxifraga

A large and very important, primarily alpine, genus with about 480 species in the Northern Hemisphere and South America. The genus contains some of the jewels of the rock garden world, and various species have led to a plethora of colorful hybrids that are widely available. The species range from coarse herbs to small tufted plants, mat- or cushion-formers, some with delightfully lime-encrusted rosettes (the so-called silver saxifrages), others with bulbils, still others with slender runners. The majority bear leaves in discreet rosettes that are often crammed together in the cushion and mat-forming kinds. The flowers are solitary or, more usually, arranged in cymes or panicles and have a wide color range; they generally have five sepals, five petals, and 10 stamens. The fruit is a two-parted capsule containing dust-like seed.

Although some saxifrages thrive in cool, shaded situations in a moist humus-rich compost, the majority require a sunny aspect and a

well-drained gritty compost, especially those that form cushions. The silver saxifrages make perfect specimens for rock crevices or growing in blocks of tufa. Few genera are more suited to growing in raised beds or troughs.

Propagation is by seed when ripe or sown in late winter and early spring, division after flowering, or cuttings of single rosettes taken in late summer. When a number of species are grown in close proximity hybridization is very possible and the resultant offspring may be quite variable. Cuttings are a far safer and more reliable method of increasing the best named clones.

Saxifraga ×anglica

An important triple hybrid involving *S. aretioides*, *S. lilacina*, and *S. media* that has resulted in some outstanding cultivars. The hybrids form domed or rather flat cushions that may be lime-encrusted or not; flowers are borne in early spring. 'Cranbourne' rather flat cushions of gray-green rosettes, the leaves linear-oblanceolate, recurved at the tip, the flowers solitary on a stalk to 15 mm (⅗ in) long, wide-opening,

rose-pink; 'Myra' glaucous green flattish cushions of small rosettes and stems to 3 cm (1⅕ in) bearing up to three deep red flowers; 'Winifred' deep green flat mats of linear, recurved leaves and solitary deep carmine flowers borne close to the foliage.

Saxifraga ×*apiculata*

A popular, easy, and adaptable hybrid between *S. marginata* and *S. sancta* that produces spreading, rather pale green, firm hummocks to 30 cm (1 ft) across, sometimes more. Rosettes composed of linear-lanceolate leaves; yellow flowers borne on leafy stems up to 10 cm (4 in) tall bearing up to 12 yellow flowers, each 15–20 mm (⅗–⅘ in) across; late winter to spring. 'Albert Einstein' deep green cushions and yellow flowers on red stems; 'Gregor Mendel' glossy foliage and pale yellow flowers; 'Primrose Bee' similar to the last but with flatter cushions and larger flowers.

Saxifrage ×*boydililacina* 'Penelope'

Plant forming a neat, small, rather lax cushion to 5 cm (2 in) at the most. Leaves quite dark glaucous green, linear-lanceolate. Flowers solitary on stems to 2.5 cm (1 in) tall, amber yellow with a rosy base and veins, fading gradually; early spring.

Saxifraga callosa

Central and southern Europe. A fine, rather variable, silver saxifrage forming spreading mats of lax rosettes, 30 cm (1 ft) tall in flower. Leaves linear-spathulate, thick and with recurved tips, varying in length according to provenance from 2.5 to 9 cm (1 to 3⅗ in) long,

....

Saxifraga ×*anglica* 'Cranbourne'

Saxifraga callosa

heavily lime-encrusted. Numerous white flowers, each 12–16 mm (½–⅔ in) across, produced in arching panicles, petals often red-spotted at the base; early summer. A limestone rock inhabitant in the wild, like the silver saxifrages *S. cochlearis* and *S. longifolia*.

Saxifraga cochlearis

Southwestern Alps. A silver saxifrage forming tight, rather hard, mounded cushions to 25 cm (10 in) tall in flower. Crammed rosettes composed of heavily limed, spoon-shaped leaves, 12–25 mm (½–1 in) long. The panicles of small white flowers, 12–18 mm (½–⅔ in) across, are borne on erect or arched red stems; early summer. The best and most compact form is var. *minor*, which is widely available and makes an excellent, long-lived trough plant.

Saxifraga longifolia

A specialty of the Pyrenees and southern Spain, this fascinating monocarpic species forms a single, large, lime-encrusted rosette that expands over several years before flowering. Thick and stiff gray-green linear leaves, up to 10 cm (4 in) long, expanded slightly at the tip. Spectacular pyramidal, arching inflorescences, to 70 cm (28 in) tall, carry hundreds of white flowers, each 12–15 mm (½–⅗ in) across. This fascinating and handsome species needs to be regularly grown from seed to ensure a succession. The cultivar 'Tumbling Waters', a cross between this species and *S. callosa*, gives a plant with most of the qualities of *S. longifolia* but the perennial, multirosetted habit of the other parent.

. . . .

Saxifraga longifolia

Saxifraga oppositifolia

Saxifraga oppositifolia

A quite variable species widely distributed in circumpolar regions of the Northern Hemisphere, southward into the higher mountains of Europe, including Britain. It forms lax to quite dense green or gray green mats not more than 2.5 cm (1 in) tall, bearing paired oval to obovate leaves just 2–6 mm (¹⁄₁₂–¼ in) long, with one to five lime pores at the top. Solitary pale pink to deep purple flowers, 12–25 mm

(½–1 in) across, nestle on top of foliage on very short leafy stems; late winter and early spring. Many cultivars have been named, although few are readily available today; the best have extra-large deep purple flowers borne on a compact mat.

Mossy saxifrages

Among the easiest and most colorful saxifrages available today is a race often referred to as the "mossies." They are of complex origin involving various species, most notably *S. cespitosa*, *S. granulata*, *S. moschata*, and *S. rosacea*. Whatever their origin, these are accommodating and cheerful plants that will thrive in a wide range of soils in sun or part shade, but dislike being kept too dry. They are readily increased by cuttings or division. The pale to deep green mossy cushions of dissected leaves contrast with the erect stems of lax flowers, up to 25 cm (10 in) tall, sometimes more. Numerous cultivars are available in a wide range of colors, including 'Bob Hawkins' silver-variegated foliage and white flowers; 'Cloth of Gold' golden foliage and white flowers; 'Diana' medium tall, to 15 cm (6 in), pale pink; 'Highlander Red' tall, to 25 cm (10 in), bright green cushions and deep carmine-red flowers to 2 cm (⅘ in) across; 'James Bremner' extra-large white flowers to 25 mm (1 in) across; 'Peter Pan' low plant with crimson flowers; 'Winston S. Churchill' large clear pink flowers.

Scoliopus

Despite being a monocot (it is a member of the *Trillium* family, Trilliaceae), this unusual plant is often overlooked in books on bulbs; however, it is a fascinating plant and well worth a place in the rock garden. This North American genus contains two species, only one of which is freely available.

It is a plant for a shaded position in a moist, humus-rich soil. Propagation is from seed sown the moment ripe or shortly thereafter or by division of establish clumps into single-

Saxifraga 'Cloth of Gold'

Saxifraga 'Peter Pan'

crown portions; this latter is best undertaken in late summer when the plants are dormant.

Scoliopus bigelowii

California. A clump-forming herbaceous perennial to 20 cm (8 in) tall, with basal pairs of elliptic to oblong, rather fleshy leaves to 20 cm (8 in) long, these deep green veined and mottled with purple. Flowers solitary to 30 mm (1⅕ in) across, borne on long slender, triangular stalks equaling the leaves, three-parted, olive green with reddish purple-veined sepals, petals linear, erect and horn-like; late winter and early spring. A plant not to everyone's taste but, nonetheless, intriguing. It needs to be looked at closely to see its true beauty, but beware, the flowers emit a very unpleasant odor.

Scutellaria

A genus of almost 300 species scattered in many parts of the world and including annual, perennial, and shrubby plants, several of the small montane ones making outstanding rock garden subjects. Scutellarias are members of the salvia or deadnettle family (Labiatae), with somewhat square stems and opposite leaves and whorls of flowers with a two-lipped corolla. A defining feature in *Scutellaria* is the presence on the upper lip of the calyx of a rounded appendage or scutellum, which has given rise to the common name skullcap.

The mountain skullcaps are a colorful group of plants much loved by bees and suitable for the rock garden in general, mostly requiring a gritty, well-drained compost and plenty of sunshine. Propagation is from seed

sown in late winter or early spring, division in the autumn or before growth commences in the spring.

Scutellaria alpina

Mountains of central and southern Europe. A tufted to clumping perennial to 25 cm (10 in) tall, with ovate to lanceolate, toothed leaves. Flowers purple with a white or paler lower lip, about 25 mm (1 in) long, ascending in terminal

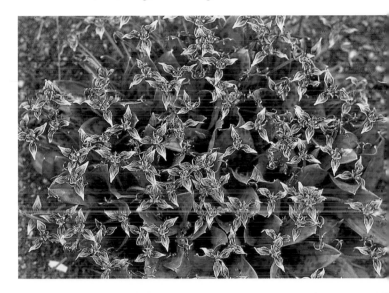

Scoliopus bigelowii

Scutellaria alpina

clusters; late spring and early summer. 'Arcobaleno' rose with a white lower lip; 'Moonbeam' compact, pale yellow.

Scutellaria indica

China, Japan, and Korea. A tufted, rhizomatous species with erect to ascending, rather slender stems to 30 cm (1 ft). Leaves deep green, ovate to triangular-ovate, to 20 mm (⅘ in) long, downy, blunt toothed on the margin. Flowers are borne in dense terminal racemes, each 30–35 mm (1⅕–1⅖ in) long and an attractive shade of purple; summer. 'Alba' pure white.

Scutellaria orientalis

Northwestern Africa and southern Europe eastward to western China. A variable tufted perennial, rather woody at the base, with spreading stems forming patches to 50 cm (20 in) across, half that in height. Leaves gray-green, ovate-oblong, to 2.5 cm (1 in) long, deeply toothed along the margin to pinnately lobed, deep green or gray-green above, gray-downy beneath. Flowers usually yellow, sometimes with red spotting or markings, but they can on occasion be entirely pink, red, or purple (according to location in the wild), borne in square-sectioned racemes, each flower up to 30 mm (1⅕ in) long; summer. Subsp. *pectinata*, from western Turkey, has striking yellow and maroon flowers; however, the usual form seen in cultivation is the yellow-flowered one. 'Eastern Sun' bright yellow.

Sedum

A large genus of succulent plants, commonly referred to as stonecrops, with some 350 species primarily concentrated in the Northern Hemisphere and on the higher mountains in Africa. They are a diverse assemblage of species with thick, fleshy leaves ranging from cylindrical to flat and toothed. The typical star-shaped to bell-shaped, hermaphrodite flowers generally have five or six free petals, occasionally as many as 12, borne in cymes or panicles, sometimes almost racemose. The fruit consists of five or six, occasionally more, follicles forming a star-shape overall and containing numerous seeds.

Most stonecrops thrive in a somewhat dry, well-drained soil in full sun, although there are a few that prefer damper, partly shaded places in the garden. Propagation is by seed sown in the spring or, more readily, from cuttings in summer and autumn. For those with larger leaves, leaf cuttings are possible. They make excellent plants for warm or hot dry gardens, especially those where watering is restricted for one reason or another. They can be attractive in both flower and foliage.

Scutellaria orientalis

Sedum acre

Europe to western Asia and North Africa. The wallpepper is a neat, rather bright green, little perennial to 5 cm (2 in) tall, but spreading to 30 cm (1 ft). Leaves egg-shaped, alternate, not more than 5 mm (⅕ in) long. Flowers bright yellow, starry, 9–12 mm (⅖–½ in) across, borne in small terminal cymes; summer. A very easy plant to grow, suiting poor stony places and wall and roof tops with equal ease. Small pieces that break off the parent plant will root readily when they touch the ground. 'Aureum' ('Variegatum') young shoots tipped yellow; 'Elegans' leaves suffused with creamy silver; 'Yellow Queen' extra-large bright yellow flowers on a vigorous plant.

Sedum album

Europe to western Asia and North Africa. A laxly tufted to matted perennial, 10 cm (4 in) tall and up to 40 cm (16 in) across. Leaves sub cylindrical, very fleshy, gray-green, often suffused with red, to 8 mm (⅓ in) long, sometimes more. Flowers in lax cymes, starry, white, about 8 mm (⅓ in) across; summer. Can be invasive but attractive in full flower. 'Coral Carpet' compact, low grower with foliage flushed cherry red, especially in full sun, and pink flowers.

Sedum ewersii

Afghanistan to Mongolia. A handsome species forming tumbled mats from a somewhat woody base, to 50 cm (20 in) across, about 25 cm (10 in) tall in flower. Leaves paired, rounded, to 2.5 cm (1 in) long, pale gray-green, with a clasping heart-shaped base and slightly toothed margin. Flowers pink, about 10 mm (⅖ in)

across, borne in rather dense rounded heads; late summer and autumn. Often wrongly sold under the name *S. pluricaule*, a rare species in gardens.

Sedum spathulifolium

Western North America; British Columbia to California. A mat-forming succulent, rather brittle, to 30 cm (1 ft) across, only 5 cm (2 in) tall, with lax rosettes of glaucous, flat, spathu-

Sedum ewersii

Sedum spathulifolium 'Cape Blanco'

late leaves to 2 cm (⅘ in) long. Flowers yellow, 12 mm (½ in) across, numerous in branched, rather flat heads; summer. 'Aureum' whole plant suffused yellow in the spring; 'Cape Blanco' (often misnamed 'Capa Blanca') tight silvery gray rosettes with a bloom forming compact clumps; 'Purpureum' a coarser plant with purple-suffused leaves that intensifies in very dry conditions.

Sempervivum

The houseleeks genus contains about 40 species distributed primarily in the mountains of Europe and western Asia. Related to the stonecrops (*Sedum*), they are very distinctive in their neat regular succulent rosettes of leaves that are crammed together into mats or hummocks. The inflorescences arise from the center of the rosettes on a thick stem with overlapping scalelike leaves, the flowers starry with 9 to 13, commonly 10, narrow pointed petals; individual rosettes die after flowering.

Houseleeks are excellent plants for dry stony places, succeeding in very little soil. Indeed some make fine plants for the tops of old walls and roofs. They are indispensable plants for those gardeners concerned about water saving and global warming and splendid plants for those starting to grow rock plants for the first time. A trough or container filled with various houseleeks can make a very interesting feature in the garden. They are easily propagated, almost at any time in the year, from offset rosettes pulled away from the parent clump.

Sempervivum arachnoideum

Mountains of central and southern Europe. The cobweb houseleek is so-called because the green leaf rosettes, to 1.5 cm (⅗ in) across, are crisscrossed with a web of fine white hairs. Leaves obovate, to 12 mm (½ in) long, stem leaves generally rather smaller and often red-tipped. Flowers borne in tight clusters, on a stem to 12.5 cm (5 in) tall, bright pinkish red, about 20 mm (⅘ in) across; summer. 'Stans-

. . . .

Sempervivum cultivars

Sempervivum arachnoideum

fieldii' rosettes flushed with plum-red at certain times of the year; subsp. *tomentosum* (syn. 'Laggeri'), from southern France and Spain, has more substantial, flatter, rosettes to 2.5 cm (1 in) across, abundantly cobwebbed.

Sempervivum montanum

Mountains of central and southern Europe east to the Carpathians. A variable but often rather neat houseleek to 20 cm (8 in) tall in flower. Rosettes 2.5–7.5 cm (1–3 in) across, rather dull green, producing numerous offsets; leaves oblanceolate, finely hairy overall. Flowers wine red, to 4 cm (1⅗ in) across, borne in fairy dense clusters, each with up to 13 petals; summer. 'Lloyd Praeger' rather flat rosettes with reddish brown tipped leaves.

Sempervivum tectorum

Mountains of central and southern Europe. The common houseleek is quite a variable species with substantial rosettes to 17.5 cm (7 in) across, bluish green, leaves tipped with red often, or the entire rosette flushed or suffused red or purple. Leaves sharply pointed, obovate to oblong, to 9 cm (3⅗ in) long, often with white ciliated margin. Inflorescence substantial, to 50 cm (20 in) tall, bear a lax cymes of up to 100 purple or dull pink flowers, each about 20 mm (⅘ in) across. This is the houseleek sometimes seen established on old rooftops and walls. Unfortunately, it has been much confused with a plethora of modern lookalike hybrids. 'Atrorubens', 'Atroviolaceum', 'Nigrum', 'Red Flush', and 'Violaceum' are all cultivars with varyingly colored leaf rosettes, as the names imply.

. . . .

Sempervivum montanum

Cultivars

There are a large number of *Sempervivum* cultivars available today, and the list seems to extend almost by the month. These come in an exciting range of colors and can be a striking feature in the garden, especially when planted en masse, such as sandwiched between rocks or arranged in an old stone trough. These hybrids have arisen by chance, indeed some are found in the wild. However, in more recent times extensive breeding programs have resulted in many fine new hybrids. The number of *Sempervivum* hybrids available today is breathtaking and has created a great upsurge of interest in these fascinating plants. The plants listed here are a slight sample of those available and are simply presented to show the range of color and form being sold by nurseries and garden centers. 'Aldo Moro' rosettes green with shades of orange and red; 'Apache' downy rosettes, green at first, strongly suffused deep pink toward the latter half of the year; 'Black Prince' dark purple, near black rosettes, silvery with marginal hairs; 'Blue Boy' bluish gray, small rosettes; 'Boromir' blue-green flushed

crimson; 'Butterbur' outer leaves greenish brown, inner purple-red; 'Carmen' large rosettes, pale green flushed with brownish red; 'Cherry Tart' largish rosettes of flat leaves, shiny, rich wine red, keeping its color for much of the year; 'Chocolate' dark chocolate for much of the year; 'Commander Hay' large flattish rosettes, green suffused red, fading as summer progresses; 'Crimson Velvet' downy rosettes of crimson; 'Director Jacobs' large rosettes of deep red leaves margined with silvery hairs; 'El Tora' apple green and red rosettes; 'Emerald Giant' emerald green flushed pink, large; 'Flaming Heart' rosettes dark red with a green center; 'Gazelle' multicolored rosettes of yellow, pink, red, and green, fading gradually; 'Glowing Embers' medium rosettes, glowing red at the height of summer; 'Greyfriars' medium rosettes gray, heavily suffused with pinkish red; 'Jack Frost' green, outer leaves flushed bronze, margins silvery-ciliated; 'King George' rosettes deep maroon for much of the year; 'Lavender Old Lace' small to medium rosettes of soft rose-lavender, margined with silvery cilia; 'Lipstick' medium rosettes of shiny, bright glowing red

leaves, fading to dull green in winter; 'Mount Hood' flattish rosettes of pinkish red, flushed with purple and gray; 'Pippin' medium rosettes of dark reddish brown, deeper in winter; 'Pumaros' small compact rosettes of dark reddish brown, tipped with whitish hairs; 'Raspberry Ice' rather small rosettes pink flushed, adorned with silky hairs; 'Sioux' globular rosettes of orange-red flushed pink toward the leaf tips; 'Spice' large velvety rosettes, green at first, then flushing with maroon; 'Stuffed Olive' medium rosettes, olive green with a red center; 'Traci Su' glossy, large, red-brown, rather flat rosettes; 'Zackenkrone' medium-sized rosettes of greenish gold with a dark purple center.

Silene

A large genus with more than 500 species that is especially prominent in the Northern Hemisphere but also present in temperate South America and southern Africa. Popularly known as catchflies because many have sticky stems and calyces, the species range from annuals to herbaceous and evergreen perennials or subshrubs. They have in common opposite simple leaves and tubular to campanulate calyces and clawed petals, usually with scales in the mouth of the flower. The many-seeded fruit is a capsule splitting at the top into 6 or 10 teeth, twice as many as the number of styles.

Although many are too weedy or large for the rock gardener, the genus does contain some delightful gems, some from surprisingly low altitudes in the wild. Those included here thrive best in scree conditions in sun or part shade. Propagation is from seed sown in late

Silene acaulis

winter or early spring or cuttings of vegetative shoots in late summer.

Silene acaulis

Circumpolar in the Northern Hemisphere, reaching the higher mountains further south. Known as moss campion because of its moss-like mats or domes of bright green foliage, this gem is ideally suited to troughs and raised beds or for growing on blocks of tufa. The leaves are tightly amassed, awl-shaped, and not more than 12 mm (½ in) long. Flowers solitary pink or reddish purple, 5–12 mm (⅕–½ in) across, sitting on top of the foliage; late winter and spring. 'Alba' white; 'Flore Pleno' double, pink; 'Frances' yellow domes and sparse pink flowers; 'Mount Snowdon' tight neat cushions and very small deep pink flowers.

Silene alpestris

Eastern and southeastern Europe. A laxly tufted, colony-forming perennial to 20 cm (8 in) tall, spreading by slender rhizomes. Leaves narrow-obovate to almost linear, to 3 cm (1⅕ in) long. Flowers white, 10–12 mm (⅖–½ in) across, petals neatly four- to six-lobed; summer. 'Flore Pleno' fully double flowers.

Silene hookeri (syn. *S. ingramii*)

Oregon and California. A small tufted plant not more than 15 cm (6 in) in height, with lower stems often prostrate and rooting at the nodes. Leaves gray-green, obovate to spathulate, hairy, 4–7 cm (1⅗–2⅘ in) long. Flowers variable in shape and color, 2–3 cm (⅘–1⅕ in) across, petals red, purple, pink, or white, with two broad and two narrow, shorter, lobes;

late spring and summer. Best grown in scree, raised bed, or rock crevice, but not always easy to please; however, it will often flower during the first year from seed.

Silene schafta

Caucasus to northern Iran. A lax tufted perennial to about 20 cm (8 in) high in flower, spreading with decumbent stems to 40 cm (16 in) across, sometimes more. Leaves obovate to

Silene hookeri

Silene schafta (Photo courtesy of Alpine Garden Society)

ovate, to 2 cm (⅘ in) long. Flowers in lax cymes, pink to rose-magenta, about 25 mm (1 in) across; summer and autumn. An excellent plant for dry stone walls and banks. 'Shell Pink' is a fine cultivar.

Sisyrinchium

A genus of perhaps 60 species from the Americas of fibrous-rooted perennials and annuals

with small tufted fans of grassy leaves and fleeting flowers with six spreading tepals borne on flattened scapes, several housed in bract-like green spathes. Although each flower only lasts a day, they are produced in succession to give a colorful display over many weeks.

Those listed here are readily grown in most well-drained soils and are best displayed in groups or drifts. Some may self-seed around, indeed they can do so very freely, but it is easy to pull up unwanted seedlings. Propagation is by division in the spring as plants come into growth or seed sown at the same time.

Sisyrinchium californicum (includes *S. brachypus*)

Southwestern Canada south to California. A tufted perennial to 30 cm (12 in) tall, often less, with broadly winged stems. Leaves glaucous, shorter than the stems and about 6 mm (¼ in) wide. Flowers bright yellow with darker veining, 2.5–3.5 cm (1–1⅖ in) across; late spring and summer. Plants sold as *S. brachypus* are only 15 cm (6 in) tall in flower, with brighter green leaves.

Sisyrinchium idahoense (syn. *S. macounii*)

Central United States. A tufted perennial to 40 cm (16 in) tall, often half that height, with simple, somewhat twisted stems; spathes paired, one much larger than the other. Leaves deep green, somewhat glaucous, to 6 mm (¼ in) wide. Flowers rich purple-blue with a yellow eye, 20–25 mm (⅘–1 in) across; summer. Var. *bellum* (syn. *S. bellum*) from California is distinguished by its branched stem and rather larger purple, blue, or lilac, occasionally white,

. . . .

Sisyrinchium idahoense 'Album'

Sisyrinchium macrocarpum

flowers. 'Album' (syn. var. *macounii* 'Alba') dwarf white form.

Sisyrinchium macrocarpum

Argentina. A bright green or gray-green, tufted, short-lived perennial to 20 cm (8 in) tall in flower with slightly flattened, narrowly winged stems. Leaves shorter than the stems, about 5 mm (⅕ in) wide. Flowers yellow, 20 mm (⅘ in) across, each petal attractively marked with an inverted V-shaped brown mark near the base; summer. Dislikes excessive winter wet.

Sisyrinchium montanum

Central and eastern North America and Greenland. A variable tufted perennial to 50 cm (20 in) tall in flower with winged stems and rather pale glaucous green leaves to 4 mm (⅙ in) wide, reaching the flowers or shorter. Flowers rich purple, to 25 mm (1 in) across, stamen filaments partly fused together; summer. Sometimes sold under the name *S. graminoides*, a distinct species from eastern North America.

Cultivars

Of those of hybrid origin the finest four are *Sisyrinchium* 'Californian Skies', 'Devon Skies', 'E. K. Balls', and 'Sapphire', all growing to about 15 cm (6 in) tall and with good-sized flowers of varying intensities of blue.

Soldanella

A small genus of about a dozen species concentrated in the mountains of central, southern, and eastern Europe. They are characterized by rounded cyclamen-like leaves and bear one or

Sisyrinchium 'E. K. Balls'

Sisyrinchium 'Sapphire'

several fringed, nodding bells on a slender scape above the foliage.

The majority are snow-melt plants from high in the mountains and are quite difficult to maintain and flower in cultivation. However, the one included below is relatively easy, requiring a moist humus-rich compost in dappled shade. Propagation from division every other year after flowering helps keep the clumps

growing vigorously. Seed is best sown the moment it is ripe.

Soldanella villosa

A charming, neat plant that inhabits the foothills of the western Pyrenees, favoring damp shady habitats. A small tuft-forming evergreen perennial with simple, deep green basal leaves, rounded with a heart-shaped base, 2–7 cm (⁴⁄₅–2⁴⁄₅ in) across, and with a glandular-hairy petiole. Three or four nodding, bell-shaped, purple-blue flowers, 15–20 mm (³⁄₅–⁴⁄₅ in) long, neatly and deeply fringed, are borne on a common glandular-hairy stem to 20 cm (8 in) tall in fruit; spring. The elongated fruit capsule contains numerous seeds.

. . . .

Soldanella villosa

Solidago virgaurea 'Goldzwerg'

Solidago

A genus of some 100 perennials, mostly North American in origin but with a few species scattered in South America, Europe, and Asia. Most are rather hefty perennials too large and unsuitable for the rock gardener. Goldenrods have a tendency to hybridize freely and seed around even more freely in the garden; however, a few of the smallest are fine rock garden plants.

Goldenrods require no special treatment and will succeed on any well-drained soil. Regular division of the parent plant, in early spring or after flowering, will keep plants growing and flowering well. The flowers are attractive to a host of insects, particularly various kinds of flies and beetles.

Solidago virgaurea

Europe, Asia, and North Africa. A quite variable plant to 60 cm (2 ft) tall, often far less, with a tufted habit and erect stems bearing elliptic to lanceolate, generally toothed, leaves up to 10 cm (4 in) long. Flowerheads small, yellow, 5–10 mm (⅕–⅖ in) across, borne in condensed to lax racemes in late summer and autumn. 'Goldzwerg' (GOLDEN DWARF) only 10–20 cm (4–8 in) tall, with compact clusters of flowerheads; 'Minutissima' even dwarfer and ideal for troughs and raised beds.

Stachys

A large genus with some 300 species of annuals, perennials, shrubs, and subshrubs distributed almost throughout the world except for Australasia. Most are far too large and coarse for the rock garden, but there are a few little gems worthy of consideration. The species have paired (opposite) leaves borne on square stems and tubular, two-lipped flowers in whorls at the upper stem nodes, forming a spike-like inflorescence overall. The fruit is typical of labiates (Labiatae), with four small nutlets hidden at the base of the persistent calyx.

The one described here thrives best in a gritty, well-drained soil in full sun. Propagation is from seed sown in late winter.

Stachys lavandulifolia

Turkey eastward to Iraq, Iran, and the southern Caucasus. A charming little tufted subshrub not more than 30 cm (1 ft) tall in flower. Leaves gray-green, basal oblong-lanceolate to oblanceolate, 2.5–6 cm (1–2⅖ in) long, usually with an entire margin, silky with hairs; stem

. . . .

Stachys lavandulifolia

leaves broader and relatively shorter. Flowers borne in rather dense oblong heads, purple or mauve, about 15 mm (⅗ in) long, partly enveloped in the leathery calyces; late spring and early summer. A mountain plant of rocky slopes and screes in the wild.

Symphyandra

A small genus of 15 species closely related to the true bellflowers (*Campanula*) found from eastern Europe to central Asia and Korea. They are very similar in general appearance to *Campanula* in their bell-shaped flowers, differing primarily in the stamens, which are fused into a tube around the style. Technical details aside, the symphyandras are a colorful and very garden-worthy group well worth a niche in any rock garden, the smaller ones are also excellent for troughs and various containers.

They require a moist, gritty, well-drained compost with a little added humus and partial shade. Propagation from seed sown in late winter or early spring affords the best means of increase, particularly as a number of the

species are short-lived perennials or monocarpic plants; however, they do self-sow in some gardens.

Symphyandra hofmannii
Northern Balkans. A usually monocarpic plant to 60 cm (2 ft) tall in flower, with a large lax basal rosette of ovate to lanceolate, coarsely toothed leaves, to 15 cm (6 in) long, tapered at the base into a long petiole; stem leaves increasingly smaller and sessile. Flowers numerous in a broad panicle, creamy white, corolla tubular-campanulate, 25–30 mm (1–1⅕ in) long; summer.

Symphyandra wanneri
Northern Balkans, Bulgaria, Romania. A biennial or monocarpic plant to 30 cm (1 ft) tall in flower. Basal leaf rosette deep green, leaves lanceolate to narrow-oblong, 5–10 cm (2–4 in) long, toothed and with winged petiole; stem leaves smaller and sessile. Flowers violet-blue, many in an erect leafy panicle, the bells tubular-campanulate, 2–3.5 cm (4/5–1⅖ in) long; summer.

Teucrium

A cosmopolitan genus of labiates (Labiatae) with some 100 species of evergreen perennials, shrubs, and subshrubs, found particularly in the Mediterranean region. They usually have square stems, opposite leaves, and tubular, one-lipped flowers borne in whorls at the upper nodes, sometimes forming spike-like inflorescences.

The alpine species, commonly called germanders, are excellent plants for the rock garden or larger raised bed, requiring plenty of sunshine and a gritty well-drained compost. Propagation is from seed sown in late winter and early spring or from cuttings of vegetative shoots taken either in the spring or in the autumn. Teucriums are first-class plants for attracting bees and butterflies into the garden.

Teucrium ackermannii
Turkey. A low mounded, rather dense subshrub to 60 cm (2 ft) across, but scarcely 20 cm (8 in) tall. Leaves gray-green, ovate to oblong, to 2.5 cm (1 in) long, finely corrugated and with a crennate margin that is rolled under,

Symphyandra wanneri

gray-woolly beneath. Flowers in dense, rounded or oblong heads, grayish in bud but opening to deep purple, about 6–10 mm (¼–⅖ in) long; summer and early autumn. An excellent and rather underrated plant that repays with its bountiful show of bloom through the summer months.

Teucrium montanum

Central and southern Europe. Mountain germander is a mat-forming perennial to 50 cm (20 in) across, or more, with a woody base to the stems. Leaves medium green, narrow-elliptic to linear, to 3 cm (1⅕ in) long, toothed, hairy beneath but glabrous above. Flowers in disk-like heads or short spikes, cream, white, or bicolored, to 20 mm (4/5 in) long; summer. A fine plant for paving crevices or a niche in the rock garden between two rocks.

Thalictrum

This genus has about 85 species of often rather airy perennials, particularly in the mountains of the old world, but with representatives in the tropical African and South American mountains. They are generally clump-forming or rhizomatous, with compound leaves reminiscent of those of columbines (*Aquilegia*). The petalless flowers sometimes sport large and showy persistent petal-like sepals, but in the majority these are small and soon fall away, leaving a boss of showy stamens as the main feature. The flowers are often borne in substantial panicles. Most of the showy species, although excellent garden plants, are too large for the average rock garden.

. . . .

Teucrium ackermannii

Thalictrum kiusianum

They thrive in moist humus-rich soils in part shade. Propagation is from seed sown the moment ripe or in late winter or by division of the parent clump in spring before growth commences or in the autumn.

Thalictrum kiusianum

Japan. A charming little tufted, colony-forming perennial no more than 15 cm (6 in) tall in flower, with neatly divided biternate leaves;

leaflets ovate with three to five lobes, to 15 mm (⅗ in) long, bluish green, often suffused with purple. Flowers in small frothy inflorescences, rose-purple, with purple or whitish sepals only 3 mm (⅛ in) long; late spring and summer. An excellent companion to small ferns in an acid, shaded trough.

Thalictrum orientale
Greece and Turkey. A more substantial plant

than *T. kiusianum*, to 30 cm (1 ft) tall in flower. Leaves bi- or triternate, mostly borne on the wiry stems; leaflets almost rounded, toothed or lobed, about 20 mm (4/5 in) long. Flowers borne in airy panicles, about 20 mm (4/5 in) across, with relatively large spreading oval sepals, lilac (Turkish origin) or white (Greek origin); late spring and summer.

Thymus

A familiar genus of highly aromatic herbs, some of which are widely used in culinary dishes. The genus is rather large, with about 350 species widespread in the Northern Hemisphere old world. They are evergreen shrubs or subshrubs, some mat-forming, with small linear to elliptic, entire leaves borne in pairs on squared stems. Flowers two-lipped with a short or long tube, often with the stamens protruding, borne in whorls or heads, sometimes in spike-like inflorescences.

Thymes generally require a warm and sunny situation in a gritty well-drained compost. The carpeting types are first-rate plants for paving and the front of raised beds, while the tufted ones make excellent rock garden or container plants. Seed can be sown in early spring or cuttings taken in late summer and overwintered in a cold frame. Division of the mat-formers, which generally root down freely, provides a quick and satisfactory means of increase. They are excellent plants for attracting bees and butterflies into the garden. Apart from those listed here there are many other excellent rock garden thymes available; all are aromatic to varying degrees.

Thalictrum orientale

Thymus cilicicus

Thymus cilicicus

Turkey. A charming and colorful little cushion- or tussock-forming subshrub to 15 cm (6 in) tall. Leaves lanceolate or awl shaped, 7–10 mm (⅓–⅖ in) long, ciliate in the lower part, gray-green. Flowers borne in short spike-like heads, with prominent ovate, yellowish bracts adorned with numerous oil glands, the corolla lilac to purplish, about 8 mm (⅓ in) long; late spring and early summer. A very good and rather unusual trough plant, which may require protection from excess winter wet.

Thymus kotschyanus

Turkey to Iran and Iraq. Similar dimensions to *T. cilicicus*, but with larger, more generally hairy, gray or whitish leaves, 10–13 mm (⅖–½ in) long. Flowers in dense heads, pale pink to white, about 7.5 mm (⅓ in) long; summer. Requires protection from excess winter wet.

Thymus longiflorus (including *T. membranaceus*)

Southeastern Spain. A charming bushy thyme forming rounded, twiggy tufts to about 25 cm (10 in) tall. Leaves linear, to 15 mm (⅗ in) long, with downturned margins, velvety pubescent overall. Flowers purple or white, borne in rounded, terminal heads, with a ruff of prominent ovate, purplish or whitish bracts, corollas cylindrical, to 15 mm (⅗ in) long, with very short lips; summer and early autumn. A gem suited to sunny, sheltered sites, especially on a raised bed or in a stone trough. Probably best protected from excess winter wet.

Thymus longiflorus

Thymus polytrichus 'Porlock'

Thymus polytrichus (syn. *T. praecox* subsp. *polytrichus*)

Europe. Similar to *T. serpyllum* and much confused with it in cultivation, however, *T. polytrichus* can be distinguished quite readily by leaves with marginal lateral veins toward the top and stems hairy on two opposing sides. Up to 10 cm (4 in) tall in flower, often spreading to 60 cm (2 ft) across, lanceolate to obovate leaves, uppermost merging with bracts that are often

purple-flushed. Flowers purple or mauve, 6–7 mm (¼ in) long. 'Porlock' deep green cushions and abundant pink flowers; 'Thomas's White' a good white.

Thymus serpyllum

West and central Europe eastward to Ukraine. The common wild thyme is a mat-forming plant not more than 10 cm (4 in) tall in flower but often spreading to 60 cm (2 ft) across, more in some forms. It is quite variable with gray or green, linear to lanceolate leaves, 5–10 mm (⅕–⅖ in) long, ciliate at the base. Flowers pink, mauve, or purple, 6–7 mm (¼ in) long, borne in small cylindrical heads, often in great profusion; late spring and summer. Numerous cultivars exist, including 'Albus' white; 'Annie Hall' flesh pink; 'Coccineus' crimson-pink; 'Coccineus Major' purple-red; 'Elfin' forms small bun-shaped cushions, generally flowerless, but an excellent accent plant in a trough; 'Goldstream' purple, leaves blotched yellow; 'Minor' neat and slow-growing, pink; 'Pink Chintz' flesh pink with gray-green leaves; 'Rainbow Falls' pale purple, with yellow variegated foliage, flushed red; 'Ruby Glow' ruby red, deep green leaves; 'Russettings' deep mauve, with bronzy foliage; 'Snowdrift' the best white.

Townsendia

A genus of about 20 species restricted to western North America generally at quite high altitudes. Most are exquisite little daisies with clustered rosettes of leaves. The proportionately large aster-like flowerheads are nestled in the center or somewhat above the foliage, with white, pink, violet, or blue rays surrounding a yellow disk.

The species are much confused but several make fine plants for troughs and raised beds or for pan culture, requiring a gritty, well-drained compost and plenty of sunshine. Scree conditions suit them well in the open garden, although not all are easy to please, particularly disliking excess winter wet. Although often rather short-lived, townsendias are reasonably

Thymus serpyllum 'Albus'

Thymus serpyllum 'Minor'

easy to grow from seed, which is best sown the moment ripe. Like the seed of many composites, a proportion will prove to be sterile, generally only the plump seed being fertile and worth sowing. Townsendias are considered by many growers to be the elite among the many genera of rock garden daisies.

Townsendia alpigena (syn. *T. montana*)

Western United States; Utah to southwestern Montana and Wyoming. Plants form low clusters of rather dense leaf rosettes; leaves narrow oblanceolate, with uprolled margins, generally hairy. Flowerheads almost sessile or borne on stalks to 5 cm (2 in) long, 30–40 mm (1⅕–1⅗ in) across, with white to pink, bluish, or deep purple rays; summer. It is more perennial than most in cultivation: the form normally sold has deep purple flowerheads.

Townsendia hookeri

Western United States; Montana to Utah and Colorado. Very similar to *T. rothrockii*, but the leaves have the margins rolled upward while the flowerheads have white rays; summer.

Townsendia rothrockii

Colorado. A low perennial scarcely 5 cm (2 in) tall in flower, forming tufts of gray-green leaf rosettes. Leaves thick and leathery, narrow-oblanceolate, entire, slightly shiny, to 6 cm (2⅖ in) long. Flowerheads nestling close to the leaves, pale blue or somewhat mauve, 25–35 mm (1–1⅖ in) across, with a prominent golden disk; summer.

. . . .

Townsendia rothrockii

Trollius

A small genus of about 20 species of buttercup-like plants, but readily distinguished by the absence of sepal-like structures: in fact the sepals are large and colored, petal-like, while the true petals are modified into small, tubular nectaries. Known popularly as globeflowers, the species are found in the temperate Northern Hemisphere. They have rounded leaves that are variously lobed and dissected, while the flowers bear 5 to 15 petal-like sepals. Unlike the buttercups (*Ranunculus*), the fruit consist of a collection of multiseeded follicles.

The larger species are too big, but several smaller one are good subjects for the rock garden as well as troughs and raised beds, thriving in a moist humus-rich soil in sun or part shade. Propagation is by division in late summer or, more practically for the smaller species, from seed sown in late winter.

Trollius acaulis

Western Himalaya. A small tufted herbaceous perennial to 25 cm (10 in) tall in flower. Leaves

rather bright green, with five or seven toothed lobes. Flowers solitary, deep yellow, saucer-shaped, about 5 cm (2 in) across, with 5 to 10 sepals; stamens slightly longer than the petals; late spring and early summer. A plant of grassy alpine slopes and meadows in the wild.

Trollius pumilus

Eastern Himalaya and southwestern China. Rather larger than *T. acaulis*, to 30 cm (1 ft) tall, the leaf segments each trilobed and acutely toothed. Flowers solitary, yellow, 2.5–4 cm (1–1⅗ in) across, opening flat, generally with only five or six rounded sepals; petals and stamens equal; late spring and early summer.

Tropaeolum

A South American genus with some 90 species that include the garden nasturtium (*Tropaeolum majus*). The species are rather succulent with spreading or clambering stems, the climbing ones attaching themselves with coiling petioles. Leaves disk-like (peltate) or variously digitately lobed. Flowers five-parted, solitary from the leaf axils, with clawed, often fringed petals that are often unevenly developed, usually prominently spurred. The fruit consist of one or several berry-like seeds.

Only one species is suitable for the average rock garden. It can become invasive, yet is, nonetheless, delightful, thriving in a deep gritty soil with added humus. Propagation is from seed when available or from division or offsets of the tubers. These latter are often difficult to locate and remove, as they delve down deep into the soil. Seed can be temperamental in germination, with fresh seed giving the best results.

Tropaeolum polyphyllum

Chile and Argentina. A sprawling, prostrate plant with thick pale stems. Leaves rather pale blue-gray, sometimes suffused purple, rounded, with five to seven obovate, entire, upfolded leaf-

Trollius acaulis

Tropaeolum polyphyllum

lets. Flowers numerous at the middle and upper leaf axils, forming a raceme-like, one-sided structure, bright yellow or orange-yellow (pinkish gray in bud), petals toothed and wavy, the upper two rather larger than the others; early summer.

Verbascum

The mulleins, as they are popularly called, represent a large and very complicated genus with more than 350 species in Europe and Asia, particularly Greece and Turkey. They are annuals, perennials, or subshrubs, many forming large and handsome leaf rosettes initially and often adorned with a thick felt of stellate hairs. Flowers are regular, five-parted, and borne on spikes, racemes, or panicles; petals are rounded equal or subequal. The fruit is a two-parted, many-seeded capsule.

The two species presented here are excellent rock garden or container plants for full sun in a sheltered site and a well-drained gritty compost. Propagation is from seed, if produced, and sown in late winter or from root cuttings taken during the summer; only thick healthy sections of root should be used. Verbascums are subject to invasion by moth caterpillars, and these need to be guarded against on occasion.

Verbascum dumulosum

Turkey. A grayish, mound-forming subshrub to 80 cm (32 in) across eventually, but only 15–30 cm (6–12 in) tall in flower. Leaves elliptic to lanceolate, to 5 cm (2 in) long, with an entire to slightly crenate margin, densely gray-woolly. Flowers in short racemes, bright yellow,

about 15 mm (⅗ in) across, the stamens with violet- or yellow-haired filaments; summer. Although not as hardy as some, this plant makes a fine subject for vertical rock crevices and dry walls, especially if it can be given some protection during the winter months.

Verbascum 'Letitia'

An excellent hybrid derived in cultivation from *V. dumulosum* and the Cretan *V. spinosum*.

Verbascum dumulosum

Verbascum 'Letitia'

Plants form small hummocks to 50 cm (20 in) across with bluish gray, oblong-lanceolate, pinnately lobed leaves to 7.5 cm (3 in) long, grayish white with down. Flowers in short, branched spikes, butter yellow, about 15 mm (⅗ in) across, some filaments with violet hairs; late spring and summer. An outstanding hybrid that is surprisingly hardy and long-flowering. Although sterile, plants are readily raised from root cuttings.

Veronica

A large and colorful genus noted particularly for its blue flowers, although other colors are found. There are some 250 species primarily confined to the northern temperate zone. They range from weedy annuals to bold perennials and neat cushion-forming alpine plants. The leaves are opposite, simple, or variously lobed. The flowers are borne in lateral or terminal racemes and are four-parted, the petals joined

. . . .

Veronica austriaca 'Knallblau'

Veronica austriaca 'Shirley Blue'

near the base into a short tube. There are only two stamens. The fruit is a flattened two-parted capsule, which is often lobed.

The choicer veronicas or speedwells for the rock garden generally require a well-drained gritty, moderately fertile soil and a sunny site, although *V. peduncularis* will thrive in partial shade. Propagation is by division in autumn and early spring, from late spring or summer cuttings, or, when available, seed sown in late winter.

Veronica austriaca

Central Europe eastward to Turkey and the Caucasus. A clump-forming, often rather lax perennial spreading to 60 cm (2 ft), with decumbent stems. Leaves grayish green, to 5 cm (2 in) long, finely bipinnately divided, with linear, hairy lobes. Flowers bright blue, in paired,

long-stalked, tapered racemes to 15 cm (6 in) long; late spring and summer. 'Crater Lake Blue' gentian blue, to 30 cm (1 ft) tall; 'Ionian Skies' bright sky blue; 'Knallblau' rich deep blue; 'Shirley Blue' deep blue, the best dwarf form, to 20 cm (8 in) tall.

Veronica caespitosa

Turkey, Syria, and Lebanon. A matted or hummock-forming plant to 30 cm (1 ft) across, with crowded linear leaves to 13 mm (½ in) long, with revolute margins, often glandular-hairy overall. Flowers sky blue to purple blue, 8–13 mm (⅓–½ in) across, two to five in a cluster just above the foliage; summer. An excellent raised bed plant.

Veronica cinerea

Turkey. A mat-forming plant to 40 cm (16 in) across, with whitish hairy prostrate branches. Leaves linear to oblanceolate, to 16 mm (⅔ in) long, thinly downy, with revolute margins. Flowers deep blue to purple-blue with a white eye, 8–10 mm (⅓–⅖ in) across, up to 25 in paired racemes; summer. A very fine and floriferous species providing plenty of summer color.

Veronica montana

Europe eastward to the Caucasus and south to North Africa. A mat-forming plant to 60 cm (2 ft) across, with spreading stems, to 15 cm (6 in) tall in flower. Leaves broad-ovate, to 3.5 cm (1⅖ in) long, toothed, grayish green, and softly hairy. Flowers in lax racemes, pale lilac-blue with darker veins, 7–10 mm (⅓–⅖ in) across; late spring and summer. 'Corinne Tre-

. . . .

Veronica cinerea

Veronica montana 'Corinne Tremaine'

maine' rich blue flowers contrasting with yellow foliage.

Veronica peduncularis

Turkey and the Caucasus. A rather untidy, yet easy and attractive, species to 70 cm (28 in) across, but not more than 20 cm (8 in) in height in flower. Leaves ovate to lanceolate or rounded, to 3 cm (1⅕ in) long, coarsely toothed, sometimes shallowly pinnately lobed, often flushed

with bronze. Flowers pale to medium blue with purple veining, 8–13 mm (⅓–½ in) across, up to 20 in lax racemes that are freely produced; late spring and summer. 'Alba' white; 'Georgia Blue' bright blue; 'Oxford Blue' deep blue with bronzed foliage. When clipped back after flowering, plants will generally respond with a second crop of flowers.

Veronica prostrata

Europe. A mat-forming evergreen perennial to 50 cm (20 in) across, with prostrate to decumbent stems. Leaves deep green, ovate to oblong, 1–3 cm (⅖–1⅕ in) long, densely hairy and with an almost entire to toothed margin. Flowers rich blue, occasionally pink, about 10 mm (⅖ in) across, borne in dense racemes; summer. 'Alba' white; 'Blue Sheen' wisteria blue; 'Kapitan' silvery blue; 'Mrs Holt' soft pink; 'Nana' blue, dwarf, and compact; 'Rosea' pink; 'Royal Blue' deep blue; 'Spode Blue' pale blue; 'Trehane', medium blue contrasting with yellow foliage.

Viola

One of the most charming and popular groups of plants, the pansies and violets have long been favorites among gardeners and many are first-rate plants for the rock garden. The genus is a large one, with around 500 species almost throughout the world, ranging from nondescript annuals to bright and floriferous perennials, and fascinating alpines of high altitudes, especially in South America. The pansy flower is familiar to many, consisting of five small sepals and five large colorful petals, with two uppermost in the flower, while the lowest forms a lip that is extended behind into a pouch or spur. Many species have attractive marked faces. The fruit is a five-parted capsule containing numerous seeds.

Those species listed here are all good, relatively easy plants for the rock garden, the smaller ones for raised beds and troughs, all requiring a moisture-retentive yet well-drained compost. They will often seed around in the garden, but the offspring are likely to be quite variable because of their tendency to hybridize. Propagation is by seed when ripe or sown in early spring or by cuttings of strong leafy shoots taken during the summer.

Viola biflora

Northern Hemisphere. A tufted mountain plant to 10 cm (4 in) tall in flower, with kidney-shaped, bright green leaves, to 4 cm (1⅗ in) wide, with a neat crenate margin. Flowers held just above the leaves, small yellow violets, about 15 mm (⅗ in) across, with purple-brown lines on the elliptical lip; spring and summer. Will thrive in semi-shade.

Viola biflora

Viola calcarata

Alps and Jura to Slovenia. A tufted to clump-forming perennial to about 15 cm (6 in) tall in flower. Leaves in lax rosettes, rounded to lanceolate, to 4 cm (1⅗ in) long, with a crenate margin. Flowers violet, blue, yellow, or white, often bicolored, 2.5–4 cm (1–1⅗ in) across, with a slender spur to 15 mm (⅗ in) long; spring and early summer.

Viola cornuta

Pyrenees and Apennines. An elegant, clump-forming perennial to 40 cm (16 in) across, up to 25 cm (10 in) tall in flower. Leaves bright green, ovate to elliptic, to 3 cm (1⅕ in) long, with a crenate margin. Flowers violet to blue-violet, to 5 cm (2 in) across, often somewhat smaller, with well-spaced petals and a slender spur 10–15 mm (⅖–⅗ in) long; spring and summer. 'Alba' white; 'Alba Minor' the white equivalent of 'Minor'; 'Lilacina' lilac mauve; 'Minor' a dwarf variant half the height (10 cm, 4 in), forming denser clumps with medium violet-blue flowers; 'Victoria's Blush' pale pink with magenta markings. *Viola cornuta* is a parent of many tufted garden violas. Because they vary somewhat in color, many are put into colored groups such as the Alba Group, Lilacina Group, and Purpurea Group.

Viola doerfleri

Northern Balkans. An attractive tufted perennial to 12.5 cm (5 in) tall in flower, short-hairy in most parts. The leaves range from ovate to oblong, not more than 2.5 cm (1 in) long, with a slightly crenate margin. Flowers deep violet, about 2 cm (4/5 in) across, with a deflexed spur about 6 mm (¼ in) long; late spring and early summer.

Viola dubyana

Italian Alps. Rather similar to *V. doerfleri*, but more robust, to 20 cm (8 in) tall in flower with somewhat larger flowers of violet with a yellow base to the lip; summer.

Viola cornuta

Viola doerfleri

Viola riviniana (syn. *V. labradorica* of gardens)

Europe, Azores, and North Africa. A patch-forming plant with spreading stems. Leaves in basal clusters and on lateral stems, heart-shaped to ovate, to 7.5 cm (3 in) long, occasionally larger. Flowers violet-blue, small violets 15–20 mm (⅗–⅘ in) across, with a pale, occasionally yellowish spur; spring. 'Ed's Variegated' cream-speckled leaves; Purpurea Group (*V. labradorica* 'Purpurea') is the usual form seen in gardens with varying amounts of purple suffusion on the leaves; it seeds around freely in the garden and will thrive in sun or dappled shade.

Viola sororia (syn. *V. papilionacea, V. septentrionale*)

Eastern and central Canada and United States. A patch-forming herbaceous perennial to 30 cm (1 ft) across, 15 cm (6 in) tall in flower, sometimes more, with creeping greenish aboveground stems. Leaves rather bright green, heart-shaped, toothed, to 5 cm (2 in) long. Flowers variable in color from violet-blue to pale violet or white with violet veining or zoning, about 2 cm (⅘ in) across; spring. Thrives in sun or partly shaded areas. 'Albiflora' (syn. *V. cucullata* 'Alba', 'Snow Princess, 'White Sails') pure white; 'Alice Witter' white with purplish red throat; 'Freckles' white heavily freckled violet; 'Red Giant' reddish purple.

Viola zoysii (syn. *V. calcarata* var. *zoysii*)

Southeastern Alps and western Balkans. Very similar to *V. calcarata*, but a more compact plant only half the height with broad ovate to rounded leaves and solitary bright yellow flowers; spring and early summer. An excellent raised bed or trough plant.

Cultivars

Many hybrid violas have been produced over the years, and these are extremely popular today. Many were first bred by crossing the sweet violet, *V. odorata*, with the little seen *V. suavis*. Further crosses with multistemmed species

Viola riviniana Purpurea Group

Viola sororia

like *V. conuta* resulted in plants with a wide range of form and color. While the choice of cultivar or selections available is too large to include here, some are well worthy of a mention, being first-rate plants to brighter the rock garden in late spring and summer. They are easily raised from cuttings, using strong leafy shoots. Most of those listed here have flowers in the range of 3–4 cm (1⅕–1⅗ in) wide. 'Andros Gem' dark blue, blotched yellow on the lower lip; 'Bowles' Black' near black flowers; 'Eastgrove Blue Scented' medium blue, long-stalked, well-scented flowers; 'Etain' white with a violet margin and yellowish center, scented; 'Foxbrook Cream' lemon yellow; 'Huntercombe Purple' deep purple-violet, long-stalked flowers; 'Irish Molly' a curious mixture with maroon brown upper petals and yellow-green flushed khaki lower petals, blotched and lined darker, and with a yellow throat; 'Jack-

anapes' yellow with the upper petals dark crimson brown; 'Jeannie Bellew' very fragrant cream flowers; 'Maggie Mott' silvery mauve, scented; 'Molly Sanderson' black flowers with a yellow eye; 'Moonlight' creamy yellow, scented; 'Prince Henry' deep violet-blue with golden markings in the throat; 'Rebecca' cream, frilled flowers, scented; 'The Czar' deep purple violets, scented; 'Tiger Eye' golden yellow, scented.

· ·

Right: *Viola zoysii*

Bottom left: *Viola* 'Andros Gem'

Bottom right: *Viola* 'Prince Henry'

Vitaliana

A single species restricted to Europe, today often included in the genus *Androsace*, but distinct and perhaps best considered on its own. Despite this, plants can be cultivated in a similar manner to the easier androsaces, with a gritty, well-drained soil and a sunny position being the foremost requirements. As plants tend to root down freely, ready rooted pieces (Irishman's cuttings) can be separated from established clumps and grown on. Vitalianas are also readily raised from seed sown when ripe or in late winter. Seedlings can vary a lot, and only the best—those with the larger flowers freely borne—should be retained. Like *Primula* species, plants exhibit two types of flower, long- and short-styled (pin and thrum), these being borne on separate plants; to get a good seed set, both are required and growing in close proximity.

Vitaliana primuliflora (syn. *Androsace vitaliana, Douglasia vitaliana, Primula vitaliana*) Mountains of central and southern Europe. A green or gray-green, low, mat- or cushion-forming plant to 20 cm (8 in) across, occasionally more, with leaves crowded and overlapping on the stems, linear, 5–10 mm (⅕–⅖ in) long. Flowers solitary, bright yellow, 10–20 mm (⅖–⅘ in) across, with a somewhat inflated tube to 15 mm (⅗ in) long, and spreading elliptic lobes; spring. Subsp. *praetutiana* from the Apennines forms lax mats with blunter, oblong-lanceolate leaves that are white-downy beneath and at the tips.

Wahlenbergia

A genus of about 150 species of annuals and perennials confined mainly to southern Africa, Madagascar, and Australasia. They are closely related to *Edraianthus* but have solitary, unbracted flowers and capsules that open at the top by short valves.

They are fairly easily grown, but tend to be rather short-lived in the open garden; they will sometimes prove more permanent in a trough, or indeed within the confines of an alpine house or cold frame. Spring-sown seed or division in the autumn afford the best means of increase. Cuttings taken in late summer are also possible.

Wahlenbergia albomarginata

New Zealand. A quite variable rhizomatous perennial, 10–20 cm (4–8 in) tall in flower. Leaves in basal rosettes, oblong to lanceolate or almost linear, to 5 cm (2 in) long, with a thickened, white margin. Flowers borne on slender, erect stems, campanulate, lavender to white, often with pale green veining, 15–25 mm (⅗–1 in) long; summer. The easiest and most reliably

Vitaliana primuliflora

perennial species in general cultivation. 'Blue Mist' is a particularly well-colored clone.

Wahlenbergia gloriosa

Southeastern Australia. A laxly tufted perennial to 20 cm (8 in) tall in flower, with lax rosettes of obovate to spathulate leaves to 3 cm (1⅕ in) long, those on the stem few and opposite, wavy margined. Flowers borne on long, slender stems that are leafless in the upper half, deep violet-blue, 20–30 mm (⅘–1⅕ in) across, with widely flaring lobes; summer. A beautiful and easily grown species, although only surviving mild winters in the open garden.

Zaluzianskya

A genus of some 35 species found in the mountains of eastern and southern Africa in the figwort family (Scropulariaceae). They have flowers with long tubes and spreading, generally deeply notched, petal-lobes. The flowers tend to open in the evening and are richly perfumed.

These are plants for a well-drained soil and sheltered sunny site in the garden. Plants can be propagated from seed when available or from late summer cuttings protected under glass or away from frost. This and related species are being increasingly sold as container plants by garden centers.

Zaluzianskya ovata

South Africa, primarily in the Drakensberg Mountains. A woody-based evergreen perennial of bushy habit, to 30 cm (1 ft) tall in flower, although generally less, with gray-green, lanceolate to elliptic, toothed leaves, 2.5–6 cm (1–

2⅖ in) long. Flowers catchfly like, maroon in bud and on the reverse, but opening glistening white, the limb 15–18 mm (⅗–⅔ in) across, with deeply notched lobes and a long slender tube 35–40 cm (14–16 in) long, opening in the evening or during dull weather, sweetly scented; borne from spring until autumn.

Wahlenbergia gloriosa

Zaluzianskya ovata

Zigadenus

Some 15 species of rhizomatous, often tufted perennials from North America and central and eastern Asia, with basal clusters of linear, grass-like leaves. Inflorescences borne on stiff, erect stems, racemose, often branched, the flowers starry, six-tepaled with one or two glands at the base of each tepal. Fruit a small three-parted capsule.

Although monocots, these delightful plants are often omitted from books on bulbs, hence their inclusion here. Plants require a well-drained, fertile soil and a sunny position, but are generally too big except for larger rock gardens. Propagation is by seed sown when ripe or in late winter; division is sometimes possible in the autumn, although this needs to be undertaken very carefully.

Zigadenus species, like common ragwort (*Senecio jacobaea*), are very injurious to cattle. For this reason, plants are eliminated from regularly grazed meadows in North America. They are very unlikely to colonize meadows elsewhere.

Zigadenus elegans
Western North America; Alaska to New Mexico. A tufted perennial to 70 cm (28 in) tall, with bluish green, narrow, strap-shaped, tapered leaves to 30 cm (12 in) long. Flowers borne in branched, lax racemes, white to cream with a greenish reverse, 16–24 mm (⅔–1 in) across, each tepal with a greenish yellow, kidney-shaped, gland at the base; summer.

Zigadenus fremontii
Western United States; southern Oregon and California. Very similar to *Z. elegans*, but inflorescence often unbranched and tepals more pointed, with an oval yellowish gland at the base of each tepal; summer.

Zigadenus fremontii

Rock Garden Plants for All Aspects

Sunny dry walls

Arabis caucasica

Aubrieta deltoidea, A. ×cultorum cultivars

Aurinia saxatilis

Campanula cochlearifolia, C. portenschlagiana, C. poscharskyana

Erigeron mucronatus

Erinus alpinus

Lewisia cotyledon

Onosma alborosea

Penstemon fruticosus

Saponaria ocymoides

Saxifraga cotyledon, S. longifolia, S. 'Tumbling Waters', and any silver saxifrage

Sedum acre, S. album

Sempervivum species and cultivars

Shady or semi-shaded crevices and ledges

Arenaria balearica

Asarina procumbens

Corydalis ochroleuca

Erinus alpinus

Haberlea rhodopensis

Horminum pyrenaicum

Iris cristata

Lewisia tweedyi

Penstemon rupicola

Pratia pedunculata

Primula auricula

Pseudofumaria lutea

Ramonda myconi

Also a host of small hardy ferns not included in the A to Z section, including: *Adiantum pedatum, Asplenium adiantum-nigrum, A. ceterach, A. dareoides, A. septentrionale, A. trichomanes, Polypodium hesperium, Woodsia alpina, W. polystichoides*

Scree

Aethionema grandiflora

Alyssum montanum

Androsace sempervivoides, A. studiosorum

Anthemis montana

Armeria juniperifolia

Campanula carpatica, C. pulla

Carlina acaulis

Dianthus alpinus

Edraianthus pumilio, E. serpyllifolius

Erodium reichardii

Gentiana acaulis, G. verna

Gypsophila repens

Leontopodium alpinum

Linaria alpina

Linum 'Gemmel's Hybrid'

Morisia monantha

Papaver alpinum

Phlox adsurgens, P. subulata

Pulsatilla grandis, P. halleri, P. vulgaris

Saponaria pumilio

Sempervivum arachnoideum, S. montanum, numerous cultivars

Viola cornuta

Sunny troughs and raised beds

Anchusa cespitosa

Androsace hirtella

Aquilegia flabellata var. *pumila*

Asperula sintenisii

Dianthus alpinus

Draba aizoides

Gentiana acaulis, G. verna

Globularia repens
Linum suffruticosa var. *salsoloides*
Oxalis adenophylla, O. 'Ione Hecker'
Phlox douglasii
Potentilla nitida
Primula marginata
Rhodohypoxis baurii hybrids and cultivars
Saxifraga cochlearis, S. cotyledon, S. panicu-lata, and many others
Sempervivum arachnoideum, S. montanum, numerous cultivars
Silene acaulis

Shady and semi-shady situations

Arenaria balearica
Corydalis ochroleuca
Cyclamen coum
Gentiana sino-ornata
Haberlea rhodopensis
Hepatic nobilis
Houstonia caerulea
Iris cristata
Jeffersonia dubia
Pratia pedunculata
Primula vulgaris
Ramonda myconi
Veronica peduncularis

Tufa

Anchusa cespitosa
Campanula zoysii
Draba bryoides
Edraianthus pumilio
Leontopodium alpinum subsp. *nivale*
Petrocallis pyrenaica
Physoplexis comosa
Ramonda myconi
Saxifraga cochlearis, Saxifraga 'Faldonside', *S.* 'Myra', *S.* 'Tumbling Waters', *S.* 'Winifred', and numerous other small cultivars

Acid humus beds (cool semi-shade)

Corydalis flexuosa
Cyclamen coum
Dodecatheon media, D. pulchellum
Gentiana sino-ornata, hybrids between *G. sino-ornata, G. farreri,* and *G. veitchiorum*
Haberlea rhodopensis
Hacquetia epipactis
Jeffersonia dubia
Meconopsis quintuplinervia
Phlox divaricata
Primula rosea, P. vulgaris, numerous cultivars
Ramonda myconi
Sanguinaria canadensis
Soldanella villosa
Also a host of small hardy ferns not included in the A to Z section, such as: *Adiantum pedatum, Asplenium adiantum-nigrum, A. ceterach, A. dareoides, A. septentrionale, A. trichomanes, Polypodium hesperium, Woodsia alpina, W. polystichoides*

Containers, specimen plants for alpine house and cold frame

Anchusa cespitosa
Androsace species and hybrids
Asperula arcadiensis, A. sintenisii
Campanula zoysii
Clematis marmoraria
Dianthus alpinus
Gentiana verna
Lewisia cotyledon, L. rediviva, L. tweedyi
Linum suffruticosum var. *salsoloides*
Morisia monantha
Phlox douglasii, P. mesoleuca
Physoplexis comosa
Potentilla nitida
Primula species and cultivars (smaller species especially)

Saxifraga species and cultivars
Sempervivum species and cultivars

Drought-resistant plants

Chiastophyllum oppositifolium
Delosperma species and cultivars
Rhodiola rosea
Sedum species and cultivars
Sempervivum species and cultivars

Dwarf shrubs and subshrubs

Daphne arbuscula, D. cneorum, D. petraea,
　D. retusa, numerous dwarf cultivars
Deutzia gracilis 'Nikko'
Dianthus erinaceus

Dryas octopetala
Erigeron glaucus
Erinacea anthyllis
Genista lydia
Helianthemum nummularium, cultivars
Hypericum olympicum
Iberis sempervirens
Juniperus communis 'Compressa'
Linum arboreum
Lithodora diffusa, L. oleifolia
Origanum 'Barbara Tingey', *O. rotundifolium*
Polygala chamaebuxus, P. vayredae
Rhodanthemum hosmariense
Salix lanata, S. reticulata
Verbascum dumulosum, V. 'Letitia'

Nursery Sources

This is a partial list of nurseries in the United Kingdom, the Netherlands, the United States, and Canada that specialize in rock garden and alpine plants. Catalogues or lists are available from most (hard copy and via websites). No endorsement is intended by their inclusion, nor is criticism implied by those not listed.

European Nurseries

Aberconwy Nursery
Graig
Glan Conwy
Wales LL28 5TL
United Kingdom
Tel. 01492 580875

Ardfearn Nursery
Buchrew
Inverness IV3 6RK
United Kingdom
Tel. 01463 243250
www.ardfearn-nursery.co.uk

Craig Lodge Nurseries
Balmaclellan
Castle Douglas DG7 3QR
United Kingdom

D'Arcy & Everest
P.O. Box 78
St Ives
Huntingdon
Cambridgeshire PE27 6ZA
United Kingdom
Tel. 01480 497672
www.darcyeverest.co.uk

Edrom Nurseries
Coldingham
Eyemouth
Berwick TD14 5TZ
United Kingdom
Tel. 01890 771386
www.edromnurseries.co.uk

Ger van den Beuken
Zegersstraat 7
5961 XR Horst (L)
Netherlands
Tel. 0031 7739 81542

Graham's Hardy Plants
'Southcroft'
North Road
Timsbury
Bath BA2 0JN
United Kingdom
Tel. 01761 472187

Inshriach Alpine Plant Nursery
Aviemore
Inverness-shire PH22 10S
United Kingdom
Tel. 01540 651287
www.drakesalpines.com

Jim Almond
5 Coolock Close
St Peter's Park
Shrewsbury SY3 9QD
United Kingdom
Tel. 01743 242271

Kevock Garden Plants
16 Kevock Road
Lasswade
Midlothian EH18 1HT
United Kingdom
Tel. 01314 540660
www.kevockgarden.co.uk

Lamberton Nursery
No. 3 Lamberton
Berwickshire TD15 1XB
United Kingdom
Tel. 01289 308515
www.lambertonnursery.co.uk

Norden Alpines
Hirst Road
Carlton
Nr. Selby DN14 9PX
United Kingdom

Pottertons Nursery
Moortown Road
Nettleton
Caistor
Lincolnshire LN7 6HX
United Kingdom
Tel. 01472 851714
www.pottertons.co.uk

Slack Top Nursery
Hebden Bridge
West Yorkshire HG7 7HA
United Kingdom
Tel. 01422 845348
www.slacktopnurseries.co.uk

Thuja Alpine Nursery
Glebelands
Hartpury

Gloucester GL19 3BW
United Kingdom
Tel. 01452 700548

Tile Barn Nursery
Standen Street
Iden Green
Benenden
Kent TN17 4LB
United Kingdom
Tel. 01580 240221
www.tilebarn-cyclamen.co.uk

Tough Alpine Nursery
Westhaybogs
Tough
Alford
Aberdeenshire AB33 8DU
United Kingdom
Tel. 01975 562783

U.S. Nurseries

Arrowhead Alpines
P.O. Box 857
Fowlerville, Michigan 48836
Tel. 517 223 3581
www.arrowheadalpines.com

Edelweiss Perennials
29800 S. Barlow Road
Canby, Oregon 97013
Tel. 503-263-4680
www.edelweissperennials.com

Evermay Nursery
84 Beechwood Avenue
Old Town, Maine 04468
Tel. 207 827 0522
www.evermaynursery.com

Laporte Avenue Nursery (Rocky Mountain
    Alpines)
1950 Laporte Avenue
Fort Collins, Colorado 80521
www.laporteavenuenursery.com

Mt. Tahoma Nursery
28111 112th Avenue East
Graham, Washington 98338
Tel. 253 847 9827

Siskiyou Rare Plant Nursery
2115 Talent Avenue
Talent, Oregon 97540
Tel. 541 535 7103
www.siskiyourareplantnursery.com

Wild Ginger Farm
24000 S. Schuebel School Road
Beavercreek, Oregon 97004
Tel. 503 632 2338
www.wildgingerfarm.com

Canadian Nurseries

Alpine Mont Echo
1182 Parmenter Road
Sutton, Quebec J0E 2K0
Tel. 450 243 5354
www.alpinemtecho.com

Cushion Creek Nursery
175 Stewart Road
Salt Spring Island, British Columbia, V8K 2C4

Pacific Rim Native Plant Nursery
44305 Old Orchard Road
Chilliwack, British Columbia V2E 1A9
Tel. 604 792 9279
www.hillkeep.ca

Wrightman Alpine Nursery
RR#3 1503 Napperton Drive
Kerwood, Ontario N0M 2B0
Tel. 519 247 3751
www.wrightmanalpines.com

Societies and Clubs

Alpine Garden Society
www.alpinegardensociety.net

Dutch Alpine Garden Society
(Nederlandse Rotsplanten Vereniging)
www.rotsplantenvereniging.net

New Zealand Alpine Garden Society
P.O. Box 2984
Christchurch, New Zealand

North American Rock Garden Society
www.nargs.org

Rock Gardener's Club Prague
(Klub skalničkářů Praha)
www.soldanella.cz/eng

Scottish Rock Garden Club
www.srgc.org.uk

Glossary

achene small, dry, one-seeded fruitlet, generally in tight clusters

acid having a soil pH less than 7

alkaline having a pH more than 7

alternate arranged, often spirally, along a stem; generally refers to leaves

auricle ear-like appendage

basal growing at the base of the plant

calyx (calyces) outer whorl of flower parts, often green and usually smaller than the petals

capsule dry fruit containing often numerous seeds; capsules split in many different ways, from slits to pores

ciliate fringed with hairs or bristles

crucifers members of the cress or cabbage family, Cruciferae (Brassicaceae), with characteristically four-petaled, cross-shaped flowers

cultivar plant maintained and propagated in cultivation; many cultivars have distinguishing names

cyme regularly branched inflorescence with each branch terminating in a flower

deciduous shedding leaves at the end of the season, not simply dying down (as opposed to evergreen)

decumbent branches spreading horizontally but turning up toward the tip

dioecious with distinct male and female flowers borne on separate plants

double having numerous extra petals, often replacing all or most of the other flower parts

epicalyx extra calyx, often smaller, to the outside of the prime calyx

filament stalk of a stamen

flowerhead tight collection of florets borne on a common flat or elongated axis, as in daisies and sea hollies

gesneriad member of the saintpaulia family, Gesneriaceae

glaucous bluish gray, sometimes with a bloom

herbaceous in reference to perennials, those that die down to ground level annually; often wrongly termed deciduous

hermaphrodite flowers with both male and female organs

inflorescence structure (spike, raceme, panicle, etc.) bearing the flowers

labiates members of the deadnettle or sage family, Labiatae (Lamiaceae), with characteristic two-lipped flowers

lanceolate shaped like a lance, elliptic but broadest below the middle

linear narrow and with parallel sides like a grass leaf

monocarpic plants that grow for several years, often as a leaf rosette, before flowering, fruiting, and dying

nectary gland that secretes nectar

neutral (in reference to soils) having a pH of 7

node point on stems where the leaves join

oblanceolate opposite to lanceolate, broadest above the middle

obovate opposite to ovate, broadest above the middle

opposite arranged in pairs along a stem; usually refers to leaves

ovate broad-lanceolate, widest below the middle, egg-shaped but flat

palmate shaped like the hand

panicle branched raceme

pedicel stalk of a flower

petiole stalk of a leaf

pinnate compound leaf with leaflets in opposing pairs aligned along an axis, with or without a terminal leaflet; bipinnate when the main axis is itself divided

prostrate flat on the ground

raceme spike-like, unbranched inflorescence in which the individual flowers are stalked

rays (ray florets) outer flowers in the flowerhead, often much extended as in daisy flowerheads

revolute with margin rolled under; refers primarily to leaves

rhizomatous having rhizomes

rhizome swollen, horizontal or inclined stem with lateral buds, at ground level or below

rosette cluster of leaves, flat or otherwise, generally at ground level

scape flower or inflorescence stem without leaves

semi-double flowers with extra flower parts (petals especially) but generally still with stamens and ovaries intact or mostly so

sessile without a stalk; in the case of leaves without a petiole

spathe bract- or leaf-like structures that enfold a flower or inflorescence in bud

spathulate paddle-shaped

spike unbranched inflorescence in which the individual flowers are unstalked or sessile

spur extension of petal or sepal, often cylindrical and usually with a nectary inside at the tip

staminode infertile stamen, often modified into a nectary

stellate star-shaped; often refers to hairs

stipule structure located (often in pairs) at the base of the petiole; stipules can be very small to large and leaf-like

stolon creeping stem or aerial stem, sometimes called a runner, often rooting down and terminating in a plantlet, sometimes branching

stoloniferous bearing stolons

subshrub small bushy plant, generally woody at least in the lower part

tepal petal-like flower parts not clearly differentiated into sepals or petals, often brightly colored

ternate leaves with three leaflets, as in the trefoils

trilobed with three lobes

tufa porous rock composed primarily of calcium carbonate, formed where highly alkaline waters are checked and sometimes building up into substantial deposits

umbel inflorescence in which all the stalks come off at the same level, as in the spokes of a wheel or umbrella

umbellifer member of the carrot or parsley family, Umbelliferae (Apiaceae)

whorl leaves, bracts, or flowers borne in a circle around the stem, sometimes tiered one above the other

Further Reading

Beckett, K., ed. 1993. *Alpine Garden Society Encyclopaedia of Alpines*. Alpine Garden Society, Pershore, UK.

Elliott, R. C. 1963. *Alpine Gardening*. Vista Books, London.

Farrer, R. 1928. *The English Rock Garden*. T. C. & E. C. Jack, London.

Good, John E. G., and David Millward. 2007. *Alpine Plants: Ecology for Gardeners*. Timber Press, Portland, Ore.

Grey-Wilson, C., ed. 1989. *A Manual of Alpine and Rock Garden Plants*. Christopher Helm/Timber Press, London and Portland, Ore.

Grey-Wilson, C. 1994. *The Alpine Garden*. Conran Octopus, London.

Grey-Wilson, C., and M. Blamey. 1995. *Alpine Flowers of Britain and Europe*. HarperCollins, London.

Heath, R. 1964. *Collectors' Alpines*. Collingridge, London.

Ingwersen, W. 1978. *Manual of Alpine Plants*. Will Ingwersen and Dunnsprint Ltd., London.

Jermyn, Jim. 2005. *Alpine Plants of Europe: A Gardener's Guide*. Timber Press, Portland, Ore.

Lowe, D. 1991. *Growing Alpines in Raised Beds, Troughs and Tufa*. Christopher Helm/A. & C. Black, London.

Mineo, Baldassare. 1999. *Rock Garden Plants: A Color Encyclopedia*. Timber Press, Portland, Ore.

Nicholls, Graham. 2002. *Alpine Plants of North America: An Encyclopedia of Mountain Flowers from the Rockies to Alaska*. Timber Press, Portland, Ore.

North American Rock Garden Society. 2003. *Rock Garden Design and Construction*. Ed. Jane McGary. Timber Press, Portland, Ore.

Royal Horticultural Society. 1997. *Rock Plants*. Dorling Kindersley, London.

Various. 1939–. *Alpine Garden Society Bulletin* (*The Alpine Gardener*). Alpine Garden Society, Pershore, Worcestershire, UK.

Index